CONSTRUCTING NEOLIBERALISM

Economic Transformation in Anglo-American
Democracies

Constructing Neoliberalism

Economic Transformation in Anglo-American Democracies

JONATHAN SWARTS

UNIVERSITY OF TORONTO PRESS
Toronto Buffalo London

ISBN 978-1-4426-4646-9

Printed on acid-free, 100% post-consumer recycled paper with vegetable-based inks.

Publication cataloguing information is available from Library and Archives Canada.

University of Toronto Press acknowledges the financial assistance to its publishing program of the Canada Council for the Arts and the Ontario Arts Council.

Canada Council   Conseil des Arts
for the Arts   du Canada

ONTARIO ARTS COUNCIL
CONSEIL DES ARTS DE L'ONTARIO
50 YEARS OF ONTARIO GOVERNMENT SUPPORT OF THE ARTS
50 ANS DE SOUTIEN DU GOUVERNEMENT DE L'ONTARIO AUX ARTS

University of Toronto Press acknowledges the financial support of the Government of Canada through the Canada Book Fund for its publishing activities.

To Neovi and Giovanni

Contents

Contents

Acknowledgments

This book would simply not have been possible without the support and assistance of numerous people and organizations over many years. I would first like to thank the many men and women who so generously gave of their time to be interviewed for this project. In the course of an interview program spanning several years and three continents, I never failed to be amazed and gratified by the openness and warmth with which I was received by so many. I cannot express adequately my thanks to them for taking the time to be interviewed – and, in the process, helping me to make this book possible.

The support of many other people along the way was also invaluable and deeply appreciated. I would like to thank Anthony Mughan and Richard Gunther, my mentors and friends at The Ohio State University. They were unstinting in their support for this project and in their encouragement to take on and complete what seemed at times to be an impossibly large research plan. I would also like to express my appreciation to Frank Castles and Barry Hindess, both of the School of Politics and International Relations in the Research School of Social Sciences at the Australian National University (ANU). They graciously arranged for me to be affiliated with their department during my stay in Canberra. I cannot overstate how beneficial it was for me to have access to the library, offices, and other resources of the ANU. Also on the campus of the ANU, the director and staff of the Australian-American Educational Foundation helped in numerous ways to make my time in Australia very rewarding, both professionally and personally.

Given the scope of this project, a key element was the financial support I received to conduct my research in the four countries analyzed here. At The Ohio State University, support came from the Graduate

School, the University Center for International Studies, the Office of International Studies, the Mershon Center for International Security Studies, and the Department of Political Science. Their generous awards made possible my research in Britain and New Zealand and the initial writing of this book. Research in Canada was funded by the Canadian Government's Graduate Student Fellowship. In Australia, an extended stay was fully supported by a Fulbright Fellowship from the Australian-American Educational Foundation. I offer a sincere thank you to each of these organizations for their generous support. Finally, Purdue University North Central made a very generous contribution to underwrite the production of this book. For this, my very sincere thanks go to Karen Schmid, Vice Chancellor for Academic Affairs; Kumara Jayasuriya, Associate Vice Chancellor for Academic Affairs; S. Rex Morrow, Dean of the College of Liberal Arts; and Michael R. Lynn, Chair of the Department of Social Sciences.

This research program was not only an invaluable intellectual experience, it also netted me a number of dear friends. I wish to thank all of them for every instance of support and friendship they showed me during my time in the field. In London, Norah and Frank Mughan were delightful friends, and I remember with appreciation their warm hospitality. In Australia, I had the good fortune to meet a number of wonderful individuals whose friendship and hospitality made my time there a real joy. I thank all of them sincerely for their friendship. Among them, Darren, Michelle, and Parhyse May were – and are – the most generous and hospitable of friends. Stefanos Nicolaou and his family were fantastic – they befriended me and did innumerable acts of kindness for me that I cannot forget. Finally, John Kalokerinos and his family deserve special thanks for their warm and constant friendship – then and since. Each of these people made me feel like Canberra was my second home, and I express to them my sincere thanks.

At the University of Toronto Press, Daniel Quinlan has been simply wonderful, and I thank him most sincerely for his patience, insight, and sage advice in shepherding this project through to completion. I also appreciate the significant time and effort expended on this book by two anonymous readers. Their comments were comprehensive, penetrating, and insightful – and contributed greatly to strengthening the manuscript. Any errors or shortcomings, of course, remain my own.

Finally, and most importantly, I cannot adequately express my love and appreciation to my family – those who, more than any others, made this book possible. I wish first to thank my mother, Patricia Swarts, for being a never-failing source of encouragement and love. Throughout every part of this research project, she has supported me and my work, patiently awaiting the day when "it will all be finished." Some of my fondest memories are of her visits to London and to Ottawa, where we had a wonderful time together.

I now turn to the two people who are truly the loves of my life. First, to Neovi, without whom this book certainly would never have happened. She has been beside me for every stage of this project, and I cannot begin to express how much this book is a result of her love and support – whether it was during the early days of this book's formulation in Columbus; the long absences during the years of field work; her visits to London, Ottawa, and Canberra; or the seemingly endless rounds of revisions in South Bend. She has enthusiastically supported and encouraged me every step of the way, never failing when a boost of confidence was needed or when I asked her to read the manuscript for the hundredth time. She kept her faith in me and in this project – even when I did not. I cannot express enough to her my love and appreciation.

The other love of my life is Giovanni. Though he was not yet born when the research for this book was done, nor did he read a word of the manuscript as it was written, he has nonetheless contributed a tremendous deal to this project – especially the fun. His infectious enthusiasm and excitement with life, his dauntless optimism and resilience, never failed to encourage me, pleasantly distract me from my work, and spur me on to this book's completion. I am very thankful for his love – and proud of him indeed.

Thus, to Neovi and to Giovanni, I gratefully dedicate this book.

CONSTRUCTING NEOLIBERALISM

Economic Transformation in Anglo-American
Democracies

1 The Construction of Political-Economic Imaginaries

In 1950, future British prime minister Harold Macmillan proclaimed, "The excessive individualism of the *laissez-faire* age under-emphasised man's duty to his neighbour, and exaggerated the rights of the individual man and family."[1] A generation later, another Conservative prime minister, Margaret Thatcher, would declare, "There is no such thing as society. There are individual men and women, and there are families."[2] In Australia, on the Labor side of politics, a similar shift took place. In 1947, Prime Minister Ben Chifley proposed the nationalization of Australian banks, declaring, "The Labor Party throughout its existence has never left any doubt in the public mind that the complete control of the financial and monetary system should be in the hands of the people."[3] But, by the end of the century, another Labor prime minister would disavow state ownership saying, "Through time ... people have adopted [positions] which they regard as fundamental but which to me seem absolutely irrelevant. ... [For instance, Labor] had commitments that we had to operate a bank; that we had to own and operate an airline. Bullshit."[4]

How did these transformations occur? The short answer is that over the course of the 1980s and 1990s, in countries governed by parties of both the right and the left, traditional policies of Keynesian demand management and active state economic intervention gave way to policies – variously dubbed "neoliberal," "economically rationalist," and "New Right" – privileging the role of the deregulated, "free" markets. Quoting Colin Hay's thorough definition, *neoliberalism* (or economic rationalism) as used in this book is an economic philosophy characterized by the following central tenets:

1. A confidence in the market as an efficient mechanism for the allocation of scare resources.

2. A belief in the desirability of a global regime of free trade and free capital mobility.
3. A belief in the desirability, all things being equal, of a limited and non-interventionist role for the state.
4. A conception of the state as a facilitator and custodian, rather than a substitute for market mechanisms.
5. A defence of individual liberty.
6. A commitment to the removal of those welfare benefits that might be seen as disincentives to market participation (in short, a subordination of the principles of social justice to those of perceived economic imperatives).
7. A defence of labour market flexibility and the promotion and nurturing of cost effectiveness.
8. A confidence in the use of private finance in public projects and, more generally, in the allocative efficiency of market and quasi-market mechanisms in the provisions of public goods.[5]

In the course of little more than a decade, this set of ideas became entrenched as normative in an increasing number of industrialized democracies. In what has been labelled a "counter double movement,"[6] the very policies and state institutions that had been the cornerstones of the post-war, interventionist mixed economy were "systematically delegitimated and dismantled."[7] The worldwide wave of market liberalization was dramatic. Government economic intervention, market regulation, tariff protection, and labour-friendly policies were drastically scaled back. Deregulation, attempts to control government expenditure, reduce debt loads, eliminate inflation, free up world trade, and reduce the influence of traditionally powerful trade unions, became widespread. Moreover, the collapse of communism accelerated this trend by further discrediting any kind of interventionist alternative. As a result, in large numbers of countries the perception became firmly entrenched that some form of liberal, free market economics is the *only* basis on which efficient and successful economies can operate.

Given the global spread of neoliberal economic policies, and especially their adoption by left- and right-wing parties alike, this book explores the neoliberal policy phenomenon through an examination of neoliberalism as adopted and promoted by four governments: two of the right, in Great Britain and Canada, and two of the left, in Australia and New Zealand.[8] In all four countries, governments effected a significant reorientation of economic policy – away from traditional methods of active state economic intervention and regulation toward policies emphasizing the alleged superiority of "free market" outcomes. Each country's previously dominant policy pattern was dramatically altered – away from the post-war interventionist "consensus" to a new set of policies oriented toward growth through market liberalization. As neoliberal economics became a new policy consensus, the imperatives of the market – efficiency, productivity, and output – came to eclipse such long-held social goals as full employment and social solidarity. In this shift, both left and right played key roles: the Conservative Parties of Britain and Canada inaugurated their countries' neoliberal revolutions, while the Labor Parties of Australia and New Zealand drove economic rationalism there. Later, the opposition in these countries would sign on to the neoliberal agenda themselves: on the "left," Labour in Britain and the Liberals in Canada, and, on the right, the Coalition parties in Australia and National in New Zealand, would all pick up where their predecessors had left off. The shift to neoliberalism was common to both sides of politics in all four countries – what one side of politics initiated in the 1980s, the other side consolidated and entrenched when it acceded to power in the 1990s.

This book analyses neoliberalism in these four countries as a prime example of the social construction of political and economic change. In this account, neoliberalism is presented as, in large part, an ideational and discursive construction – what I shall call a "political-economic imaginary" – promoted by elites as part of a strategy to reset the basic parameters, expectations, and shared norms of the relationship between the state, society, and the (inter-)national economy. Operating within a set of political and economic structures that both facilitated and constrained their policy advocacy, these norm entrepreneurs successfully persuaded and coerced other social actors to either agree with or at least acquiesce to their proposed "reforms." The long-term result was the shift toward a new set of intersubjective norms about appropriate economic policies, the role of the state in the economy, and the proper expectations and aspirations of citizens, indeed the very nature of an advanced industrial democracy in a globalizing world – in short, a new *political-economic imaginary*.

The ways in which that new political-economic imaginary came to prominence in Britain, Canada, Australia, and New Zealand is the subject of this book. Applying ideas primarily drawn from the constructivist literature in international relations and sociology to what were largely domestic political processes, I deploy a constructivist model of the interplay between economic ideas, norm entrepreneurs, and the economic and political environment.[9] That is, in addition to a showing *why* elites in these countries pursued neoliberalism as a radically new policy approach, I also focus on *how* elites successfully constructed neo-liberal economic ideology as a set of allegedly inescapable, ontological facts to which no credible alternatives existed. In doing so, I emphasize the critical importance of norm entrepreneurs in creating, promoting, and reproducing social norms or imaginaries. Without denying the important role played by other actors and institutions, this book's con-ceptual and empirical focus is on the politicians and bureaucrats most central to the construction of neoliberalism.

As will become clear in the pages that follow, I make three main arguments about how elites go about the business of constructing (and reconstructing) norms. First, I emphasize how these norm entrepre-neurs employ coercion, not just persuasion, as a strategic instrument in their construction of new imaginaries. Moving beyond a rather benign Habermasian model of communication and persuasion as the engine of ideational change, I show how elite constructions can also be coercive, forcing reluctant actors to at least acquiesce to the new normative cre-ation. Second, I attempt to untangle – at least partially – the intertwined thicket of material "reality" and ideas, arguing that a nuanced con-structivist account of ideational change must interrogate the connection between material and ideational forces and effects. Specifically, I dis-aggregate persuasion and coercion into material and ideational forms, showing how norm entrepreneurs in the Anglo-American democra-cies employed all four permutations (persuasion/coercion, material/ ideational) in their construction of a new economic reality. In so doing, material incentives and even compulsion were deployed in the service of both new public policies and long-term ideational change. Then, as reluctant individuals were either coerced or materially induced to con-form to the new economic structures, experience and habituation led the new ideological and policy paradigm to become "taken-for-granted" by many and even accepted by increasing numbers as objectively "true" and necessary. In this way, then, material influences were put to the service of ideational change. Finally, I seek to bring "politics back in" to the analysis of norm construction. That is, this book systematically integrates an analysis of domestic political institutions and processes – and in particular the unique opportunities and constraints presented by each country's structure of political institutions – with a keen awareness of the strategic choices made by partisan politicians seeking their own political advantage. In so doing, I focus my analysis of normative change on the role played by strategic political processes in each country and, in so doing, contribute to the engagement of the study of economic policy change with the conceptual purchase offered by constructivist analyses.

Imaginaries, Norm Entrepreneurs, and the Ideas-Praxis Linkage

This book adopts the view that much of political and social life – especially such significant political change as wholesale economic reorientation – can be understood only with reference to the ideas about those spheres that human beings bring to them. While politics and society are more than ideas – they are not, in that now well-known phrase, "ideas all the way down"[10] – ideas provide the core meanings that structure and regulate social and political behaviour and attitudes.[11] Because "behavior is pervasively a function of norms," as Cass Sunstein puts it,[12] large-scale changes in political (or social) systems cannot be explained without reference to changes in ideas about politics (or society). Whether the phenomenon to be explained is the end of slavery, the banning of landmines, or the rise to prominence of new economic dogmas, constructivist accounts such as mine emphasize that "idea shifts and norm shifts are the main vehicles for system transformation."[13] Political systems change as human beings change (consciously or not, purposively or not) their dominant ways of thinking, as their views of what is appropriate and desirable change, and as their behaviour and interaction with others change accordingly.

Indeed, it is only by examining the ideational shift that took place in Britain, Canada, Australia, and New Zealand that we can understand why and how their economic policies changed so dramatically. In each case, former policies of state regulation and intervention were replaced with ones promoting privatization, deregulation, and "the market" as the final arbiter of economic outcomes. Thus, these countries' experiences are instructive examples of a larger ideational shift underway in much of the world. As regulation and protection fell into disfavour, a new paradigm based on neoliberalism began to take hold in much of the world as strategic norm entrepreneurs sought to instantiate a new political-economic imaginary. The cases I consider here are important examples of how that shift manifested itself in a variety of forms in quite different economic and institutional settings.

Indeed, a remarkable feature of this common neoliberal shift in the Anglo-American democracies is that it occurred in countries that differed so significantly across a wide range of "material" factors, including population and geographic size, total economic output, degree of integration in the world trading system, levels of state own- ership of industry, the structure of labour market regulation, and so on. As is discussed in some detail later in this chapter, each country adopted neoliberal policies and underwent a neoliberal ideational shift despite varying in important material ways. Britain has a large econ- omy with a long history of industrial production, global financial cen- trality, and extensive international trading links. Canada, by contrast, is a country characterized by a much smaller economy traditionally dependent on trade with a single foreign partner – first Britain, later the United States. Australia and New Zealand, meanwhile, are former colonies once heavily dependent on trade in primary commodities with the imperial power but that, in the twentieth century, sought through state regulation and control to insulate themselves from the vagaries of the international economy. Yet, despite these significant differences in the size, nature, and international integration of these economies, economic policy – and, indeed, the very ideological foundations of that policy – shifted to the point that, by early twenty-first century, both sides of politics in these countries had to a large extent converged on the new pro-market paradigm.

These similar changes across such structurally dissimilar economies cannot be understood without an analysis of ideational change. Put simply, there was no material change or factor common to all four coun- tries that can fully explain the common shift to neoliberalism. For such an explanation, one must examine how these new economic ideas were constructed as necessary, appropriate, and ultimately "true." In ana- lysing this construction, the ideas themselves must play a central ana- lytical role – they constitute neither "a vague, residual category" to be invoked when other explanations fall short, nor are they "an undissect- able background condition whose influence is pervasive in principle but undemonstrable in detail."[14] Rather, what we shall see in this study is that changing ideas about the proper relation between the state, the market, and society played a key role, to paraphrase Biernacki, on their own – though not by themselves – in creating new material practices.[15] In short, we need a constructivist, as opposed to a purely rationalist, account of policy change in these countries.

What we see in these countries, in my view, are the local, adaptive man- ifestations in specific political, economic, and social settings of a larger global ideational shift – put somewhat differently, the Anglo-American cases can be considered particular species of a larger ideational genus developing internationally in this period. In this respect, the "unexpected isomorphism" of the British, Canadian, Australian, and New Zealand neoliberal shifts can be traced in large part to the local construction and implementation of an emergent, increasingly "universalistic (global) model" of neoliberal economics.[16] As John Meyer and his colleagues in the "world society" literature have argued, the isomorphism we see in states' political, economic, and social institutions and policies – despite the fact that these states vary on a wide variety of other material scores – is often the consequence of common cultural or ideational forces that diffuse from the global to the national level. As states increasingly define their fundamental purposes, identities, and goals in ways consonant with the values of the emerging "world society," their policies, ideational orientations, and institutional structures begin to converge around the global norm.[17] In this view, then, the "wider [global] system defines, legitimates, and supports the identities of [individuals, organizations and nation-states]; constructs appropriate purposes and technologies for them; and helps enforce their sovereignty, responsibility, and control capacities."[18] From this perspective, Anglo-American neoliberalism can be seen as the local working-out and implementation of an emerging global set of economic ideas and norms.

This view, however, must be immediately qualified and complicated. Even supposedly universalistic global norms and cultural trends are instantiated in specific national settings, and, as Martha Finnemore emphasizes, the ways in which this does (or does not) occur are likely to be characterized by contestation, (re)interpretation, and agency – in a word, by politics.[19] In her terms, isomorphism does not imply equifinality: "different and shifting solutions will be tried in different places, and local context becomes important in identifying the particular solutions that will be tried in each place."[20] Each society is likely to filter, interpret, and construct (and reconstruct) the common set of global norms through its own institutions, political and partisan configurations, policy traditions, and a host of other critical "mediation points."[21] As Colin Hay has argued – identifying a number of factors that, as we will see, made for diversity within Anglo-American neoliberalism – pressures for convergence will not produce truly isomorphic results since they

   are likely: (1) to impinge upon domestic economies in rather different
   ways; (2) to challenge or reinforce distinctive national "models" and

practices to different degrees and in often divergent ways; (3) to be understood and interpreted differently in different national/regional contexts;
and (4) to be responded to differently, even where common understandings are reached, since different states have rather different strategic
capacities for implementing responses.[22]

Put simply, even if we accept the existence of tendencies toward isomorphism deriving from a world society, we must investigate the contingent, site-specific, eminently contestable, and political ways in which
these global influences manifest themselves at the local level to produce
diversity and heterogeneity. What we will see in this book is just this:
within an increasingly global trend toward neoliberalism – a trend to
which Britain and New Zealand, in particular, were early contributors –
the specific neoliberal programs of each differed in important ways. In
both respects – both in the common move toward neoliberalism and
in the variations within that framework evinced in each country – ideational factors proved key. We now turn to a more detailed discussion
of these ideational frameworks, how they help create social "reality"
(particularly new economic policies), and how political and social elites
can act as significant change agents, seeking to reorient these ideational
structures while at the same time operating within and being constrained by them.

The Political-Economic Imaginary

A *political-economic imaginary*, as I define it, is a set of interrelated ideas
concerning the proper relationship between the state, society, and
the economy, particularly the appropriate extent and form of state
regulation of socioeconomic life and the legitimate objectives of state
economic policy. In structuring ideas about the appropriateness, desirability, and efficacy of government actions vis-à-vis society and the
market, a political-economic imaginary provides the "well-established
meanings and social relations out of which representations" of the state
and economy are constructed.[23]

A political-economic imaginary is, in many ways, a species of what
Cornelius Castoriadis has called the "social imaginary":

> [that construction] which gives a specific orientation to each institutional
> system, ... which is the creation of each historical period, its singular man-
> ner of living, of seeing and conducting its own experience, its world, and

its relations with this world, this originary structuring component, ... the source of that which presents itself in every instance as an indisputable and undisputed meaning.[24]

The concept of the social imaginary forms the centrepiece of Castoriadis's argument that the social world cannot be understood solely as a series of rationalist responses to a variety of a priori, inherent human needs. Such a purely functionalist understanding of human society ignores the fact that beyond such obvious basic human needs as food and shelter, virtually all of the rest of life's pursuits and "needs" are ones we ourselves create together – that is, ones we socially construct as valuable, desirable, and worthy of our time and effort. In fact, even the ways people go about satisfying their basic needs – for instance, the infinite ways people choose to satisfy their hunger, often to the total rejection of other people's ways – reveal the limitations of a purely functionalist explanation.[25] Even in cases in which social norms and practices can be seen as rational means to particular ends, the questions arise: which ends, and determined by whom? As Castoriadis puts it, "[T]he whole of social life cannot be understood as a system that is purely functional, an integrated series of arrangements geared to satisfying the needs of society. For every interpretation of this type immediately leads to the question: functional in relation to what and to what end? ... Every society up to now has attempted to give an answer to a few fundamental questions: *Who are we as a collectivity? ... What do we want; what do we desire; what are we lacking?*"[26] Simply put, the answers to these questions are generally provided by the social imaginary.

In this book I build upon these notions of the imaginary to address the relationship between state, society, and economy. Without denying the potential usefulness of rationalist analysis, my contention is that a particular social construction – a political-economic imaginary – plays a crucial role in structuring the norms and ideas that govern economic policy.[27] Specifically, my argument is that the ideas inhering in a political-economic imaginary constitute an image of the political and economic worlds that acts as a powerful conceptual lens, constituting actors and their identities, prescribing and proscribing the behaviour of state and non-state actors based on conceptions of appropriateness and efficacy, and, perhaps most importantly, constraining and guiding what can (and cannot) be thought about the proper ends of the state and economy.[28] A political-economic imaginary contains the answers – whether explicitly acknowledged or not[29] – to those fundamental questions

Castoriadis argues are asked by each society. In fact, Castoriadis's questions are particularly susceptible to a political-economic cast. Who are we as a collectivity? (And, it might be added, *are* we truly a collectivity?) What are our responsibilities to one another? What do we desire as a society? What are our economic and social goals? What role should the state – or private markets – play in the pursuit of these goals? What values and norms inform these choices – and our preferred means of attaining them?[30] These questions are eminently political-economic in nature.

In fact, as I will be at pains to point out in this book, seemingly value-free, objective decisions over purportedly technical aspects of economic policies embody (whether actors recognize it or not) implicit norms and values deriving from the dominant political-economic imaginary. As Mark Blyth cogently argues, even such seemingly "objective" and non-ideological factors as money and "material resources ... are powerful only to the extent that they can be mobilized to specific ends. However, neither material resources nor the self-interest of agents can dictate those ends or tell agents what future to construct. Ideas do this, and this is ultimately why they are important."[31]

The fascinating irony, however, is that those norms and values, because they derive from a largely unconscious, unstated political-economic imaginary, can appear eminently rational, objectively true, and thus beyond contestation. As Castoriadis puts it, "it is the economy that exhibits most strikingly the domination of the imaginary at every level – precisely because it claims to be entirely and exhaustively rational."[32] As we shall see, neoliberal policies in Britain, Canada, Australia, and New Zealand were presented – and pursued – with a certainty and conviction usually reserved for settled religious dogma. Neoliberal norm entrepreneurs in these countries essentially constructed neoliberalism as economic "fact" – and thus attempted to immunize their policy approach from ideological debate or partisan contestation by claiming that opposition to the "facts" was nonsensical. As Australian prime minister Bob Hawke would dismissively retort, when challenged by opponents of his program of economic rationalism, "What are they in favor of – economic irrationalism?"[33] Yet, as Jacqueline Best argues, "economics is not, in fact, a neutral set of techniques that can simply be applied to different situations. It is instead a profoundly contested field of knowledge. Different economic theories not only reflect and empower different economic and political values but are also based on different ontological assumptions about the nature of economic actors."[34] Put differently, economic theories are very much social, constructed phenomena.

Thus, these fundamental questions – the Castoriadian "who are we?" and "what do we want?" or questions regarding the proper role of the state vis-à-vis the market – are not answered in a political or social vacuum. It is for this reason that I employ the term *political-economic imaginary* to highlight the ineluctable *political* aspects of imaginaries. Put simply, economic answers to these questions cannot be had without a direct engagement with the political. "What we want" and "what is appropriate and desirable" from an economic point of view involve a political-economic nexus that cannot be unwound. What sort of economy a society should have, how the state should regulate that economy, what levels and kinds of state interventions should exist, what economic and social goals are deemed desirable and appropriate, and what values the economic and social choices of citizens in a particular locale have are inextricably bound up with political institutions, political contestation, and political actors. Thus, the term *political-economic imaginary* highlights that any economic imaginary contains within itself an embedded set of norms, values, expectations, and ideas about politics as well as economics and, in particular, about the nature and extent of the intersections between the political and economic worlds.[35] The term is thus *political* and *economic* in nature.

While I hope to show the utility of the political-economic imaginary concept to the study of economic policy orientations, it is important to deal with an important potential critique. One consistent criticism of constructivist accounts of norms, ideas, and their constraining influence is that they often end up being highly structuralist, wittingly or not erasing any real agency. Thus, while constructivism prides itself on the idea of the co-constitution as a way to break through the agency-structure logjam,[36] constructivism's treatment of ideational constructs often seems to produce over-mighty structures and under-powerful agents. What appears to be a solution to the agency-structure problem can all too easily overspecify the constraining effects of ideational structures, undertheorizing the ability of agents to act with some degree of relative autonomy within those structures.[37] The problem is potentially even more severe with respect to structural change. If constructivist accounts end up privileging the ideational construct to the detriment of agency, then it becomes very difficult indeed to explain changes within or to the ideational construct. One particularly unsatisfying option is to ignore the sources of ideational change, treating them as exogenous and perhaps not terribly important.

The same problem is potentially present when using the heuristic concept of the imaginary, of whatever sort. As a set of foundational ideas about the very nature, form, and meaning of social life, the imaginary could easily be conceived in terms that diminish or even exclude the possibility of change to those ideas and the structure they instantiate. Castoriadis's analysis of imaginaries, for instance, has no place for change or agents of change. Imaginaries are assumed to *be*, and while, of course, they are held to be social constructions par excellence, there is no real analysis of how they came into existence or, more to the point of this book, how they might change. From norms of war and peace to the appropriate level of state ownership of industry, how any of these ideas might change often remains unspecified.

The difficulty in analysing and accounting for change is not insurmountable, however. First, the concept of the imaginary – perhaps to a greater extent than the notion of norms more generally – implies ideas and values of a broad, first-order nature. Thus, we should expect them to be "sticky" over time, relatively less changing and mutable than other, less primary ideas. Musical preferences, one presumes, are more mutable than political-economic imaginaries – Australians could evince a predilection for new musical styles more quickly than they could change their conception of the proper role of the state in regulating industrial relations. Yet, the stability – the stickiness – of imaginaries is a relative, rather than absolute, one. Imaginaries, as foundational ideational constructs, may be more stable and consistent over time than other sets of more ephemeral, less deeply held ideas (*relatively* more sticky), but this in no way implies that they are immutable and resistant to the forces of change and change agents (that is, *absolutely* sticky). Were imaginaries entirely resistant to change, a whole range of formerly normative structures and resultant practices – from slavery and apartheid[38] to the post-war economic policy "consensus" discussed in chapter two – would still be intact. Change does in fact take place – and it is one of constructivism's great challenges, and promises, to explain it. It is here that politics and political contestation make their appearance.

The Ideas-Praxis Linkage

The shift to new ideas and norms is often purposive and intentional: it often occurs as the result of conscious action by individuals (or groups) committed to normative change. Human beings are not automatons, captives of an overarching structure of ideas and institutions they are incapable of influencing. Rather – in what is perhaps the central argument of the entire constructivist school of analysis – agents and structures are part of a recursive, never-ending cycle of mutual influence, of co-constitution.[39] While the effects of structure are thus inescapable and a sine qua non of social life, at the same time, "[a]ctors are not simply the bearers of social roles and enactors of social norms; they are also the artful and active interpreters of them."[40] One might add that actors not only actively interpret extant roles and norms, they seek to re-interpret and re-construct them as well. Actors can find themselves at odds with existing normative structures and consciously work to reorient them wholesale (as opposed to conforming to them, attempting to escape them, or working to alter them only marginally). As Finnemore and Sikkink put it in their seminal work on the topic, these "norm entrepreneurs" are "agents having strong notions about appropriate or desirable behavior in their community" who set out to reorder extant practices through a restructuring of relevant, commonly held (that is to say, intersubjective) norms.[41] As a wide variety of case studies of normative change have shown,[42] norm entrepreneurs work to change the dominant values operative in a society or system – what I here call the imaginary – consciously attempting to reorient these values in a direction they believe more appropriate and desirable.

In the pages that follow, I seek more fully to delineate the role of norm entrepreneurs in the altering of a society's political-economic imaginary. Specifically, I develop a heuristic of ideational change, focusing on various possible ways in which norm entrepreneurs may be able to change political-economic imaginaries through both persuasion and coercive constructions, and through them to policy change and change in political and economic systems – what I call the "idea-praxis linkage." Here I resist the temptation to label this relationship a "process." As will become clear later, the nature of the link between ideas and praxis is recursive and often nonlinear. *Process* often connotes a clearer cause-effect relationship than I intend to describe here. Moreover, I do not claim that this heuristic representation is in any way universally generalizable – that is, that it is some sort of nomothetic assertion of what must apply in all cases. Rather, my notion of ideational change is indicative of *some* of the *possible* ways in which normative structures change, acknowledging the futility in fully accounting for the multiple

Figure 1. The Ideas-Praxis Linkage

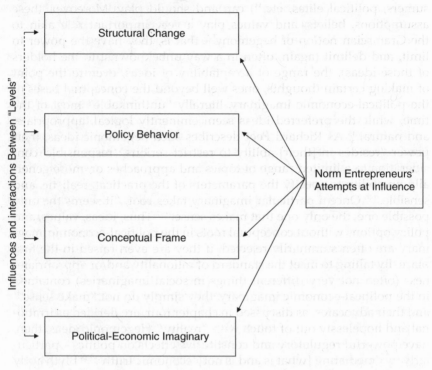

ways in which change can occur and fully appreciating the role that contingency and variation play in such phenomena.

Figure 1, illustrates a schematic conception of this linkage, showing the relationship between the political-economic imaginary, interpretations of "objective reality," the policy options and prescriptions decision makers employ, and the effect this linkage has on the nature of material economic and political structure.[43] While this linkage should be applicable to a wide range of state policies and actors, I limit my discussion primarily to that of economic policy and the role played by norm entrepreneurs in that particular regard.

At the base, so to speak, of this linkage is the political-economic imaginary itself. Here, as discussed previously, we encounter those core values, orientations, usually unspoken (even unconscious) assumptions and beliefs about how political and economic systems should be structured and the roles that various actors (states, corporations, consumers, political elites, etc.[44]) can and should play. Moreover, these assumptions, beliefs, and values play a very important role akin to the Gramscian notion of hegemony – that is, they have the power to limit, and delimit (again, often in a way unbeknownst to the holders of those ideas), the range of acceptability of ideas, even to the point of making certain thoughts, ones well beyond the conceptual bases of the political-economic imaginary, literally "unthinkable" most of the time, while the preferred ideas seem eminently logical, appropriate, and natural.[45] As Richard Peet describes such hegemonic ideas, their power "resides in [their] ability to restrict serious, 'responsible' consideration to a limited range of topics and approaches or, more generally, an ability to specify the parameters of the practical, realistic, and sensible."[46] Once a particular imaginary takes root, "it seems the only possible one, the only one that makes sense."[47] Thus, ideas, values, and policy options without conceptual roots in the political-economic imaginary are often summarily rejected, if they are even raised in the first place. By failing to meet the standard of rationality and/or appropriateness (often not very different things in social imaginaries) contained in the political-economic imaginary, they simply do not "make sense," and their advocates, as discussed in chapter four, are derided as irrational and hopelessly out of touch with "reality." Hegemonic ideas, then, have powerful regulatory and constitutive effects on politics – particularly by "mediating [what is and is not] 'economic truth'."[48] Blyth aptly describes the impact of such ideational priors: "Economic ideas ... [act] as interpretive frameworks that describe and systematically account for the workings of the economy by defining its constitutive elements and providing a general understanding of their 'proper' (and therefore improper) interrelations. Such ideas provide agents with both a scientific and a normative critique of the existing economy and polity, and blueprint that specifies how these elements *should* be constructed."[49] The result is that imaginaries can have "a constitutive power in shaping economic orders and the manner of their embedding in wider ensembles of social relations" – that is, imaginaries "can involve not only construal but construction."[50]

Next, based on that core imaginary, a particular view of "reality" can emerge. Cognitive psychology has long attested to the filtering and structuring effects that prior conceptions and ideas can have.[51] In a similar way, the core ideas in the political-economic imaginary serve to help actors make sense of the world around them by organizing a complex set of information and facts, limiting and filtering external "stimuli" and perceptions, and interpreting that "data" in a way that maintains consistency with – and in so doing, reinforces the apparent rationality and legitimacy of – the political-economic imaginary. Political-economic imaginaries play an important role in what Bob Jessop refers to as "complexity reduction" – that is, dealing with "the hypercomplexity of the natural and social worlds and the impossibility of observing and explaining these worlds (and their interaction) in real time."[52]

Imaginaries thus help actors construct conceptual frames, ones that simplify and interpret reality. These frames, operating at a more specific, contextualized level than that of the imaginary, consist of "specific metaphors, symbolic representations, and cognitive cues used to render or cast behavior and events in an evaluative mode and to suggest alternative modes of action."[53] They "render events of occurrences meaningful, ... organiz[ing] experience and guid[ing] action, whether individual or collective."[54] In this way, the conceptual frame based in the political-economic imaginary takes the general values and orientations of the political-economic imaginary and embeds them into specific "realities," all the while representing reality in ways consistent with the political-economic imaginary, constructing interpretations of that reality using the basic normative "building blocks"[55] provided by the political-economic imaginary, and discounting or attempting to block perceptions incongruent with the fundamental precepts of the political-economic imaginary. The result, as in the cases of the neoliberal norm entrepreneurs, is that if actors are able to persuade others to accept their "definition of the situation" – that is, their particular frame – they gain a great deal of control, as the definition of a problem usually implies a particular solution.[56]

Take, for example, the relationship between a particular political-economic imaginary and the conceptual frame that is rooted in it. A society whose imaginary deems it a state responsibility to own and manage significant parts of national industry will likely view the subsidization of unprofitable state-owned companies – and the preservation of jobs in them – very differently than a society whose core imaginary emphasizes the inherent superiority of private enterprise. If inefficiencies and fiscal shortfalls in these industries emerge, the society with the interventionist imaginary is likely to frame the public policy problem very differently than the society with the pro-market imaginary. Calls for privatization, for instance, will "play" quite differently between the two societies as the central elements in each society's core imaginary produce quite different frames of interpretation of actual events – and indeed quite different representations of "reality."

The practical result of this different framing and representation is obvious: a different conceptual frame can often produce dramatically different behaviour on the part of social and political agents – the third "stage" in Figure 1. Thus, a particular frame facilitates (indeed impels) policy-makers to generate a set of policy options consistent with that frame (and, beyond it, with the relevant political-economic imaginary). Just as conceptual frames inconsistent with the core political-economic imaginary are often "unthinkable" and ideas counter to it "irrational," so public policy options inconsistent with the chief elements of the political-economic imaginary are likely to be ignored, discarded, ridiculed, or even, in perhaps most cases, never even "thought about." This is what we will see with respect to the Anglo-American democracies. Neoliberal ideas were used as "cognitive locks"[57] by norm entrepreneurs who claimed that "there is no alternative" to the neoliberal "reality" of economic "facts." Once this argument from "facticity" took hold, economic rationalism served to cast any policy alternatives as, in the quote from Bob Hawke mentioned earlier, quite literally irrational.

Thus, "norms shape actors' awareness and acceptance of the methods and technologies on which they might rely to accomplish their objectives."[58] The connection is clear: frames provide a means by which social problems are refracted through the key normative elements of the imaginary. Thus, in the search for ways to address the social problem – indeed, whether something is even held to be a problem – the way the problem is framed is of central importance in the shaping of a response.

The fourth "stage" in the linkage depicted in Figure 1 is the structural change brought about by public policy. All public policies have at least some form of structural influence. Even seemingly minor policy changes alter, in their own ways and to varying degrees, the edifice of the institutions that structure political life. Their effect may not be large; these changes may not reform the entire edifice. But their effect is present nonetheless. This is even truer with respect to wholesale policy changes. As we shall see with neoliberalism in Britain, Canada, Australia, and New Zealand, a large number of significant (and many less significant) pro-market policy reforms had the cumulative effect of dramatically reordering key social and economic institutions and the constraints they placed on the behaviour of social actors.

Having briefly reviewed the connection between the four elements in the ideas-praxis linkage – Imaginary, Frame, Policy Behaviour, and Structural Change – it is imperative to point out that the linkages posited here and shown in Figure 1 are not to be construed in any strictly causal or even necessarily linear way. While I position the imaginary at the base of this linkage, and while I discuss frames and policy behaviour deriving from previous stages (and ultimately from the imaginary), there is nothing necessary or even particularly causal about the linkage. Instead, as indicated by the linked arrows on the left-hand side of the figure, the connections are recursive, interactive, and characterized by multiple effects of co-constitution and mutual influence. Each element in the linkage can potentially have important effects on the other elements, linking the "levels" in a highly complex, contingent way that goes beyond strict, linear causation.[59]

Thus, changes in the core imaginary will likely effect change in the representational frame, perhaps leading to policy change, which over time can lead to structural change. However, such effects can only be discussed in a probabilistic, contingent way – as changes that *may* happen in *certain* cases. Recognizing the contingent nature of this interaction, we cannot state that (a) the linkages are necessary or (b) that "reverse-direction" effects will not occur. That is, the linkages posited here are not inextricably linked in a causal way such that change x in imaginary I can be said to lead to corresponding change y in frame F, to change z in policy P, and so on. At best, one can only hypothesize in a probabilistic way that such changes will occur. It is entirely possible that change x in imaginary I leads to change y' in Frame F, or no change at all, or perhaps an unforeseen change in some other frame implicated in the imaginary. One cannot exactly specify a priori the effect that a change at one "level" will have on others, nor can the effects of change at that level be isolated or limited to only that location. Thus, a shift from a statist to a neoliberal political-economic imaginary is likely to affect how public ownership of industry is framed, as discussed previously, but to argue that it *must* do so leads to a form of ideational determinism that most constructivists, myself included, would wish to avoid. In particular, to do so eliminates the exercise of agency and contestation – two features of political life that, I argue, are important elements in the social construction of politics.

Moreover, effects can be seen in the "reverse" direction. The model is a recursive one: changes at "higher" stages of the schematic can have important impacts on "lower" stages. In fact, in the case of

Anglo-American neoliberalism, changes at different points of the link-age played important roles in reinforcing and ultimately legitimating changes at other points. Policy changes can become so institutional-ized – so taken-for-granted as part of the policy landscape in a coun-try – that they eventually come to be part of the political-economic imaginary itself, even for those who may have opposed them initially. Deregulationist labour market policies in Britain, Australia, and New Zealand, for instance – changes at the Policy Behaviour and Structural Change points of the schematic – ended up reconstituting the rights and identities of workers in such a thoroughgoing way that they con-tributed to workers' (at least partial) acceptance of the new political-economic imaginary of neoliberalism. In this case, then, a complex, recursive pattern can be seen: A newly emergent political-economic imaginary provided the basis for significant labour market policy change – workers, for instance, were coerced by legal requirements to "freely" participate in a deregulated labour market. Over time, how-ever, as these changes became taken-for-granted as "normal" and even appropriate, any talk of returning to the regulated labour markets of old – indeed, any widespread public support for such a move – virtu-ally vanished. In other words, the effects of the policy changes proved recursive as they served to further legitimate and reinforce the underly-ing neoliberal political-economic imaginary that provided their initial rationale and justification.

Contestation and Normative Change

This leads to the role of norm entrepreneurs. As just mentioned, the effects in the ideas-praxis linkage are neither necessary nor determin-istic. To imply otherwise would be to deny what is at the heart of this analysis: agency, contestation, and their effects on social construction. At each point in the linkage of co-constitution, norm entrepreneurs can exercise their influence in the service of normative change. In other words, the impact of norm entrepreneurs is multispacial and multitem-poral. Their influence – as represented by the arrows connecting the various boxes in Figure 1 – can be brought to bear at a variety of points and times. Reflecting something often implied but not often explicitly articulated, norm entrepreneurs are not solely interested in, or limited to, attempts to change the central imaginary. While most extant studies reflect this level of influence – the fight against apartheid, for instance, is an attempt to change a central element in a society's moral imaginary –

norm entrepreneurs actually attempt to effect change at multiple sites. While a change in the core imaginary may be the ultimate goal – in that norm entrepreneurs recognize the effects that changes in the imaginary are likely to have "down the line" in policy and structure – they are by no means limited to this strategy alone. Instead, as will be shown in the case of neoliberalism, norm entrepreneurs seek to make changes at multiple sites, reflecting their (perhaps not always conscious) recognition of the ultimately recursive nature of social constitution. Thus, a savvy neoliberal norm entrepreneur is unlikely to concentrate solely on changing the central political-economic imaginary – a site that is usually quite resistant to change much of time anyway – while neglecting attempts at influence elsewhere. Rather she will be entrepreneurial at multiple levels, working at the level of the frame to repackage and re-represent "reality" as "market-driven," seeking at the policy settings level to effect deregulatory policy "reforms," all the while aiming at institutional and structural change, implicitly aware of the recursive effects these changes can and often do have on the ultimate target: the political-economic imaginary.

This emphasis on the multiple ways in which norm entrepreneurs can make their influence felt is further reinforcement of the previous argument that the linkages between these levels are not automatic or deterministic, but rather highly contingent. Simply put, contestation is possible – and generally pervasive – at all sites. As Sum and Jessop put it, ideational constructs and "discursive practices are always contestable and open to the play of agency."[60] Not only between contesting normative structures, but even within a single political-economic imaginary, corresponding frames, policies, and institutional structures are not inherently given or necessary. Political-economic imaginaries *make possible* particular frames, policies, and agent actions; they do not determine them – in Craig Parsons' words, "actors who share one idea as the 'master frame' … do not necessarily agree on more detailed actions therein."[61] As a result of this indeterminacy, space is opened for political contestation: the "outcomes of policy debates [are] inextricably also contestations of social power within the broader … imaginary."[62] A neoliberal political-economic imaginary may imply certain frames and policies, but as discussed later in this book, significant variations occur nonetheless. From the way inflation and unemployment were framed, to the ways parties dealt with trade unions, to the specific settings of monetary policy (and, indeed, whether monetary policy was even important), all varied among the neoliberal programs discussed here.

Thus, whether due to past policy traditions and institutional structures, partisan competition, international influences, even the personality of leaders (and surely a host of other factors), variation is not only possible, it is ubiquitous – and almost always a locus of contestation and "politics" in the most general sense of the word.

Such contestation is of course part of "normal politics" in most societies most of the time. This is particularly true when it comes to the framing and policy options stages. Here contestation is ongoing. In fact, virtually all of the political contestation we observe during a period of "normal politics" is dispute and debate over how to frame reality and what policy settings should be pursued. This "normal" contestation is deemed normal because it takes place within a relatively settled and undisputed political-economic imaginary. Debates, for instance, over the level of taxation, the generosity of social welfare benefits, or the wisdom of fiscal stimulus or austerity can and do generally take place without bringing into question the fundamental principles of the political-economic imaginary itself. As emphasized by Castoriadis, imaginaries usually operate behind the scenes, unseen and not directly apprehended – but all the while exercising their important influence, setting the terms of debate, and limiting the options agents perceive as possible and desirable. In these circumstances, the imaginary remains beyond debate. There are times, however – often times of crisis, as discussed in chapters two and four – when norm entrepreneurs move beyond such "normal politics," going beyond challenges to specific frames or public policies to the very taproot of how a particular set of norms and values constructs social reality.[63] It is in these rather unusual instances that norm entrepreneurs attempt to alter the very imaginaries themselves.[64]

A final important point arises from this discussion of contestation. A key element in the efforts that norm entrepreneurs expend in attempting to change elements in the ideas-praxis linkage – and in whether their efforts meet with success or failure – is the nature of the political "organization of power" of the society and polity in which they operate.[65] As is discussed in some detail in chapters four and five, norm entrepreneurialism does not occur within a political and institutional vacuum.

First, the success or failure of these attempts at normative change are not due solely to the persuasiveness – or lack thereof – of the ideas themselves. As various analysts of norm entrepreneurs have pointed out, the success or failure of these attempts is in large part dependent on a variety of factors affecting the ability of norm entrepreneurs to make their voices heard, to mobilize public support for their efforts, and to directly influence policy-makers and the policy-making process. As Parsons puts it, "ideas matter most when espoused by those with power – presumably because they can press other actors to align on their ideas."[66] Or, in Judith Goldstein's somewhat stronger formulation, "ideas influence policy only when they are carried by individuals or groups with political clout."[67] Norm entrepreneurs lacking such political resources are likely to find their efforts stymied – not because of the merits of their arguments per se, but due to their lack of access, resources, and political capital. In contrast, well-placed norm entrepreneurs – those with political power, media exposure, and institutional and bureaucratic support at their disposal – are much better placed (though by no means ensured) to effect the normative shifts they desire. One need only contrast the efforts to effect normative change of Margaret Thatcher to that of Theodore Kaczynski, the Unabomber. While the actual substance of their ideas surely affected their chances of general acceptance, the fact remains that the political resources available in the service of normative change differed considerably between a prime minister with a solid parliamentary majority in a democratic polity and a lone Luddite living in the wilderness and committing eccentric acts of terror. As politicians from time immemorial have recognized, the message one brings may prove secondary to the ability one has to propagate and implement it.

Second, an analysis of the structure of political competition must also consider the impact of partisanship and partisan ideology on the efforts of norm entrepreneurs. Most extant analyses of norm entrepreneurs have largely "black-boxed" the domestic partisan political environment,[68] ignoring the often intense political battles that take place over the construction of new normative structures – battles that oftentimes reflect partisan divisions and partisan competition that take place within a particular society and polity. What is clear in the case of Anglo-American liberalism is that partisanship did indeed matter when it came to the adoption of a new neoliberal political-economic imaginary. However, its impact was not uniform, consistent, or entirely in keeping with standard expectations of partisan behaviour. In short, by considering both the resources available to norm entrepreneurs, as well as the partisan environments in which they operate, this book thus pays particular attention to the political opportunity structures in which neoliberal change was effected in all four countries.

How to Be a Norm Entrepreneur: Persuasion or Coercion (or Both)

Given this structure of interactions between different levels of ideas and public policies, between norm entrepreneurs and the normative structures they seek to construct and re-construct, how, then, do norm entrepreneurs actually *do* the task itself? How do norm entrepreneurs go about changing dominant norms and values?

Traditionally, the literature on norm entrepreneurs has focused on *persuasion* as the primary instrument by which entrepreneurs effect ideational change.[69] For these analysts, a Habermasian perspective on the persuasiveness of ideas informs their views – the emphasis is on "[c]ommunicative action [which] requires exchange of views in a common 'lifeworld' that involves an absence of coercion but with some amount of empathy and the ability to see matters from the other party's point of view."[70]

For Finnemore and Sikkink, in their central work on norm entrepreneurialism, persuasion "is the mission of norm entrepreneurs: they seek to change the utility functions of other players to reflect some new normative commitment." If their attempts at persuasion prove successful, the result is that "agent action becomes social structure, ideas become norms, and the subjective becomes the intersubjective."[71] This process of persuasion involves the kind of framing discussed previously: norm entrepreneurs "call attention to issues or even 'create' issues by using language that names, interprets, and dramatizes them." These resulting cognitive frames are an "essential component of norm entrepreneurs' political strategies, since, when they are successful, ... [they] are adopted as new ways of talking about and understanding issues."[72] Key to this process of persuasion is convincing a critical mass of other actors that the new normative perspective is appropriate, desirable, and preferable to the norms and values that currently obtain. In what is often a very calculated, strategic project in a contested political environment, norm entrepreneurs attempt to persuade this critical mass that their views are preferable – they engage in "strategic social construction."[73] "Coercive power is important to being *heard*," but primarily in that it provides "the opportunity to *persuade*" – that is, power is conceived fundamentally as one of the "important facilitators of persuasion."[74]

Recently, however, some scholars have begun to question the analytical attention paid to persuasion as the fundamental mechanism of normative change. These critics argue that too heavy an emphasis on persuasion underestimates, in Craig Parsons's words, the role of "agency, conflict and power" in what is inevitably and "properly [a] political story."[75] It overlooks instances in which "ideas as weapons" is a more accurate description of normative shifts than persuasion.[76] Most notably, Krebs and Jackson have launched a very important critique of the dominant emphasis on persuasion within the literature on normative change.[77] They argue that a process in which "political actors deploy resonant rhetorical forms and thereby *persuade* their interlocutors of the correctness of their preferred course of action ... undoubtedly occurs in the political arena, [but] it is also rare."[78] Since "power and rank are omnipresent in the political sphere," to speak of changing normative structures without assessing the "[r]ules of exclusion and employment [that] dictate which argument can be proffered, under what conditions, and by whom" is to fundamentally misapprehend the true nature of the discourse in question.[79] Because relations of power are always present, instances of "pure" persuasion are actually the exception, rather than the rule. Instead, Krebs and Jackson argue, analysts need to be particularly attuned to "*all* speech, no matter how interlaced with power relations."[80]

Specifically, they argue that a very powerful exercise of rhetorical power is what they label "rhetorical coercion." Rather than deploying cogent arguments framed in such a way as to convert the hearer to the speaker's point of view, actors instead attempt to "maneuver each other onto more favorable rhetorical terrain and thereby close off routes of acceptable rebuttal." Because rhetoric is shaped and structured by shared meanings, understandings, or rhetorical commonplaces – intersubjective understandings that "both enable and constrain speakers' rhetorical possibilities" – not all arguments are equally plausible or likely to convince.[81] Only those arguments congruent with the structure of the existing discourse are acceptable, legitimate, or even seem rational. Thus, savvy rhetorical contestants can use the elements of the standard discourse to manipulate the discursive battle in such a way that their opponents have little choice but to accept the argument itself, no matter how reluctantly. As Krebs and Jackson describe the mechanism of rhetorical coercion, a "claimant" (C) competes with the "opposition" (O) observed by a "public" (P).

> Rhetorical coercion is successful when C's rhetorical moves deprive O of materials out of which to craft a reply that falls within the bounds of what P would accept. In the end, O finds itself, against its better judgment, endorsing (or at least acquiescing in) C's stance *regardless* of whether O

has been persuaded or believes the words it utters. ... [Thus], one argument "wins" not because its grounds are "valid" in the sense of satisfying the demands of universal reason or because it accords with the audience's prior normative commitments or material interests, but because its grounds are *socially* sustainable – because the audience deems certain rhetorical deployments acceptable and others impermissible.[82]

They show, for instance, how the Druze of Israel successfully manipulated the elements of national discourse to their advantage. By drawing on Israelis' commitment to the norm that citizens' rights derive from and are legitimated by fulfilling one's obligation of service to the state and community, the Druze successfully parlayed their record of service in the Israel Defense Forces (IDF) into a successful claim for greater citizenship rights. In a way that Christian and Muslim Arabs – who are not liable to be conscripted into the IDF – could not do, the Druze rhetorically coerced a reluctant Israeli Jewish community to accept their arguments for more equal political and social status. In effect, Israeli Jews had no other realistic options – they had been trapped "in a rhetorical cul-de-sac."[83] Normatively committed to the reciprocity of citizen rights and obligations, and unwilling to admit to the second-class status of non-Jewish citizens, Israeli policy-makers found themselves rhetorically coerced into granting greater rights to the Druze. Christian and Muslim Arabs, without the rhetorical weapon of military service, were consequently unable to exercise coercion in a similar way.[84]

Krebs and Jackson's contribution is a very important refinement to our understanding of how norm entrepreneurialism works. When this notion of coercion is combined with the more traditional focus on persuasion, a much broader range of analysis is opened and a number of new theoretical possibilities are identified – ones that I explore later in this chapter.

The recognition that both persuasion and coercion are potential instruments in the norm entrepreneur's tool kit invites us to broaden our analysis a step further. Recognizing that a fuller analysis of normative change has to include both persuasion and coercion, I submit that we should also introduce the distinction between rhetorical and material forms of persuasion and coercion into the mix. Specifically, as diagrammed in Figure 2, I believe that we can fruitfully distinguish not only between persuasion and coercion, but between rhetorical and material aspects of these practices. That is, persuasion and coercion should be disaggregated into rhetorical and material components, thus

Figure 2. Rhetorical and Material Forms of Persuasion and Coercion

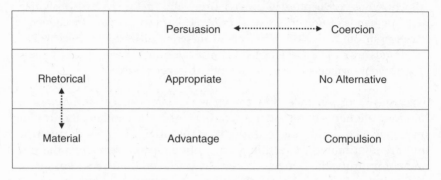

	Persuasion ◄·····················► Coercion	
Rhetorical ▲ ┆ ▼ Material	Appropriate	No Alternative
	Advantage	Compulsion

arriving at the four combinations shown in Figure 2 – rhetorical persuasion, material persuasion, rhetorical coercion, and material coercion.
These four, then, represent four *possible* strategies that norm entrepreneurs can utilize in the service of ideational change. It should be noted
that these four combinations in no way represent an exhaustive catalogue of the tools available to norm entrepreneurs. Rather, they serve
to help us explore the ways in which their various constituent elements
can interact. For this reason, no claim is made for comprehensiveness or
universality – as with Figure 1, this figure is indicative and suggestive
of conceptual possibilities.

Rhetorical persuasion and rhetorical coercion have just been discussed. The former represents the frame in which norm entrepreneurialism has traditionally been discussed. The latter is, of course, the
more recent concept deriving from Krebs and Jackson's 2007 analysis.
However, it is potentially useful to also consider the other two combinations – material persuasion and material coercion – and how they
interact with the rhetorical forms of influence.

Let us first consider material persuasion and its relationship to rhetorical persuasion. Material persuasion, as I conceive it, is encapsulated
in the notion of *advantage*. If rhetorical persuasion involves convincing
the audience that one's norms and values are "appropriate," then material persuasion involves making the new norms and values "advantageous."[85] Simply put, this involves an appeal to the kind of rational
self-interest that rationalist analysts promote and constructivist analysts tend to critique. Norm entrepreneurs, however, are not limited to
the confines of social science debate. They are acutely aware that to the

extent that new normative constructions can be made to appeal to self-interest, to the extent that adoption of these new norms can be framed as advantageous when compared to the old, then their chances of success are proportionately greater.

Many constructivist analyses of norm entrepreneurialism have focused on cases in which people adopt new norms either indifferent to or in opposition to what would seem to be their own interests. There was (and is) a good social science reason for this focus on cases of "pure" persuasion: constructivism's value as an analytical tool is based in large part on its ability to explain instances in which the dominant rationalist explanations fail – that is, when people do things apparently against their own interests. Thus, it makes a good deal of sense to focus on such phenomena as states voluntarily giving up sovereignty to supranational organizations in the name of international cooperation[86] or willingly divesting themselves of certain weapons in the name of morality and human rights.[87] These are the "hard cases" for rationalism – and constructivism has been remarkably successful in demonstrating how these cases can be understood as exemplars of normative shifts.

However, there is no reason to believe that normative shifts cannot be accompanied – even facilitated – by an appeal to material advantage. In fact, introducing material inducements and, as we shall see, coercion into a constructivist account does not make it less constructivist. Rather the inclusion of material factors makes a constructivist analysis more sensitive to the range of tools norm entrepreneurs have at their disposal. A nuanced – and ultimately, potentially more accurate – constructivist account thus must at least consider strategies that go beyond rhetoric and argumentation. As argued previously, practical-minded norm entrepreneurs seem to have long recognized this linkage between rhetorical and material and have exploited it to further their own normative goals. Religious leaders promote virtue and denounce sin as *both* good (in and of itself) *and* good for you (a better life and perhaps an eternal reward). Margaret Thatcher's arguments for free markets were couched both in terms of norms (entrepreneurialism and self-reliance are more virtuous than reliance on the state) *and* in terms of self-interest (deregulation will produce economic growth and a higher standard of living). The two arguments, far from standing in opposition to each other, are actually complementary in a way that practical politicians have long understood. Thus, if one asks whether the promotion of freer markets was the result of rational calculations *or* normative commitments, the real answer is probably both, not just for different people, but for the same individual. While there are certainly instances of actions motivated exclusively by one or the other,[88] successful attempts at persuasion often involve appeals to both, framing the "appropriate" moral choice as also the "advantageous" self-interested one (and vice versa).

This connection between appropriate and advantageous can be extended a step further. As the arrows linking the rhetorical and material in Figure 2 indicate, there can be a particular temporal linkage between the two. That is, the connection between rhetorical and material appeals is not limited to the fact that both kinds of appeals can be made, and happily coexist, simultaneously. Rather, one kind of persuasion can help produce the other: specifically, compliance with a new set of norms for self-interested reasons can, over time, actually emerge as a truly held set of moral or normative commitments. Individuals who, for some purely self-interested reason, adopt a particular set of behaviours often end up committing to the normative structure underlying and justifying them. The experience of acting within a new normative framework, even if one is initially uncommitted to it, can have the effect (particularly if that experience is a significantly positive one) of acclimatizing and eventually converting actors to the merits of those norms, in and of themselves.[89]

Some studies of democratic transition and consolidation, for instance, contend that a process of "learning" can take place, particularly through positive experiences with democracy and negative experiences with the alternatives. In her work on Greece, for example, Karakatsanis has shown that both leftist political elites and military officers – groups whose commitment to democratic values was, at best, doubtful for much of the 1950s and 1960s – came to internalize[90] democratic norms and practices as appropriate in principle and not just as a tactical manoeuvre. Both groups initially acquiesced to democratic practices as a self-interested expedient – the left to gain political influence when extra-parliamentary tactics proved unpopular and ineffective, and the military to extricate itself from the disastrous 1967–74 junta. However, as both leftist politicians and military officers began to appreciate the benefits of democracy and the dangers of the alternatives, their self-interested experiment with democratic participation turned into a true normative commitment. Their "persuasion" based on material advantage was eventually internalized as a part of their own normative structure.[91]

Moreover, the arrow can also run in the other direction. Those with strong normative commitments generally perceive distinct material advantages flowing from them. While many people experience rhetorical conversions – basing their behaviour on their own moral structures – they generally believe that good material results often come as well. Thus, even if motivated primarily by standards of appropriateness and not rational self-interest, their actions often produce (at least in their estimation, belief, or hope) positive material benefits. To use the examples mentioned previously, the sinner may become a saint for solid normative reasons. But she will likely believe that her new lifestyle has brought numerous earthly, not just spiritual, benefits in this life – to say nothing of the hoped-for benefits in the next. The neoliberal may base his advocacy solely on his own beliefs in the virtues of self-reliance. But he is likely also to believe that such self-reliance will reap real material rewards as well. Whether or not this belief in the material benefits of normative commitments is empirically sound – maybe the neoliberal will lose his job to global competition – is not, at this stage, particularly relevant. What matters is that actors *believe* such connections between the normative and the material to exist – which helps them to both legitimate (and psychically reward) their own actions and to proselytize the unconverted.

A similar distinction and interaction obtain, I believe, with respect to coercion (see Figure 2). Here, too, we can distinguish rhetorical and material forms. Rhetorical coercion is that discussed previously, characterized here by what I call the logic of "no alternative." As we shall see in the case of Anglo-American neoliberalism, norm entrepreneurs in these countries successfully coerced large numbers of reluctant and initially disbelieving actors by arguing that there was no alternative to the neoliberal reform program. As with the case of the Druze discussed by Krebs and Jackson, neoliberal norm entrepreneurs effectively pulled the rhetorical rug out from under their opponents, whose only initial response was to argue for the maintenance of an increasingly unpopular status quo. By successfully framing their own preferred policies as the only rational, legitimate options in a time of economic crisis, these elites successfully wrong-footed their opponents, rhetorically coercing them into acquiescing to their agenda.

Besides the concept of rhetorical coercion of Krebs and Jackson, however, I add an element of material coercion, or what I label *compulsion*. Scholars, of course, have long acknowledged the role that compulsion plays – either explicitly, or more often, implicitly – in political life.[92]

In most of these analyses, the image of such coercion is one in which governments command compliance with the threat of force lying just behind the command. My use of the term does not exclude the possibility of force being used to secure compliance. Such a possibility lies behind so many government mandates – from payment of taxes to road rules to the criminal code – that it cannot be ignored altogether.

That being said, the form of material coercion – or compulsion – I have in mind has to do with the more ordinary compulsion by which individuals are made to comply in practice with dictates arising from normative structures, whether they agree with those norms or not. In fact, across political and social life, in innumerable ways, the actions of individuals and groups are constrained by a set of laws and regulations whose basis resides in a particular set of normative values.[93] Regardless of whether individuals' own norms run parallel to those that inform the legal structure, they are compelled to observe these rules. Corporations may have little normative commitment to the environment but are compelled to install costly emission-reducing equipment. Libertarians who believe in strictly limited government have to pay federal income taxes anyway. Workers, to take an example that will figure later in this book, who operate in a deregulated labour market are compelled to play by the rules of that market – for instance, entering into individual contracts with employers – even if they are normatively opposed to them. While, at some level, physical force lies behind this compulsion, this conception of coercion is far too blunt for our purposes here. What matters is that compliance is ultimately secured regardless of whether one agrees with the normative basis for that compulsion. Sustained compliance – combined with a lack of credible alternatives, especially as constructed by the new political-economic imaginary – can then become taken-for-granted.

Many analysts of coercion argue that, in most cases, it is a strategy that is likely to fail.[94] Coercion generally lacks legitimacy, they argue, and in democratic systems in particular, legitimacy is critically important. Norm entrepreneurs generally cannot get their way through force – such attempts at normative shifts generally backfire and fail to produce the desired results.[95] However, this conclusion may not hold when material coercion is supplemented by rhetorical coercion. In this situation, individuals are the targets of two forms of coercion that work together in an integrated and mutually reinforcing way. Specifically, material coercion, or compulsion, is joined to a rhetorical coercion that presents a logic of no alternative. Under these conditions, the rules that

compel certain types of behaviour may not be liked, or their normative bases shared, but in the absence of credible alternatives – an effect
of successful rhetorical coercion *a la* Krebs and Jackson – no successful opposition or contestation emerges. Thus, the deunionized worker
compelled by the rules of a deregulated labour market into an individual employment contract may have a strong normative commitment
to (to say nothing of nostalgia for) the "good old days" of collective
bargaining and confrontational trade union action. However, she may
be successfully manoeuvred through rhetorical coercion into accepting
that no other option exists and that the current situation is "just the
way it is." In such a situation, the two forms of coercion reinforce each
other. On the one hand, the logic of no alternative embodied in rhetorical coercion justifies regulatory or legal compulsion: if there is no
appropriate or desirable alternative to deregulated labour markets, for
example, then this justifies laws that force workers to be "free." On the
other hand, this act of compulsion can reinforce the fundamental validity of the normative commitment – after a certain period of being "free,"
individual bargaining agents, workers may come to accept the status
quo as inevitable, as "the way it is." The old ways of doing things are
missed, but it may be accepted that they cannot return. To take another
example, no one likes to pay taxes. But, we are both materially and rhetorically coerced into paying them – materially, in that jail time awaits
noncompliants, and rhetorically, in that we acquiesce in the notion that
there are no other credible alternatives to raise sufficient government
revenue for the services we expect. Thus, material compulsion com-
bines with a rhetorical coercion to produce acquiescence.

Having considered, then, both persuasion and coercion from both
rhetorical and material standpoints, I wish to conclude this discussion
with a comment about the "bitter medicine" arrow connecting persuasion and coercion in Figure 2. This arrow points to the fact that coercion
(of either kind) and persuasion (of either kind) are potentially linked.[96]
Put simply, normative shifts that originate in coercion can, over time,
become persuasive and be accepted either rhetorically (as "appropriate") or materially (as "advantageous").[97] In particular, as the logic of
"no alternative" inherent in rhetorical coercion makes its power felt
throughout a community, particular normative structures can become
naturalized – they come to appear to be natural, organic parts of the
basic fabric of life in a way that makes alternatives difficult, if not
impossible, to conceive. They thereby acquire the quality of "taken-
for-grantedness"[98] – they become "sedimented"[99] as a naturalized part

of social, political, and economic life. As discussed previously, social imaginaries limit the range of what is considered normal, acceptable, appropriate, even rational. One of the ways they do this is by making the elements in the imaginary appear as organic, inherent parts of the "real" social world – to which alternatives cannot even be imagined.

My argument here is that, over time, norms and values, though originally arising through coercion, can eventually become persuasive as they gradually appear to be integral, organic parts of the "natural order of things." When such social constructions "have successfully defined the relationship of particular representations to reality as one of correspondence," and when "they are treated as if they neutrally or transparently reflected reality," they have become naturalized parts of political and social life – in a way akin to Gramscian "common sense."[100] As Sum and Jessop describe it, when an "imaginary is successfully operationalized and institutionalized, it transforms and *naturalizes* [its] elements into the moments of a specific economy."[101] In this way, new normative structures – ones that frequently "rest on defeated and repressed alternatives"[102] – can reach "the moment of extreme ideological closure" when contestation largely ceases and the new norms appear unremarkable, perhaps even unnoticed, parts of the social landscape.[103]

In this regard, one thinks of the normative values of equal rights inherent in the American civil rights movement of the 1950s and 1960s. Initially, this radical normative shift was accomplished primarily through material and rhetorical coercion. Materially, agents of the state physically enforced the edicts of the new norms – most obviously, troops were posted to ensure the integration of previously segregated schools. Rhetorically, civil rights leaders effectively dramatized the gap between the ideal of equal justice for all and the reality of racial discrimination with, among other things, demonstrations for basic rights that were repressed with police violence. Similar to the dilemma faced by Israeli Jews in Krebs and Jackson's account of the Druze, white Americans were rhetorically manoeuvred into admitting the validity of the demonstrators' claims for equal justice or risk denying a fundamental tenet of the American political imaginary. However, one could argue that, over time, this normative shift based on coercion has, by means of both rhetorical and material persuasion, translated (albeit incompletely and imperfectly) into a far more widespread normative commitment to equal rights for all. While the coerced integration of segregated schools and public spaces was truly a "bitter medicine" for segregationists, the long run effect was persuasion of both the rhetorical and material varieties: far larger numbers of people today likely believe that equality is both "appropriate" and socially "advantageous." What had seemed radical and pernicious, I would argue, has been naturalized as a fundamental part of a common normative commitment. Moreover, these new norms were gradually embedded into the structures and practices of political institutions, a process that further delegitimizes and excludes the old ways of thinking.[104]

As we shall see, the same process of naturalization is potentially underway with respect to neoliberalism. Over time, the coercive elements of the neoliberal political-economic imaginary shift can give way to a naturalized sense that "this is the way the world works" – that is, the original political contestation over a new and competing normative structure can be forgotten as the new structure is accepted as reasonable, desirable, and eminently organic.[105] If and when this occurs – when the formerly contested and controversial becomes seen as natural and organic, when the new norms are instantiated in the social imaginary – then norm entrepreneurs can be said to have been successful. It is the efforts of norm entrepreneurs in constructing a new neoliberal political-economic imaginary – and, as integral parts of that project, their attempts to alter the imaginary's related frames, policy behaviour, and structural changes, as shown in Figure 1 – with which this book is primarily concerned.

Analysing the Construction of Neoliberal Political-Economic Imaginaries

The analysis of the neoliberal shift presented in this book is based on a variety of data and information sources, including economic data, party documents and publications, transcripts of parliamentary debates, and journalistic and other secondary accounts. However, the primary source is an extensive series of in-depth personal interviews with political elites in all four countries. In all, more than 110 interviews were conducted over the course of several years in Britain (March–July 1997), Canada (November 1997–January 1998), Australia (March–October 1998), and New Zealand (November 1998).

Those interviewed were almost entirely former cabinet ministers from across the political spectrum in each country – including four former prime ministers – as well as a number of high-ranking economic ministry bureaucrats and trade union officials. A significant number of these respondents held important positions in the reforming governments of the 1980s. However, in an explicit attempt to explore the nature and magnitude of the break with the past that these policies represented, interviews were also conducted with a wide range of politicians from both sides of politics who had served in governments of the 1960s and 1970s. In an effort to secure the most candid and forthcoming responses – and at the explicit request of some respondents – interviewees were promised anonymity in the reporting of their comments. This commitment proved to be particularly important to current office holders and especially to politicians in Britain and Australia, as many interviews were conducted there in the run-ups to these countries' 1997 and 1998 general elections, respectively. Respondents are, however, generally identified in the text in a way that preserves their anonymity while indicating their party affiliation (when applicable) and their primary role in government, the civil service, or other organizations.

My analysis of the neoliberal political-economic imaginary shift begins in the next chapter by considering the pre-1980s state of economic policies in Britain, Canada, Australia, and New Zealand. In all four countries, the post-war period was a period of "consensus" politics, characterized by an all-party commitment to active state intervention in economic affairs. While each country faced its own particular policy challenges, a similar political-economic imaginary assuming the necessity and desirability of active state economic intervention existed in each case. Emerging from these political-economic imaginaries was the all-party commitment to full employment and the maintenance of the social welfare state. Closely linked to it was Keynesian demand management, a policy consensus that rested on the belief that the state could play a positive role in stimulating the national economy in times of economic downturn in order to maintain full employment. Governments of all parties were convinced of the overwhelming economic and moral imperative of full employment and felt duty bound to stimulate the economy when necessary, even at the eventual cost of government debt and higher inflation. Finally, there was a perceived need for active state economic intervention and regulation. In some places, such as in Britain and New Zealand, this meant that a large segment of economic activity was owned and controlled by the state through state-owned enterprises. Elsewhere, intervention took a variety of other forms – tariff protection, subsidies to farmers and industry, restrictions on shopping hours and price levels, and national wage fixation, among many others. While inter-party differences always existed over the nature and, particularly, the scope of desirable state intervention, the idea itself was so firmly entrenched in each society's political-economic imaginary that it was hardly ever challenged in principle, as it would be in the 1980s. To varying degrees and in different ways, the neoliberal norm entrepreneurs directed their policies toward shifting – some radically, others more incrementally – these elements of the prevailing political-economic imaginary.

Chapter three follows with a detailed account of the ideational and policy shifts that took place in the Anglo-American democracies over the course of the 1980s. It shows how this decade saw, in each country, a true revolution in economic policy, outlining the policy changes pursued by the four governing parties: Conservative in Britain and Canada, and Labor in Australia and New Zealand. Central to this analysis is the identification of two distinct types of policy change: one, a radical, "crash through or crash" approach that explicitly aimed to shift the prevailing political-economic imaginary toward neoliberalism, doing so as comprehensively and as rapidly as possible; and the other, a more gradual, incremental approach that nevertheless had the cumulative effect of instantiating a new neoliberal political-economic imaginary as well. Whether done in a radically doctrinaire or a more evolutionary, consensual way, the result was a scaleback of the state through a combination of deregulation, privatization, freer trade, and an opening up to the larger world economy. The chapter concludes with a discussion of how what was initiated by one set of norm entrepreneurs came to be further entrenched and consolidated by the governments – especially of opposite parties – that succeeded the early neoliberals. By focusing on the deepening neoliberalism by these governments in the 1990s and beyond, I argue that the end result has been a commitment to economically rationalist policies on both sides of politics – one that represents the victory of neoliberalism over the old consensus and a historic shift in each country's political-economic imaginary.

The role of political elites in accomplishing this neoliberal political-economic imaginary shift is the focus of chapter four. Specifically, I contend that this ideational and policy transformation was the result of the conscious efforts of strategic norm entrepreneurs to reorient key elements in their countries' prevailing economic policy orientations, doing so by strategically deploying the argument that neoliberalism was the only rational, appropriate, and workable policy approach in a rapidly changing world. The analysis in this chapter proceeds on several levels. First, it considers the influence of the norm entrepreneurs themselves, focusing on the critically important role played by elected political leaders who made neoliberal policy and ideational change a key part of their governing programs and initiated what would become a large-scale shift in the political-economic imaginary. Second, taking full account of the fact that norm entrepreneurs, no matter how personally influential or determined, must operate within certain political, economic, and institutional environments, I consider a number of important "environmental" factors that decisively contributed to the success of the neoliberal reformers. Particular attention is paid in this regard to the role played by the economic crises of the 1970s in facilitating the argument for change, to the influence exercised by economic bureaucrats in providing institutional and philosophical support to neoliberalism, and to the empowering nature of the majoritarian political institutional structures then extant in the countries discussed here. Finally, this chapter undertakes a detailed analysis of the most important rhetorical weapons employed by the neoliberal norm entrepreneurs. I specifically examine how the economic crises of the 1970s, the apparent post-war decline of these countries vis-à-vis other industrialized states, and the allegedly accelerating pace of globalization were all moulded into the overarching assertion that "there is no alternative" to a thoroughgoing neoliberal policy and ideational reorientation.

To this point, this book is primarily concerned with common aspects of the shift to neoliberalism in the Anglo-American democracies. Chapter five takes a somewhat different tack, further problematizing the neoliberal political-economic imaginary shift by focusing on important ideological and partisan differences between the four governments – especially as they coloured the nature of neoliberalism as pursued by the Labor parties of Australia and New Zealand. With their promotion of the new economic orientation, these parties courted the charge that they had sold out the best in Labor tradition and had adopted wholesale the prescriptions of the right-wing free marketeers. The truth, however, is more complex. I argue that despite this deviation from their traditional roots, the policies Labor adopted were not in all respects the policies that would have been adopted by conservative parties: that is, Labor's advocacy of a neoliberal orientation was not identical to the right's and, in fact, reveals a distinctive Labor imprint. Particularly with respect to the labour market, the Antipodean Labor parties pursued policies that were identifiably Labor. They refused to apply the neoliberal medicine to the labour market with anything like the zeal they evinced in deregulation elsewhere in the economy. Whereas most other aspects of economic policy were at one point or another subjected to a fairly typical application of neoliberal medicine, the Labor governments in the Antipodes adopted labour market policies that, while certainly liberalizing and transformative in their own right, revealed the unique imprint of parties whose origins and primary base of support lay in organized labour movements. In fact, the contrast between Labor's policies and those of the conservatives becomes even more apparent when considering the labour market policies of the governments that succeeded Labor. The Coalition in Australia and National in New Zealand took the neoliberal revolution much further than Labor was willing to do, indeed right into Labor's most sacrosanct areas, seeking to extend and ultimately entrench neoliberalism in an even more radical way. Thus, they confirm that while neoliberal political-economic imaginary shifts were common to all four governments, their specific characteristics were not immune to the traditional philosophical commitments of conservative and Labor parties.

Chapter six concludes by assessing these shifts to a neoliberal political-economic imaginary in the Anglo-American democracies. Here, I argue that the neoliberal shifts of the 1980s and 1990s are critically important, not only because these new assumptions and beliefs about state economic intervention still inform state behaviour and social norms today, but also for what they tell us about the ability of norm entrepreneurs to strategically use both material and rhetorical forms of persuasion and coercion to effect significant normative and ideational change. The neoliberal phenomenon in these countries shows that norm entrepreneurs, while not able to unilaterally impose a normative shift on complex, modern, democratic societies, can, under a propitious constellation of facilitating historical, economic, political, and institutional conditions, effect radically new and thoroughgoing changes in their countries' political-economic imaginaries. Thus, leadership is a critically important component of normative change. However, this study also shows that context and partisanship can figure greatly in the ability of norm entrepreneurs to achieve their goals. The political, economic, and institutional parameters within which norm entrepreneurs must operate can play a critical role in either retarding or advancing their programs of change. As we shall see, the neoliberal governments discussed in this book were successful largely because they operated within a political and institutional environment quite conducive to the kind of change they wished to effect.

Finally, I argue that the struggle for ideational change is one that successful norm entrepreneurs fight on many fronts, using the multiple strategies of persuasion and coercion in both rhetorical and material forms. The neoliberal revolutions in the Anglo-American democracies in the 1980s represent policy and ideational changes of the first magnitude. Yet, they did not happen inevitably or deterministically. Rather, they were achieved through a variety of means: Habermasian persuasion when possible, rhetorical coercion when necessary, appeals to material advantage and a better future, and even in some cases, legally-based coercion. In the end, the shift to a new, neoliberal political-economic imaginary was the result of changing ideas – ideas in the hands of strategic political actors who were, at least in these cases, able to successfully construct a new, and in many ways radically different, philosophical view of the proper relationship between the state, society, and economy.

2 Prelude to Neoliberalism: The Post-War Policy Paradigm and the Economic Turmoil of the 1970s

The first part of this analysis of the reshaping of their countries' political-economic imaginaries by norm entrepreneurs in the Anglo-American democracies is to consider what came before. As is discussed in detail in the next chapter, the neoliberal norm entrepreneurs effectively reversed many long-standing, venerable public policy traditions – some dating from the early post-war years, others from the founding of the countries themselves. The shift to new political-economic imaginaries was dramatic precisely because it so effectively reversed what had been considered by most to be fairly sacrosanct economic policy assumptions and approaches. In other words, considering the schematic presented in Figure 1, neoliberalism was not simply a policy adjustment or a marginal reframing, but in the end constituted a major re-construction of key elements in each country's political-economic imaginary.

In order to set the stage for the analysis to follow, this chapter focuses on two elements of the pre-neoliberal period: the nature of the interventionist imaginaries that prevailed throughout most of the post-war era in the Anglo-American democracies, and the conditions of economic turmoil that played a key role in casting doubt on those imaginaries and helping "open the door" to their replacement. First, this chapter considers the dominant features of post-war public policy in Britain, Canada, Australia, and New Zealand. Here the emphasis is on outlining the most important characteristics of what is often referred to as the "consensus" period of post-war politics – that is, that period after the Second World War in which economic policy in many countries revolved around a shared commitment to Keynesian demand management, various forms of active state economic intervention, and the funding of a sizeable social welfare state. In this chapter, I discuss these main characteristics in the context of the political-economic imaginary, showing how each country instituted various aspects of an interventionist political-economic paradigm. Naturally, however, no two of these countries were exactly alike in all respects. Facing their own peculiar problems and with unique histories, political cultures, geographies, and economic conditions, each country's political-economic imaginary and resultant policies reflected its own unique circumstances. However, despite these variations, certain common features stand out. The first part of this chapter attempts to outline the areas of similarity in approach and philosophy between the four countries, while also pointing to those areas of uniqueness that formed part of the national policy tradition that would be definitively reshaped by the experience of the 1980s.

The second part of the chapter examines the political and economic conditions that helped make the neoliberal shift possible – specifically, the period before the accession to power of the market liberalizing governments discussed in this study. What we see is that, by the time each of these governments came to office, economic conditions had significantly worsened and stood in sharp contrast to the boom times of the 1950s and 1960s. In fact, in all four Anglo-American democracies, the late 1970s and early 1980s were perceived – indeed framed – as a time of significant economic crisis. As economic conditions continued to deteriorate, it became clear that the facility with which governments had seemingly managed their economies in the past no longer obtained in this new environment. In the post-oil shock world, with the old certainties thrown into doubt and a sense of crisis dominating political life, the door was opened for neoliberal politicians to promote fundamental political-economic reorientations. Indeed, as is discussed in chapter four, the very sense of national "crisis" was constructed (at least in part) and used by neoliberal norm entrepreneurs in an attempt to discredit the old economic paradigm and to justify their own new economic program.

The Dominant Post-War Economic Paradigm

Britain

In examining the dominant pattern of post-war economic policy in the Anglo-American countries, it perhaps makes most sense to begin with Britain. Long touted as the quintessential example of "consensus politics,"[1] Britain serves as a prime example of many of the important features of the Anglo-American policy paradigm. While an analysis of the origins of this "consensus" is beyond the scope of this book, it can be said that the most proximate cause of the dominant consensus was the emergence of a new interventionist political-economic imaginary, especially during the Attlee Labour Government of 1945–51. Taking office alone for the first time in 1945 as a majority government, Labour would recast British society and economy – indeed, the very philosophical foundations of post-war policy – into forms that would structure future governments' policies for decades.[2] With few exceptions, this new imaginary and the policies arising from it (and serving to reinforce it) would be maintained as dominant elements in economic policy by both succeeding Tory and Labour governments. Despite long periods of Tory rule – under Churchill, Eden, Macmillan, Douglas-Home, and Heath (1951–64, 1970–74) – the basic pattern remained.

Specifically, this new political-economic imaginary rejected the economic liberalism of the nineteenth and early twentieth centuries, arguing – as did Harold Macmillan in the quote given at the beginning of chapter one – that it was insufficiently concerned with the needs of the entire community, understood as a collectivity with shared duties and mutual obligations. Rather, the basis of the new political-economic imaginary was that the state had a fundamental responsibility to pursue at least minimum levels of economic and social security for all members of society. Aiming at greater social justice, equality, and social harmony, the new political-economic imaginary envisioned a state actively engaged in the economy – as an employer, a regulator of private industry, a manager of the business cycle, a provider of a basic level of economic security for citizens, and an agent of at least modest redistribution in the name of social justice. In the language employed by this book (see Figure 1), the resulting frame was that such economic problems as unemployment, inflation, and poor output, and such related social phenomena as poverty, poor health, and inadequate education, were no longer seen as the unfortunate, but ineluctable results of "the market." Rather they came to be framed as problems created in large part by that market and amenable to amelioration – even perhaps elimination – by an activist, socially-concerned, interventionist state. This political-economic imaginary and resultant master frame made possible the pursuit of four fundamental policy settings in post-war

Britain, ones shared to varying degrees by the other Anglo-American cases as well.[3]

First, the British post-war model was fundamentally that of a mixed economy, involving a significant degree of public ownership of large industries. The idea that socially responsible economies involved large-scale state ownership, particularly in industry, can be traced directly to Clause IV of the 1918 Labour Party program, a provision that committed the party to public ownership of the "means of production, distribution and exchange."[4] This provision was put into effect in earnest by the Attlee Government after 1945. Building on the extensive state intervention arising from the exigencies of world war, the Attlee government proceeded, from 1946 to 1949, to nationalize the Bank of England, the coal industry, civil aviation, road and rail transport and haulage, the electricity and gas industries, and the iron and steel industry.[5] By the time the Tories returned to government in 1951, fully 20 percent of the British economy was in state hands.[6]

Reflecting how quickly and successfully the mixed economy made its way into the British political-economic imaginary, succeeding governments through to the 1970s essentially left this structure of public ownership in place. Even the Conservative Party, which occasionally opined about the desirability of private enterprise and ownership, did little before 1979 to substantially reverse this long-run shift to a mixed economy. The only significant industries it managed to privatize – or in the language of the period "denationalize" – before the Thatcher era were the iron and steel and road haulage industries, which were returned to private ownership by the Churchill government in 1953 and 1954, respectively. However, when Labour acted to renationalize steel in 1968, the succeeding Conservative government of Ted Heath not only declined to reverse the move but even acted, in the hope of saving endangered jobs, to nationalize the ailing Rolls-Royce and the Upper Clyde Shipbuilders. In a pattern that would be repeated with respect to neoliberalism in the 1980s and 1990s, policies that one side of politics initiated for largely philosophical reasons would later be entrenched by the other side of politics, as it pragmatically acquiesced to the new policies, even eventually coming to accept them philosophically over the longer term. As a result, Britain remained, until the 1980s, a very mixed economy, with large swathes of public ownership.[7]

A second major characteristic of the post-war British political economy was the widespread acceptance of the notion that the state has a significant responsibility for the provision of social welfare. At a minimum, in this view, this social welfare state was to provide and care for those in society least able to care for themselves – in particular, the young, the old, the sick, the unemployed – and, in its more generous forms, was to entitle all members of society to certain universal benefits, serving as a mechanism by which some measure of redistribution of wealth could take place.[8]

In Britain, the concept of state provision of welfare was not new. Its antecedents can be seen in such public policies as the nineteenth-century poor laws.[9] But the real emergence of the modern British social welfare state took place after the First World War. In those years, the predominant political-economic imaginary began to shift, with all political parties coming to accept the notion that the state had the responsibility to care, albeit in an initially rudimentary way, for those in direst need and with no other source of assistance. Hence, the state began to provide such benefits as pensions, health and unemployment insurance, and poor relief for these citizens.

It was the experience, however, of the Second World War that most solidified the primary component of the political-economic imaginary with respect to social welfare: that *all* citizens are entitled to at least some basic level of benefits from the state. In this regard, the key development was the publication in 1942 of Sir William Beveridge's *Report on Social Insurance and Allied Services*. In it, Beveridge's committee recommended the integration and consolidation of existing social welfare programs – ones that were inconsistent and non-universal in coverage – into a comprehensive system of national insurance that would protect all citizens "from cradle to grave." Benefits were to be provided universally by a system to which citizens would contribute; those unable to pay the national insurance premiums would receive "free" means-tested benefits.[10]

In the event, the war delayed the implementation of Beveridge's proposals, but it helped create an ethos of social solidarity and egalitarianism that resulted in all-party acceptance of this much-expanded role for the state. Upon taking office in 1945, the Attlee Labour Government set about implementing the major elements of Beveridge's proposals, of which the most significant was the creation of the National Health Service (NHS) in 1946. This system of universal, essentially free health care was notable in a number of ways: it was, and continues to be, financed out of direct taxation, reflecting the conception of health care as a social right to be enjoyed by all, not something subject to special payments or contributions; its creation was essentially supported by both Conservatives and Labour, in principle, if not in actual detail; and it quickly became the hallmark of the British welfare state, coming to be viewed as the sacrosanct cornerstone of the British system of welfare.[11] Recognizing the broad popularity of the NHS – and the extent to which health care came to be framed as a state responsibility – governments ever since have treated it with great political care and have been regularly moved to proclaim their commitment to, and generosity toward, it. Speaking of the Conservative Party's own commitment to social welfare, a former Heath and Thatcher minister put it, "[The party] had been very shaken by its defeat of 1945 which occurred largely because it was seen as the party of unemployment, separated from the lives of ordinary people. And their first reaction, which was quite skillfully done by RAB Butler and others, was to say, 'Oh, no. We believe in the welfare state and we will maintain it and we believe in good relations with labour and we will maintain them.' And they did, of course."[12]

As this statement indicates, a similar view prevailed with regard to the other areas of welfare policy largely created by the Attlee government. Across the political spectrum, the system of unemployment insurance, old age, retirement and disability pensions, and educational benefits enjoyed nearly universal support for most of the post-war period. The social policy phenomenon worked quite simply: Labour governments often took the lead in initiating welfare benefits and services, usually with an element of redistribution or "leveling" attached, and succeeding Conservative governments did virtually nothing to check or reverse the expansion of social services, thereby helping consolidate these new services as unremarkable and "taken-for-granted." In fact, social welfare proved to be such an enduring part of the post-war British political-economic imaginary that even the Thatcher government refused to introduce deep cuts and, to the contrary, boasted of its willingness to expand social spending throughout its term in office.[13]

In this set of "consensus" economic policies, a third key element was the commitment of British governments to full employment and their use of Keynesian demand management policies in order to achieve it. As Hall describes it, the British commitment to full employment was virtually unmatched anywhere else in the Western world.[14] The 1930s had, in Britain as in most of the industrialized world, been a period of high unemployment and economic orthodoxy. On the one hand, the Great Depression produced extremely high levels of unemployment throughout Britain but was particularly severe in poor, industrial areas of the North and in Wales, where unemployment rates reached levels of well over 60 percent.[15] However, governments of the time, including the Labour government of Ramsay MacDonald, pursued policies consistent with the prescriptions of the prevailing, classically liberal political-economic imaginary: tight budgetary controls and restraint of government expenditure.[16]

Two events occurred, however, that contributed greatly to a shift toward a more state-interventionist political-economic imaginary and the adoption of conscious government policy to achieve full employment. One was, simply, the Second World War. With the country straining to produce as much war materiel as possible, every able-bodied adult was seemingly put to work in war-related industries and thus unemployment simply ceased to exist. Within this context, the work of John Maynard Keynes came to the fore. In the aftermath of the onset of the Great Depression, his work – principally *The General Theory of Employment, Interest and Money* – made the case for government-led reinflation of the economy at times of economic downturn. Keynes argued that most economic downturns were consequences of insufficient economic demand – something that could be remedied by judicious government intervention. Government expenditure and taxation, in this view, could be tailored to produce the optimum level of consumer demand and, thus, provide the economy with requisite boosts or restraints as circumstances warranted. In this way, economic conditions could be more effectively controlled and unemployment – the bane of the 1930s – largely eliminated.[17]

Enjoying full employment based on war production and with a Keynesian-based employment generator seemingly to hand, the Conservative-led wartime coalition government pronounced in its 1944 White Paper on Employment that "one of the primary aims and responsibilities [of government would be] the maintenance of a high and stable level of employment after the war."[18] From that point until the accession to power of the Thatcher government in 1979, full employment was a goal consciously pursued by Tory and Labour governments alike. Reflecting the depth of the philosophical shift, a former head of the Home Civil Service declared, "In the 50s and 60s, full employment was almost the key policy."[19] As a leading minister in the Heath government described the dominant view, "We had been brought up ... when [there was] mass unemployment. Our motivation [which] took many of us into politics was to see that that sort of thing never happened again. And we were prepared to tolerate ... economic inefficiency up to a point, rather [than have] the social damage, hatreds and divisions,

[the] divisiveness in society caused by the mass unemployment of the earlier part of the century."[20] And, as a former Thatcher government minister put it, "[T]he inter-war period was summed up in the memorable words of Herbert Morrison: ... 'a paradise for profiteers, a hell for everyone else.' Those were words which resounded round the 1945 election. There was a huge determination that we were never going to go back to the mass unemployment of the 1930s. There was Keynesian economics which was, as it were, convincing people that you didn't have to."[21]

This all-party commitment to full employment through Keynesian demand management helped produce what is usually held to be the most obvious characteristic of British economic policy in the post-war period: the recurring cycle of stop-go, reflation-deflation economic policy. Since the Bretton Woods conference of 1944, a worldwide system of fixed exchange rates had been in place, with the British government committed to maintaining the role of sterling as a key currency of international exchange. This produced a difficult dilemma: when the government acted to stimulate the economy in order to protect jobs, large balance of payments deficits emerged as British consumers increasingly purchased imported goods. The result was downward pressure on the exchange rate and the need to strengthen the pound and slow the economy. This, of course, had adverse consequences on employment, and the cycle began to repeat itself.[22] This cycle of government-induced boom followed by deflation was further reinforced in the post-war period by policy based on the widely accepted (though, as Widmaier shows, socially constructed, contingent, and contestable) Phillips curve theory – the notion that there is a stable tradeoff between unemployment and inflation.[23] As the theory went, increases in demand usually produce (as Keynes predicted) a rise in both employment and prices. Weaker demand leads to lower inflation, but higher unemployment. Thus, prudent governments can apparently pick which combination of inflation and unemployment is most desirable, attempting to tailor macroeconomic policy to achieve the desired equilibrium.[24]

In reality, though, the equilibrium was difficult to achieve. Within a philosophical environment in which governments were committed to full employment, the preservation of jobs usually took precedence over low inflation, with governments speeding and slowing the economy as conditions seemed to warrant. Through the 1950s and 1960s, inflation remained relatively constant, but, in the 1970s, the seemingly stable Phillips trade-off collapsed in the wake of the world oil shocks and increased union militancy. From the late 1970s, and certainly since 1979, the commitment to full employment was effectively abandoned.[25]

A fourth closely related characteristic of the British post-war economy was the way in which governments attempted to structure the relationship between the state and trade unions. At the heart of this relationship was the tension between the desire to include trade unions as a significant player in national economic policy-making, on the one hand, and the need to ensure moderate wage increases in the presence of free collective bargaining and a government commitment to full employment, on the other. In Britain, the story of post-war industrial relations is largely one of this tension between wage demands and wage restraint. Despite conflict and tension along the way, however, the dominant pre-1979 feature of government-union relations was the conviction that trade unions had a legitimate and significant role to play in the determination and execution of national economic policy.

In the early post-war period, government-labour relations were remarkably amicable, particularly considering the overtly hostile attitude of governments toward unions in the strife-torn 1920s.[26] The tone had been set, yet again, by the wartime coalition government. With the full inclusion of the Labour Party in government, organized labour reaped the reward of unprecedented access to power and government decision-making. Former trade union officials and union-sponsored MPs now began to occupy high offices of state. Ernest Bevin, the former general secretary of the Transport and General Workers' Union (TGWU), was Minister of Labour in the coalition government and went on to become Foreign Secretary in the Attlee Labour government, one that gave full sway to union-sponsored MPs and union interests. In its time in government, the Labour Party repealed all the restrictive measures of the 1927 Trade Disputes and Trade Unions Act, ensured labour participation in government committees and supervisory bodies, and encouraged the notion that trade unions as a constituent part of the modern economy had an appropriate, legitimate role to play in economic policy-setting.[27]

This approach was to last up until the late 1970s, despite repeated tensions and conflicts between governments and unions, usually over the issue of wages. Put simply, the government commitment to maintain both full employment and the value of the pound demanded that some form of wage restraint be practiced by trade unions. With virtually free collective bargaining, and few statutory controls over union activities or pay awards, governments increasingly found themselves on the horns of a dilemma – attempting to accommodate union demands, fearful of union power if scorned, yet continually requiring wage restraint in order to avoid runaway inflation in a full employment economy.

Faced with the dilemma of wage restraint and experiencing increasing union militancy throughout the 1960s and 1970s, governments increasingly turned to incomes policies as a way of moderating wage increases and, through them, inflation. At times, governments attempted to moderate wages through argument and persuasion. At other times, statutory controls were briefly introduced. But in every case, incomes policies turned out to be short-lived and, ultimately, failures.[28] As Widmaier has argued with respect to the United States, this failure of incomes policies was less material than ideational: the philosophical ground had shifted. The earlier belief in the public benefit to be had from wage (and price) restraint had given way to the much more individualist notion that such restraint was naïve and that state controls were inappropriate. The result was a self-fulfilling prophecy in which the "common knowledge" that wage controls were unworkable actually rendered them so.[29] Governments recognized the need for wage moderation; however, they were, on the one hand, politically unwilling to risk the kind of industrial unrest that a thoroughgoing policy of wage limitation would likely provoke and, on the other, philosophically conditioned by the dominant post-war political-economic imaginary to reject such head-on confrontation. This prompted an alternative tack by governments in the late 1960s and early 1970s – the introduction of legislation designed to limit, structure, and regulate the power of trade unions.

First, the Wilson Labour Government produced a White Paper in 1969 titled *In Place of Strife*. The proposed legislation would have established cooling off periods for certain strikes, required workers' ballots for strikes deemed particularly threatening to the national interest, and established a regulatory body, the Commission on Industrial Relations, with the power to make legally enforceable judgments in union disputes. By the standards of the 1980s, the White Paper was relatively benign. But in the late 1960s, it was seen by labour as a distinct threat to its historic rights, privileges, and clout. Union organizations and their allies within the Labour Party combined to oppose the legislation and ensure that it was never enacted.[30] A second attempt, by the Heath Government in 1971, was at first more successful. Heath's Industrial Relations Act was intended to make the provisions and remedies present in civil law apply to trade union activity. Unions were registered and given clearly defined legal standing, and their immunity from prosecution was limited as they were exposed to the same legal liability as other corporate entities. Workers were also given the right to opt out of union membership and to vote in pre-strike ballots. In the event, the legislation failed to work as envisaged. Trade unions vehemently opposed this statutory limitation on their rights and made repeal of the Bill their primary goal, refusing to cooperate with the government at all so long as the legislation was in force.[31] By the election of 1974, the Conservative Party itself had largely admitted its failure, and the succeeding Labour government repealed all sections opposed by the unions.

Yet, despite growing conflict in industrial relations, the notion that unions had to be included in the economic life of the nation – essentially as an equal partner to employers – was felt by the Labour and Conservative Parties alike. While Britain never achieved the heights of tripartite corporatism seen in some continental European countries,[32] it was a part of the post-war British political-economic imaginary that some degree of union consultation and cooperation was not only necessary, but eminently appropriate. As a high-ranking member of the Heath government put it, "I believed in trade unionism all my life. There was a wing of the Conservative Party which was rightly regarded as anti-[union]. Ted and I and Geoffrey Howe and people like us were not of that ilk. We believed that unions were the proper thing and we welcomed strong trade unions."[33] So deeply held was this conviction that even after the nearly disastrous 1972 miners' strike, Ted Heath could still proclaim, "I believe that a Conservative Prime Minister must set himself to find common ground with the trade unions as well as the employers."[34]

This conciliatory view, however, fell into increasing disfavour in the late 1970s. The events of the latter part of the decade, particularly the 1978–79 Winter of Discontent, discussed in some detail later, facilitated a shift in public attitudes toward trade unions – even among many unionists themselves – such that the stage was set for the dramatic and radically thoroughgoing changes that were to be made by the Thatcher government.[35] In this aspect of the post-war "consensus" political-economic imaginary, perhaps to a greater degree than with any other, the Thatcher period marked a total and complete reversal.

Canada

As stated previously, Britain is in many ways the archetype of the post-war "consensus" political-economic imaginary. To greater or lesser degrees, the four elements seen in the British case – the mixed economy with a significant degree of public ownership, the existence of a modern social welfare state, the commitment to full employment and Keynesian demand management, and cooperation with and conciliation of trade unions – were present in all four cases discussed here. What has been presented here as a British archetype is perhaps more accurately portrayed as a general model that existed in various forms in most industrialized economies in the post-war period. Yet, despite a great degree of overall similarity, specifics in each country showed significant variation. Reacting to their own economic conditions and problems, each country fashioned a policy pattern that reflected these unique circumstances. In this, Canada was no exception. For Canada, the economic problem has always been obvious: a massive, yet sparsely populated country sitting directly on the doorstep of the world's most powerful economy, the United States. No discussion of Canadian economic policy can ignore this reality.

The problems of geography and population have largely driven the Canadian approach to government intervention. Occupying the second largest landmass of any nation in the world, Canada stretches nearly five thousand miles from coast to coast and includes such diverse regions and economies as maritime fishing communities, heavy industrial production, substantial farming and agribusiness, logging and timber production, and petrochemicals. It does so, however, with a current population of somewhat more than 30 million people. Taking into account that, at the turn of the twentieth century, Canada's population was only 5.3 million, the enormity of the task of economic development becomes apparent. As W.L. Mackenzie King once remarked, "If some countries have too much history, Canada has too much geography."[36]

Making this task particularly pressing, furthermore, was the presence of the United States. Ostensibly a friendly neighbour for most of Canadian history, the United States has nonetheless been traditionally viewed in Canada as a serious potential threat – one that, if it wished, could easily dominate or even extinguish the unique Canadian society in North America.[37]

Faced with these challenges – overwhelming geography, sparse population, and an ever-present threat from the south – two themes came to dominate the Canadian political-economic imaginary since the time of Confederation in 1867: first, a reliance on government-initiated and sponsored economic development and, second, the necessity of protectionism, both serving as safeguards against being overwhelmed by the economic might of the United States. Unlike the case of Britain, however, whose dominant patterns of economic policy largely date from the Second World War and the immediate post-war period, Canada's twin strategies of government intervention and economic protectionism have their roots much farther back, in the years immediately following the founding of modern Canada in 1867. In fact, this political-economic construction, one that would come to dominate virtually all Canadian government policy until the push for continental free trade in the 1980s, was based largely on the ideas of Sir John A. Macdonald, Canada's first premier, and his National Policy.

The National Policy was premised on the interrelated notions that national economic development depended on government protection from competition from the United States, while securing Canada's freedom of action vis-à-vis the United States depended on stimulating and protecting economic development along all-Canadian, east–west (rather than north–south) lines. Thus, the two main objectives went hand-in-hand – development required protection, and the best protection was development. The primary agent of this state-sponsored development was, initially, the Canadian Pacific Railway – a rail link that would connect east to west; stitch Canada together as a coherent, unified nation; and discourage what are in some ways more natural north–south links with the United States. Along with the railroad – eventually completed in 1885 – tariff protection was the primary means by which, as envisioned by Macdonald and others, Canada could sufficiently shield its primary producers and industrial manufacturers from southern competition, allowing them time and resources to develop truly indigenous Canadian industry and agriculture.[38]

So embedded in the Canadian political-economic imaginary did these notions of state-led development and tariff protection become that they became virtual bywords of Canadian politics and economic policy throughout most of the twentieth century. No serious challenge to these principles emerged prior to the 1980s, with one exception. In the 1911 election, Liberal leader Sir Wilfred Laurier took his party to the polls on a program of limited reciprocity, or tariff reduction, with the United States. Such an idea was rather new – the last attempt at tariff reduction had occurred prior to Confederation when Abraham Lincoln proposed that the United States and Canada reduce tariffs, and it failed to achieve any concrete gains. In the event, the thumping defeat administered to Laurier by Sir Robert Borden and his protectionist Tories became part of the conventional wisdom of Canadian politics – "truck or trade with the Yankees" was economic foolishness and political suicide. Such was the fear of a public backlash that, in 1947, when W.L. Mackenzie King went so far as to negotiate – in secret – a freer trade deal with the United States, he lost his nerve and quietly buried the plan before it could go public.[39] As a consequence, no serious attempt was made until the end of the twentieth century to reassess the developmental and protectionist role played by the Canadian state.[40] Conservatives and Liberals alike – parties usually quite difficult to distinguish on philosophical grounds[41] – accepted that the uniqueness of the Canadian situation dictated a strong role for government intervention. This penchant for state action was only reinforced by both strands of Canadian political culture – an Anglo-Canadian strand much less individualistic and liberal than that found in the United States, and a French-Canadian strand deeply influenced by state paternalism, corporatism, and dirigisme.[42]

Despite deep-seated concerns and suspicions about the economic and cultural might of the United States, it became increasingly clear in the twentieth century that the US–Canada relationship would be, of necessity, a close one. As cultural and economic ties with Britain and the rest of the Commonwealth declined,[43] ties with the United States strengthened considerably. Yet, the prevailing notion in Canada was that active protection was the only safeguard. The freer trade that did take place was strictly on a sectoral basis – that is, tariff reductions were negotiated with the Americans only on a limited case-by-case, sector-by-sector basis. Of these agreements, the most important was the 1965 Auto Pact, allowing for virtually free trade in automobiles and new parts and establishing an industry that, in some respects, was continental, rather than national.[44] Yet, despite intermittent calls for further tariff reform, protectionism remained the predominant theme.

Well into the 1980s, Canadian governments continued to make attempts to insulate Canada from American economic influence. The Trudeau government's "third option" was an early-1970s attempt at reestablishing some degree of independence by developing European and Far East trade links. This agenda was based on External Affairs Minister Mitchell Sharp's *Three Options* paper, which suggested three alternatives: option one was the status quo, option two was increased Americanization of Canadian trade, and option three was trade diversification. Because there was no support at the time for increased links with the United States, the internationalist, trade diversification option was chosen. As Martin puts it, "What struck Mitchell Sharp was the reaction to the proposal for further American integration. 'It didn't get a single vote.' ... No one in the cabinet, no one in the upper ranks of the civil service, no one in the Prime Minister's Office spoke out in favour of the option that would come to be the darling of the Mulroney decade."[45]

While this policy of trade diversification did have some success in expanding trade ties outside North America, it never developed into the full-fledged alternative to North American trade that the government had hoped for.[46] As a further part of this program of enhancing Canadian protection, the Trudeau government in 1974 created the Foreign Investment Review Agency (FIRA), an agency charged with screening proposals for foreign investment in Canada. FIRA proved somewhat successful in limiting the amount of foreign capital penetration into Canada with decreased foreign control of Canadian corporations, but at the cost of limiting the amount of capital available to Canadian entrepreneurs.[47] Still, the program reflected a century's worth of dominant attitudes about the appropriate way in which to limit American influence in the Canadian economy.

An even more radically protectionist move was the Trudeau government's introduction in 1980 of the National Energy Program (NEP). The NEP was consciously designed to limit foreign involvement in Canada's large and growing energy industry and to extend the control of the federal government over Canada's energy income and reserves. It did so by granting significant concessions and subsidies to Canadian energy corporations, imposing special taxes on foreign profits from Canadian energy, and providing for the transfer of up to 25 percent of the value of oil and gas finds on federal lands to the state-owned Petro-Canada, irrespective of exploration and development costs. The goal, simply put, was Canadian and, in particular, federal control of Canadian energy sources and industry – a goal completely in tune with both traditions of government intervention and economic nationalism.[48]

Finally, the tradition of state economic intervention in Canada manifested itself in an all-party commitment to the social welfare state. Based on a political-economic imaginary that was fundamentally sympathetic to and supportive of state activity in the name of communitarian values, the Canadian social welfare system formerly operated on the basis of universality of provision. The system largely dates from the time of the Great Depression when, in response to the pressing needs of the time, Conservative prime minister R.B. Bennett was elected on a platform promising enhanced social welfare. His 1935 "New Deal" promised farm subsidies, unemployment insurance, regulation of working conditions, and a minimum wage. Initially, his program was largely struck down by the Supreme Court of Canada on the grounds that it represented an unconstitutional infringement of provincial powers.[49] This decision, however, was largely bypassed by provisions allowing for provincial administration of federally mandated spending programs. The result has been a social welfare state providing universal benefits in health care, child and family allowances, and retirement pensions. As in Britain, state provision of social welfare in Canada has proved to be one of the most enduring aspects of the national political-economic imaginary – and one of the aspects of public policy most resistant to change. Every post-war Canadian government has professed its commitment to the universal social welfare state and has largely maintained it or allowed it to grow as a proportion of national output. As a former Liberal cabinet minister expressed, opposition to the social welfare state was deemed to be so far outside the mainstream as to be hardly worthy of consideration: "It was the ethos of the era. We had won the war. ... We had famous economists who could manipulate fiscal and monetary policy to stabilize [the economy] ... Who was going to be against extending the pension? ... A few extreme right-wing voices that were completely discredited – that was all."[50] As in Britain, social welfare proved to be the element of Canadian economic policy most resistant to change, even while the two longest-standing pillars of economic policy – active state economic intervention and protection against the United States – were significantly challenged and undermined.

Australia and New Zealand

The economic dilemmas facing Canada were not entirely dissimilar from those facing the Antipodean democracies. For Canada, the problem was the economic behemoth just across the border. While neither Australia nor New Zealand faced such an obvious, geographically proximate challenger, problems of domestic economic protection and development were critically important there as well. In both countries, small population size continually challenged governments in each country to protect themselves against foreign economic pressures and competition. This was true not only of Australia – which attempted to bolster its population through immigration, first from Britain, then from elsewhere – but especially of New Zealand, whose total population has never exceeded that of a reasonably large North American or European city. Furthermore, the problem of size, which was so problematic in Canada, was in many ways felt in Australia as well. With abundant natural resources, but with hardly the population or the infrastructural capacity to develop them, both Australia and New Zealand were impelled to seek state solutions and state initiative as the primary motors of economic development and change.[51]

In considering the unique characteristics of the political-economic imaginaries of the Antipodean countries, then, two major characteristics stand out. One is a perspective that, in the context of Australia, Castles has termed "domestic defence."[52] Flowing from the conceptual frame of defending the national economy was a policy agenda characterized by high tariff protection to protect domestic industry and a system of centrally determined wage fixation. The other dominant characteristic, visible especially in New Zealand, was pervasive state regulation of the economy. Both Antipodean economies were highly controlled by government regulation, and in New Zealand, by the time the radically neoliberal Labour government of the 1980s took office, the country was not unjustly labelled the most highly regulated and controlled economy in the capitalist world. We consider both of these characteristics in turn.

First, both Australia and New Zealand responded to similar economic challenges by constructing quite similar modes of economic defence from foreign economic penetration or domination. While the two countries differ immensely in size, both shared a number of important characteristics. Both were sparsely populated colonial outposts whose economies were dependent upon the production and export of raw materials.[53] It could rightly be said of both Australia and New Zealand that their primary export-driven prosperity in the nineteenth and twentieth centuries did indeed come "on the sheep's back." As Table 1 indicates, both at mid-century and just before the advent of the neoliberal Labor governments of the 1980s, Antipodean exports were dominated by raw and agricultural goods. Even though, toward the end of the century, their export economies had diversified beyond wool and milk, the fundamentally primary nature of Antipodean products is clear. The practical implication of this narrow range of primary, price-sensitive products was that both economies' ability to import necessary manufactured and finished goods continually depended on favourable terms of trade.[54]

Believing that without some form of domestic protection their national economies would be virtually controlled by external forces, governments in both Australia and New Zealand devised similar

Table 1. Main Exports of Australia and New Zealand (percentage of total exports)

	1952	1982
Australia	Wool (49.1)	Minerals (31.0)
	Wheat and flour (13.4)	Wool (9.7)
	Minerals (7.1)	Wheat (9.1)
	Meat (5.4)	Meat (7.3)
New Zealand	Wool (34.0)	Meat (23.2)
	Dairy (33.2)	Dairy (17.1)
	Meat (21.0)	Wool (13.6)
		Wood products (8.0)

Source: Easton and Gerritsen 1996, 26.

systems of domestic defence. The depressed conditions of the late nineteenth century had shown clearly that both countries were highly vulnerable to swings in the prices of their goods on international markets. Therefore, an alternative strategy – one consistent with the developmental and interventionist state envisioned by this political-economic imaginary – was developed in the early years of the twentieth century. First, high tariff barriers were erected in order to protect both primary and manufacturing industries.[55] While the initial motivation for high tariffs came from manufacturers and their employees – at the turn of the century still a fairly small force – primary producers increasingly came to support policies that would protect their products as well. The dominant view was that, in a volatile world market in which each country's primary commodities faced constantly changing prices, tariff protection served a number of necessary purposes. It provided a measure of protection behind which indigenous manufacturing could grow, diversify, and begin to satisfy domestic demand through import substitution – something that, as former colonies, neither country had fully developed. It also encouraged the growth of the manufacturing job base, diversified the economy to provide employment outside of primary industries, and helped soak up any excess labour underutilized in the primary sector. Protection also played a social function, as Castles points out in regard to Australia. By helping raise the rates of pay in the nascent manufacturing sector to a level comparable to those in primary industries, a certain degree of wage-based social insurance was put in place: declines in income were minimized by ensuring the profitability of firms through tariff protection.[56] Finally, tariffs – and, later, other non-tariff barriers, such as import licensing and quotas – served the same fundamental purpose of insulating the economy from external economic shocks, particularly those related to prices of primary goods.

Put simply, the role of tariff protection as a fundamental tenet of economic faith in Australia and New Zealand was virtually unchallenged until the advent of the liberalizing governments of the 1980s. For most of the twentieth century, the role of protection as the only insurance these countries had against volatile world markets was nearly universally accepted. To this way of thinking, it was simply economic madness to imagine that such small, relatively undiversified economies could survive if subjected fully to the vicissitudes of the world market. A former Liberal minister described the way in which the prevailing attitude framed alternatives as literally un-reasonable: "I can remember vividly in the Liberal Party room ... there were right from the beginning of my time, the 1960s, a few anti-tariff stalwarts who used to get up on every tariff debate. ... And as soon as they rose to their feet – they were popular people, they weren't fools – there would be a groan ... through the party room, a collective groan. The abolition of tariffs was regarded as a joke."[57] Up until the 1980s, then, the place of protection was secure, with possibly "the most protected manufacturing sector of any OECD country."[58] Australia had seen only one significant instance of tariff reduction – Gough Whitlam's surprise 25 percent across-the-board cut in 1973, a move that proved to be a rather unpopular one-off change rather than the herald of a wholesale philosophical shift in favour of open markets.[59] In New Zealand as well, some conservatives' hopes for significantly freer trade were dashed by Sir Robert Muldoon's application of even tighter controls and more active government intervention following the turbulent period of the 1970s.[60] As with so many of the other features of economic policy discussed here, it was only later in the 1980s that real policy change began to occur.

The second manifestation of domestic defence was one virtually unique to Australia and New Zealand: a system of centralized wage fixation. Originating in the late nineteenth century, the system of centrally determined national wage rates across the entire economy became both a fundamental pillar of Antipodean economic policy for most of the twentieth century and also, by world standards, one of the most unusual and most highly centralized forms of wage regulation in the industrialized world.[61]

In Australia, centralized wage fixing came into being largely in response to a wave of strikes experienced in the 1890s. Conscious that one of the central grievances of labour was that workers had little control over the wages for which they worked, and that these wages often bore little relation to labour supply and were imposed virtually at the whim of employers, the Commonwealth government moved to create a Court of Conciliation and Arbitration that could ensure a fair wage to labour. Moreover, these provisions were largely seen as the necessary consequence and complement to tariff protection. Just as manufacturers were insulated and protected from the vicissitudes of the foreign economic environment by trade regulation, so it was seen as only natural and right that workers should too be protected in a similar way. As Castles points out, this "'[n]ew protection' was new precisely because it promised both sides of industry a defence against the unfettered implication of the self-regulating market mechanism."[62]

In the development of the Australian system of wage regulation, the landmark event was the 1907 Harvester Judgment, in which the President of the Court of Conciliation and Arbitration, Henry Bournes Higgins, set out what would become the standard principle by which wage awards would be made in Australia for most of the coming century.[63] Higgins asserted that all workers were entitled to a living wage, one consonant with basic, ordinary human needs and unrelated to the level of profits or losses experienced by their employers. As he put it, there was no "other standard appropriate ... [to assess a] fair and reasonable wage ... than the normal needs of the average employee regarded as a human being living in a civilised community," and "the remuneration of the employee cannot be allowed to depend on the profits of his individual employer."[64] This, then, set the standard for future wage orders: the wage award consisted of a basic wage payable to unskilled labour and indexed to changes in consumer prices, plus incremental increases for skilled workers. At least in principle, the living wage was an Australian government guarantee to workers.

As the system developed, and despite Higgins's intentions, the profits of employers began to be taken into account. Recognizing that judgments made without consideration to profits encouraged employers to seek greater tariff protection as compensation for accepting higher wage awards, the Court increasingly came to introduce the "capacity of the economy to pay" as a principle operating alongside basic worker needs. In times of economic upheaval and strain, such as the Great Depression and during the Korean War, the Court felt free to limit awards to reflect its assessment of current economic conditions as a whole.[65] However, the fundamental principle remained intact until well into the 1990s.

Despite periodic episodes, particularly in the late 1960s and early 1970s when tight labour conditions and voluntary wage agreements seemed to outpace the centralized system, the fundamental commitment to centralized wage fixation remained, especially on the part of unions. It would not be until the 1990s that efforts were made, first by Labor, then by the Coalition, to move toward the more flexible enterprise bargaining arrangements common in other countries.[66]

In New Zealand, a similar system of wage regulation emerged, although the impetus for its development and the causes of its final demise were different. There, the initiative for centralized wage fixing came from neither employers nor unions, but from a Liberal government intent on extending the regulatory role of the state in order to ensure economic stability and control. As in Australia, the late nineteenth century had been a period of intense strike and union activity, culminating in the 1890 Maritime Strike, which ended in an overwhelming employer victory over the unions. In the wake of this upheaval the government undertook to implement a controlled and centralized system of wage fixation and dispute arbitration. Initially, the system was opposed both by employers, who feared the rebirth of union power, and by unions, who believed that independent action was likely to be more rewarding than cooptation into a state system.[67] In the end, the centralized regulation option was imposed, and New Zealand set out on a track quite similar to that of Australia.

As in Australia, an Arbitration Court made wage awards on the basis of the living wage concept and accepted the notion that wage increases should be consistent with increases in the cost of living. It too saw its role as having an important moderating effect on market forces, especially in such a small and economically vulnerable country. Unlike in Australia, however, the centralized fixation of wages did not last nearly as long, nor did it retain its credibility with organized labour. Economic conditions in New Zealand often outpaced the ability of the arbitration system to respond with awards satisfactory to workers. As happened in Australia, tight labour markets prompted workers and employers to largely bypass the centralized system and hammer out more generous agreements than they would have received through the Court. Unions had the advantage of labour shortages, and employers were willing to pay the additional premium for contented workers and industrial peace. Thus, at various times, the centralized wage system was overtaken by events and rendered less influential.[68]

The real blow to the Court's position, however – and the event that precipitated its total loss of credibility with organized labour – was its decision in 1968 to award no increase in the basic wage. This "nil order" was justified by the Court on the grounds that, while the increased cost of living indicated that a wage rise was in order, economic conditions as a whole did not permit any increase. This decision, coupled with a series of conservative Court awards over the course of the 1960s, essentially spelled an end to the role of the Court in centralized wage fixation. To dampen impending industrial strife, employer represen-tatives on the Court joined with union representatives to outvote the Judge of the Court and approve a 5 percent wage increase. Following the nil order debacle and the industrial unrest that succeeded it in the early 1970s, the National government moved to control wages through statutory incomes policies, reshaping the Court into little more than an enforcer of wage decisions made not by the Court, but by elected government officials. These policies were, as in Britain and elsewhere, largely unsuccessful. Workers generally succeeded in obtaining from employers much larger pay settlements than the government preferred. To the extent that they worked at all, incomes policies often served to simply bottle up pay demands until the controls expired and the inevi-table wage boom occurred.[69]

However, in a radical departure from what took place in Australia, the Fourth Labour Government of New Zealand did not attempt any large-scale revitalization of the notion of centralized wage determina-tion in the 1980s. As discussed in chapter five, New Zealand Labour did not achieve, as did Australian Labor, a series of government-union agreements in which wage increases and other labour issues were thrashed out in high-level meetings.[70] Rather, the government sought to introduce the principle of enterprise bargaining, a notion that would be extended with a vengeance by the succeeding National government (1990–9). In short, centralized wage fixation was an important part of the overall post-war pattern of New Zealand economic policy, as it was in Australia. But unlike Australia, the New Zealand experience ended much sooner and was, in the end, more dramatically restructured by neoliberal governments in the 1980s and 1990s.[71]

Finally, a key aspect of both Australia and New Zealand's twenti-eth century political economies was extensive government intervention and regulation in virtually all aspects of the national economy, with a view to providing the most felicitous social and economic outcomes. As one early commentator observed, the state was "a vast public utility, whose duty [it was] to provide the greatest happiness to the greatest number."[72] Of course, the most obvious and significant method of state regulation was the one discussed previously – the use of tariffs and other trade provisions to limit the import of foreign goods, thereby fostering domestic industry and protecting domestic employment. However, the regulation did not end there. In both countries, governments took an active role in promoting development through government initiative and protection.

In Australia, the main sources of regulation were in the protection of the financial markets and in a complex system of subsidies and development grants to virtually every domestic industry. Under the long-serving post-war government of Sir Robert Menzies (1949–66), wartime controls and restrictions were largely lifted, but they were replaced by a thoroughgoing system of new controls on the financial markets. Credit was rationed, the flow of capital was regulated, foreign investment in the financial sector was strictly limited, interest rates were state-controlled, access to world money markets was restricted, and the government intervened in the market to promote housing and industrial development through subsidized loans and tax concessions. Put simply, just as another sector of the economy that was vulnerable to foreign penetration and competition – manufacturing – was highly protected, so the government intervened to ensure that finance, also quite susceptible to external influences and fluctuations, was equally, if not more, protected and controlled.[73]

A second main feature of Australian regulation was an extensive system of subsidies, grants, price controls, and other regulation of product markets. With its origins in the farm sector crises of the 1930s, this system sought to ensure basic minimum prices for (primarily) agricultural commodities, and to limit and subsidize the cost of production.[74] With a particularly strong advocate in the rural-based Country (later National) Party and its leader, John McEwen, this system remained essentially intact until the 1980s. It consisted of regulatory, price-maintaining, and marketing boards that "regulated output levels, licensed different producers, bought and sold product, and stored and released reserves in policies designed to stabilise price levels."[75] Supplementing these were measures intended to guarantee uniform prices for producers, particularly of gasoline and other essential goods. The system of regulations and government intervention was so complicated that, as Catley puts it, "[t]he whole system ... known as McEwenism ... represented a myriad of cross-sectoral subsidies so complex they could not be easily identified, let alone quantified."[76] But it was that type of regulation that enjoyed such bipartisan support in Australia. In 1964, Prime Minister Robert Menzies, perhaps unaware that his views derived from a long-standing Australian political-economic imaginary, expressed the pre-vailing attitude this way: "We have no doctrinaire political philosophy. Where government action or control has seemed to us to be the best answer to a practical problem, we have adopted that answer at the risk of being called socialists."[77] Reflecting the fact that political-economic imaginaries stand philosophically prior to partisan political divides, one observer commented, "By the late 1960s [the free enterprise versus socialism debate] seemed dead. Australia had reached a period of close to consensus in economic management: in a mixed economy where there was recognition of the importance of both government and busi-ness activity, there were only marginal differences between the political parties about how governments should intervene."[78]

Finally, we come to government regulation in New Zealand, perhaps that country's defining characteristic of twentieth-century economic policy. For it was in the complexity and extensiveness of its system of government controls and regulations that New Zealand set itself apart from virtually every other country in the capitalist, industrialized world. Attempting to insulate itself as much as possible from the vagaries of the international economy, and seeking to compensate, subsidize, and regulate the activities of virtually every major sector of the economy, New Zealand built what was, in many ways, the archetypal example of the insulated, semi-autarchic, domestic defence economy. In con-structing this system of regulation, parties of both the left and right were active and supportive participants. In fact, in Sir Robert Muldoon, the putatively conservative National prime minister from 1975 to 1984, New Zealand had nothing less than a wholehearted believer in the benefits of government regulation and intervention – the very policies against which the radical policy shakeups of the 1980s and 1990s were directed.[79]

In critiquing this record of regulation, Roger Douglas, the Fourth Labour Government's most vocal advocate of neoliberal change, related this catalogue of state controls:

It is surprising how quickly people forget what life was like in the 1960s and 1970s when this was essentially a state-run, state-controlled eco-nomy. ... Daily life was a patchwork of controls, regulations and State interventions. Hotels closed at 6 p.m. Only the government was allowed to broadcast television programs. Interest rates were set by the government. If you wanted to bring in Italian tiles or German beers or an American car you needed a government license. Workers were obliged to belong to a trade union. ... In those days it took three to six weeks to have a business telephone connected. Movies took nine to 18 months to arrive here. There were just two sorts of refrigerator – both made by the same manufacturer to the same specifications. If you wanted to rent a television you were obliged by law to put down six months' rent in advance. If you wanted to invest in or set up a business overseas you had to renounce your nationality to get your money out of the country. You needed a permit to subscribe to an overseas journal. You were not allowed to truck goods more than 40 miles and then 150 kilometres without the permission of the Railways. It was illegal to sell petrol *below* a minimum price. ... It was against the law to make carpets from anything other than wool. To buy margarine, you had to have a doctor's prescription.[80]

It was this system of controls, regulation, and compensation that Douglas and his colleagues set about to destroy in the 1980s. In large measure they succeeded – by 1996 an *Economist* poll of 10 leading economists ranked the New Zealand economy as the freest of the 20 countries considered.[81]

In conclusion, this first section has attempted to outline the main post-war economic patterns in the Anglo-American democracies considered here. Certainly this list is not exhaustive, nor has space permitted the detailed exploration of subtle differences and similarities between the four cases. What has emerged, however, is the general outline of the economic policy programs against which the market liberalizing governments of the 1980s directed their attention. In Britain, the targets were public ownership of corporations, Keynesian demand management and stop-go economic cycles in the pursuit of full employment, and the traditionally conciliatory governmental approach to trade unions and industrial relations. For the Mulroney government in Canada, the goal was to reverse the holy writ of protectionism and resistance to freer trade, particularly with the United States. In the Antipodes, the Labor governments of the 1980s fundamentally altered traditional policies of domestic defence, reducing tariffs, eliminating widespread government controls and regulations, and decisively moving away from previous patterns of centralized wage determination. In fact, as is discussed in the next chapter, the fundamental pattern of post-war economics in these countries was vitally shifted, and in many cases, reversed.

Economic Crisis: Providing an Opening for Change

The roots of the policy transformations witnessed in the 1980s in the Anglo-American democracies can be found most immediately in the troubled times of the 1970s and, with the exception of Britain, in the early 1980s. In each case, these countries experienced major challenges to the dominant pattern of post-war economic policy just described. These challenges – and governments' seeming inability to cope with them – led to a vague, yet widespread perception that "something has to change." Put simply, extreme conditions in the economic environment led to policy crisis, one that would open the door to norm entrepreneurs to initiate a radical shift not simply in day-to-day policy "settings," but in the fundamental aspects of each country's political-economic imaginary. As is discussed in chapter four, the economic difficulties of the 1970s and early 1980s created a window of opportunity for norm entrepreneurs to claim the post-war consensus paradigm had failed and to argue that a new policy approach based on wholly different philosophical grounds was justified. The crises of the 1970s and 1980s clearly did not dictate a neoliberal policy response – governments in other parts of the world in this period (notably, France and Greece) initially pursued an opposite, statist approach. Yet, it was the seeming ineffectiveness of the old policy paradigm that created an opportunity for the Anglo-American neoliberals to act. Thus, to achieve a fuller understanding of how, why, and in what ways the governments of the 1980s set about altering, and reversing, previous policies, we must look at the immediate run-up to the neoliberal period.

Put simply, the 1970s in Britain were years of economic and social turmoil. Just as Britain now serves as a kind of archetype of radical neoliberal restructuring in the 1980s, its experience in the 1970s is similarly a paradigmatic (albeit extreme) case of the serious economic crises experienced in many Western, industrialized nations. Perhaps not surprisingly, the extremes of the 1970s contributed to and, in many ways, made possible the extreme policy reactions of the 1980s.

In 1970, the Conservative government of Edward Heath took office promising what many envisioned to be a new-found adherence to deregulation, smaller government, and a putatively neoliberal program. Heath was seen by budding neoliberals to be a man of the new right, one who would breathe fresh air into what they believed to be a stale, overregulated economy.[82] Almost immediately, however, these tentative steps – dubbed the "Selsdon" program after the hotel where the government's policy seminar was held – went awry.

Upon taking office, the government faced the immediate problem of rising unemployment. With the number inching ever closer to the psychologically critical figure of 1 million,[83] the government decisively backtracked on its commitments to tight economic policies and less government intervention. As a minister in the Thatcher government recalled, "When Heath announced as prime minister that unemployment was approaching a million ... [it became] the single most important objective ... to prevent unemployment from going to a million. ... An edict came down from Heath to [Chancellor Anthony] Barber ... that the government must halve unemployment in a year. And in the Treasury [as well], the whole process was consumed with halving unemployment in a year."[84]

Barber's resulting 1972 budget was nothing less than a Keynesian-style reflation of the economy, a policy U-turn that, in the short run at least, launched the "Barber boom," which reduced unemployment (Appendix 1), but, with the misfortune of the 1973 world oil shock, produced inflation rates of 16 percent in 1974 and 24.2 percent in 1975 (Appendix 2). Meanwhile, the government was also forced to backtrack on its early commitment to reduce the scope of government intervention. The 1971 budget, for example, had cut income taxes and reduced subsidies for housing and school milk, the latter cut defended in the House of Commons by the Education Minister, Margaret Thatcher. But later in the year, the government was forced into retreat. Faced with the imminent bankruptcy of Rolls-Royce, the government nationalized the company. Later, the same thing happened again – this time, the government stepped in to nationalize and, at least for a time, rescue Upper Clyde Shipbuilders.[85]

It was the area of industrial relations, however, that would prove the downfall of the Heath government, not to mention the Labour government to follow.[86] The government's attempt at forcing change on trade unions – Robert Carr's Industrial Relations Bill of 1971 – essentially went the way of the attempt of the previous Labour government, which was Barbara Castle's white paper, *In Place of Strife*. When Carr's bill became law, its provisions for pre-strike ballots, cooling off periods, and union registration were so vociferously opposed and effectively boycotted by the unions that it became a largely dead letter. However, the great labour events of the Heath government were the confrontations with the miners. The first coal strike lasted six weeks in early 1972 and proved to be disastrous for the government. With coal supplies at dangerously low levels, severe winter weather increasing the need for fuel, and the country on a three-day work week, the government conceded pay increases of 17 to 24 percent for the average miner.[87] The second miners' strike finished off the government. Called in early 1974, the strike again put the country on a three-day week. With inflation spiraling up as a result of the OPEC oil embargo, the strike forced Heath into an election run on the theme "Who Governs Britain?" As a former minister in that government recalls, "[T]he more trade union power saw that it had the upper hand, the more it grabbed and finally began to assert itself so strongly that it began switching on and off the electricity. That was the atmosphere in which the '74 election was fought. The British public didn't know what the alternative was, but they said, 'We can't go on like this'."[88] The result was that the 28 February 1974 election produced a Labour minority government.[89]

In later years, Thatcherite Tories would characterize the Heath government as a failed first step – one that fired the first shots at the old consensus, but failed to finish it off. As Norman Tebbit, one of Thatcher's committed "dries," put it,

> Looking back one can see that it was Ted Heath's campaign of 1970 and the Selsdon declaration which marked the Tory Party's first repudiation of the post-war Butskellite consensus. No one should doubt that at the time of the election in 1970 Ted Heath was committed to the end of the corporatist consensus and to the new liberal economics. ... [His] arguments at the time, and the 1970 manifesto ... were music to the ears of radical Conservatives like myself. ... At the time of the election I naively assumed that the conversion of both Ted Heath and the Party to the Selsdon programme was one of deeply rooted conviction. In doing so I overestimated Ted Heath's conviction and I underestimated the resistance to new thinking and change within the establishment of the Party.[90]

Tebbit and the other neoliberals would have to wait for the Thatcher government to finish the policy revolution they had believed Heath would inaugurate.

In the meantime, the Labour governments of 1974 to 1979 faced an economic nightmare.[91] Britain, like the rest of the industrialized world, was entering a period of post-oil embargo stagflation – one in which, contrary to previously accepted economic theory, both inflation and unemployment rose simultaneously. In 1974, inflation hit an inter-year high of more than 28 percent, while wages rose by 26.4 percent.[92] Inflation would drop from these dizzying heights, but it would remain in double-digits for most of the remaining decade. Meanwhile, unemployment broke through the million barrier in 1976 and never dropped below it again – the rate of unemployment continued to climb, from 2.1 percent in 1974 to nearly 5 percent in 1979.

With the economic situation deteriorating, the government attempted to rein in public expenditure and control the expansion of the money supply in what constituted the first real abandonment of Keynesian policies in the post-war era. James Callaghan, the then-Prime Minister, signalled the shift at the 1976 Labour Party Conference in Blackpool: "We used to think that you could spend your way out of a recession and increase employment by cutting taxes and boosting Government spending. I tell you in all candour that that option no longer exists, and that insofar as it ever did exist, it only worked on each occasion since the war by injecting a bigger dose of inflation into the economy, followed by a higher level of unemployment as the next step."[93] Also in 1976, with the pound under extreme downward pressure and interest rates climbing to support it, Britain had to take the humiliating step of taking a loan from the International Monetary Fund in exchange for a commitment to effect significant cuts in public expenditure.[94] The loan stabilized the pound and the country for a time, but was a deeply humiliating psychological blow – "Britain after the IMF crisis had an air of being a nation after the deluge."[95]

The coup de grâce of the 1970s was still in store, however, and turned out again to be the thorny British problem of industrial relations.[96] From 1974 on the government attempted to hold wage demands in check as a means of controlling inflation. As Table 2 shows, real personal disposable incomes actually fell between 1974 and 1977, but insisting on wage restraint in the context of double-digit inflation simply bottled up demands for pay increases. In September 1978, a massive strike against Ford was settled with a 17 percent pay increase for the autoworkers. This victory encouraged other workers to press their cases. While much of the resulting pay increases were lost to inflation and higher prices – and thus were in reality far less dramatic in real terms than they appeared – they did reflect the government's inability to pursue the wage control aspect of its anti-inflation program. With workers scoring victories in the private sector, it was not long before the public sector unions mobilized.

Table 2. Real Disposable Personal Incomes, Britain (percentage change)

Year	Change	Year	Change
1970	3.4	1975	−0.6
1971	2.9	1976	0.0
1972	7.9	1977	−1.8
1973	5.9	1978	6.4
1974	0.8		

Source: Parliamentary Debates (Hansard) [United Kingdom], 967:91.

A national public sector strike on 22 January 1979 was followed by "a rash of local selective strikes by health-service workers, dustmen, even the grave-diggers of Liverpool. Rotting rubbish piled up in the streets. Schools were kept closed because their caretakers stayed away, as did cleaners, cooks, and deliverers of fuel."[97] Eventually, an agreement was reached, but sporadic strikes continued throughout February and March. This was the Winter of Discontent, the event that, in many ways, produced a widespread desire for change and essentially doomed the government. In the words of one former Labour minister,

> [Consensus] broke down most clearly in the 1979 General Election. The public sector unions were not prepared to accept any form of income limitation. ... Bodies in Liverpool were not being buried and there were people demonstrating outside hospitals and trying to stop blood supplies going in. I mean, it was very macabre stuff.[98]

According to a former senior trade union official,

> [W]hen a strike took place in the manufacturing industry, be it Ford's or Vauxhall's or whatever, the only people really affected were the people who worked there. But when you got refuse people, gravediggers, and others who took strike action, it hit the public and perhaps nowhere else better than in transport. And families going away at holiday time couldn't fly out because of the dispute with the goods handlers or whatever. Now all these created a picture for Maggie to blame the trade unions.[99]

Largely as a result of this widespread social unrest, the Callaghan government lost a no confidence motion on 28 March 1979 and went on to lose the ensuing May election. With a comfortable majority of 44, the new Tory government of Margaret Thatcher was now in a position to effect her new radical economic program – an opportunity that had been made possible in large part by the dominant public view that "something has to change."

Turning to Canada, we see that the run-up to the neoliberal period of the 1980s was different from that of Britain in a number of ways. More than anything else, the 1970s in Canada had little of the sense of impending economic disaster that seemed to recur periodically in Britain. In fact, as throughout Canada's recent history, any sense of impending crisis or national peril has usually been constitutional in nature and has dealt with the issue of Québec nationalism and separatism.[100] Nevertheless, economic issues were never far from the surface. No less than other industrial nations, Canada had to respond to the world economic shocks of the 1970s, and, as we shall see, the resulting difficulties created a space for normative change that the government of Brian Mulroney from 1984 on would attempt to fill.

Unlike Britain, Canada in the 1970s was dominated by one political party and indeed one prime minister: the decade belonged to the Liberals and to Pierre Elliott Trudeau, who took office in April 1968 and held it until June 1984, with the single exception of the June 1979–March 1980 Conservative interlude. Thus, Canada's economic policy at this time largely reflected Trudeau's own personal attitude toward economics.[101] Trudeau was, according to most observers, largely uninterested in economic policy. For him, economics were fundamentally a matter of management, of public administration; he was more interested in the "big issues" of Canadian society and foreign affairs than in the niceties of economic theory. As one of his former ministers put it, "Frankly, Mr. Trudeau wasn't interested in things economic."[102] And in the words of another of his ministerial colleagues, "Sometimes we didn't care about economics. We just did whatever we felt was right. Everything we thought that should be done, we did. ... I think [Trudeau] loved doing these things which were of a progressive nature, liberal, which helped the needy, which brought culture and the arts to the people, housing. If you had a good social case in that cabinet, it was tough to lose it on money grounds."[103]

The only exception to this disinterest in things economic was the issue of the United States. Significantly more internationalist and less disposed toward the United States than his predecessors, Trudeau sought to reduce Canada's dependence on and economic penetration by the

United States. Meanwhile, the government continued an essentially Keynesian set of economic policies. As the economic crises of the 1970s began to bite, the government largely maintained a reflationary stance, attempting to stop what became an inevitable spike in unemployment. In the end, just before the 1984 election, Canada suffered a severe recession and, in budget terms, was on the verge of serious fiscal trouble.

Trudeau's efforts to reduce Canadian dependence on US markets and limit the degree of US penetration of the Canadian market have been touched upon previously. Essentially, his approach to trade was classic economic nationalism. Exercising the so-called "third option," the government sought to strengthen its ties with a variety of countries other than the United States, hoping that over time such links would diminish the seemingly overwhelming influence of the United States. In this regard, the third option's most tangible results were the Foreign Investment Review Agency (FIRA), set up in 1974, and the National Energy Program (NEP), introduced in 1980. Both were intended to provide Canada with some measure of control over its own economic affairs – the first by providing for the systematic vetting of all foreign investment proposals in Canada (which, in reality, nearly always meant US investment), and the second by attempting to more rigorously control the supply, distribution, and pricing of Canadian oil in an effort to achieve a high degree of self-sufficiency in energy. They were, simply, products of Trudeau's attempts to lessen American influence in Canada and, in turn, would be prime targets of Brian Mulroney's efforts to reverse this trend and transform Canada into a market virtually entirely open to foreign, and particularly American, economic involvement.[104]

The other economic story of the Trudeau years, however, is the success of economic policy in the 1970s and its seeming ineffectiveness in the 1980s. For most of the decade of the 1970s, Canada held its own against the world economic forces that were causing so much distress in Britain and elsewhere. As Appendix 2 shows, Canada certainly saw a jump in inflation following the 1973 oil shock, but it was well below the OECD average, below that in Australia and New Zealand, and nearly 6.5 percent lower on average than that of Britain during this period. Some of this success was undoubtedly at the cost of higher unemployment – Canada's unemployment rate in the 1970s was higher than the other three countries, as it had been in the 1960s and would remain so in the 1980s. But the real indication of Canada's weathering of the storms of the 1970s were its rates of growth. From 1973 to 1979, Canada averaged real GNP growth of 4.2 percent a year, a remarkable figure when compared to 2.7 percent for Australia, 1.5 percent for Britain, New Zealand's abysmal 0.2 percent, and an OECD average of 2.6 percent.

But this rather respectable economic performance unfortunately did not last. Following the brief minority government of Joe Clark (1979–80) whose tax-raising, expenditure-cutting budget failed in parliament,[105] the Liberals returned in time to be hit by another worldwide recession. In fact, the recession of 1982 was the worst Canada had seen since the Great Depression. By way of comparison, GDP had shrunk in real per capita terms by only 0.4 percent in 1975 and 0.2 percent in 1980, following the twin oil shocks. But in 1982, the Canadian economy contracted 5.5 percent on a per capita basis, by far the worst of the four Anglo-American countries and much worse than its nearest OECD competitor, the United States, at 3.9 percent. The response of the government, and that of Finance Minister Marc Lalonde, was to take the brakes off the economy altogether. Reversing recent attempts at restraining inflation, the government tried a Keynesian-inspired stimulus to reduce unemployment from its 1983 high of nearly 12 percent and bring the country out of recession. As a former Finance Minister in Trudeau's government would later say, "[W]e had certainly not abandoned the Keynesian approach – that you need pump priming in times of deep recession. That certainly added to the deficit … but this was the prevalent economic theory of the day still."[106]

In the event, the strategy was at least temporarily successful: real GDP rose by 5.4 percent in 1984. But the cost of the repeated fiscal stimuli, plus the revenue impact of recession, was an explosion of government debt.[107] From moderate deficits in the range of 1.5 to 3 percent of GDP in the late 1970s, deficits in the early 1980s ballooned to 6 percent, then to 7 percent of GDP – put differently, a debt/GNP ratio of 16.6 percent in fiscal 1974/5 had grown to 45.2 percent in 1984/5.[108] Unemployment, however, reacted weakly to the deficit spending. When the Tories took office in 1984, the jobless rate was still in excess of 11 percent, double what it had been in the early 1970s.

Thus, the Conservative government of Brian Mulroney came to power in the aftermath of an extraordinarily painful recession, much more so even than the relatively easily weathered shocks of the 1970s. Mulroney's strategy was a neoliberal-inspired combination of tight monetary and fiscal policies. Absent, however, from his initial policy program was any mention of opening Canada to international economic competition. The issue of foreign penetration, so near to Pierre Trudeau's heart, was to come later. Instead, seizing the opportunity afforded by the 1981–2 recession, the new Tory government claimed that the key to lasting economic recovery was a thoroughgoing entrepreneurial revolution in Canada, cutting the size of "big government" and rolling back what it claimed were the big-spending excesses of Liberal hegemony.

Having considered Britain and Canada, we now turn to Australia. There, the 1970s was a decade of unrealized ambitions for many. Without a doubt, the seminal events of the decade were the accession to power of Gough Whitlam and the Australian Labor Party (ALP) in 1972 and its dismissal from government in 1975. Having been in the political wilderness for most of the post-war period – the Liberal/Country Coalition had been in power since 1949 – the ALP came to office in 1972 with a leader committed to achieving a social vision based on equality, social justice, and a progressive attitude to moral and social issues.[109] In his grand vision for what a modern Australia should be, Whitlam was similar in many ways to Trudeau – a man who thought the "deep thoughts" and left the technicalities of economic administration to his Treasurers. As a former Labor prime minister put it, "Gough was afraid of economics. He didn't want to know about it."[110] The government's policies were not radically different from what one would expect from social democratic parties of the day, except that, in the case of Australian Labor, a prolonged period in opposition had whetted the party's appetite for the introduction of what it viewed as necessary and long-overdue reforms and social spending programs. As one former Labor prime minister expressed: "[T]hat government thought its real job as a national government was to distribute the proceeds of post-war growth not realizing that the very period they came to office that post-war growth was about to cease."[111]

In that spirit, the government introduced a raft of spending measures, largely targeted on social programs. As described by a former Liberal minister,

[The Whitlam government was able] to suddenly hop into the sweet jar and imagine they could do anything. And I give one example, and it was an extraordinary one. There's a man called Gordon Bryant, Minister for Aboriginal Affairs. And he was a very kindly, decent man ... And as he went around to the aboriginal communities and talked to them, he literally – and I'm not joking here – he went round with a suitcase of money and as he saw things that needed fixing, he shelled it out. On the spot. In cash. ... Now, in an extreme form, that was illustrative of the Whitlam government's approach to economics.[112]

The result was a significant growth in government spending – from 26.3 percent of GDP in 1972 to 32.3 percent in 1975. Fuelled in large measure by government spending, the economy weathered the 1973 oil shock nicely, growing at a real rate of 5.5 percent in 1973, falling only to 1.9 percent in 1974. The real problem, however, was inflation. In 1975 it peaked at 15.1 percent, this up from just 3.9 percent in 1970. As a result, the government decided to scale back its spending and introduced a fiscally tight "mini-budget" in late 1974.

In the end, however, it all ended in tears for the Labor Party. In what has now become a legendary event in Australian political history, then-Governor General John Kerr responded to a government-opposition deadlock in parliament in 1975 by dismissing the Whitlam government in what Labor supporters viewed as a supremely undemocratic, even unconstitutional, act.[113] Whitlam's brief government was replaced by the Liberal/National Coalition under Malcolm Fraser, a government that would last until 1983.

Here too, however, disappointment was at hand. Just as Whitlam's government had promised its supporters a progressive revitalization of Australian society before it was prematurely dismissed, so Fraser's accession to power seemingly signalled the arrival of a new economic doctrine – that of limited government, deregulation, rolling back the state, and restraining taxation and expenditure. But, despite the language, the results were hardly revolutionary. Fraser proved to be more a traditional patrician conservative than a radical economic rationalist.[114] In the words of a former Liberal minister, "There were a lot of people who were unhappy with Fraser because they felt that in 1976 Australia needed a dose of very strong medicine to recover from the Whitlam excesses. And Fraser, [who] looked like a patrician figure, everyone thought that ... he would really make life tough for us. Now that didn't happen. ... [H]e is, in fact, a softie and the soft options were the ones that he adopted."[115]

Rather than cutting back the scope of government as Liberal "dries" had hoped, Fraser actually extended it during his term in office. When he left office in 1983, total government outlays totaled 36.4 percent of GDP, a substantial increase from the 32.3 percent left after the Whitlam government's heyday. Fearful of policies that might damage the social fabric he so valued, Fraser resisted any significant attempts at neoliberal economic change. Meanwhile, Australia's economy contracted in per capita terms by 2.3 and 0.4 percent in 1982 and 1983, inflation reemerged in the 1980s and hit 11.2 percent in 1982, and unemployment doubled throughout the course of the government, to 9.8 percent in 1983.

By the time the Hawke Labor government came to power in 1983, the perception was widely – though by no means universally – held that the old economic shibboleths had failed and that a new economic direction was needed. Whitlam had taken a typically social democratic tack – dramatically increasing government spending and introducing deficit financing. For the rest of the decade and into the 1980s, as the economy worsened, Fraser stayed the course, carrying on largely as Australian governments always had – with sizeable doses of regulation, protection, and domestic defence forming the cornerstone of economic policy. The paradoxical result was that, when radical neoliberal norm entrepreneurs actually came to power in Australia, they came from the *left* of the political spectrum – not from Fraser, not from a Whitlamite Labor Party, but from one that was prepared to take the recent economic troubles as a springboard for a radically different course in the latter half of the 1980s.

While Malcolm Fraser's rather conservative, status quo–oriented hand rode the economic tiller in Australia, in New Zealand a very different kind of "conservative" governed the country. There, from 1975 to 1984, Sir Robert Muldoon presided over what has to be considered the most interventionist and regulatory of any industrialized capitalist democracy. As discussed previously, New Zealand had been a highly regulated, highly protected economy throughout most of the twentieth century. It was even more enveloped in policies of domestic defence than its neighbour across the Tasman. But in Muldoon it had a forceful proponent of this approach, a man convinced that only the most active government economic intervention could help protect a country like New Zealand from the incursions and instabilities of the world market. As put by one of his former ministers, "Although he campaigned all his life on being a party of private enterprise, he actually didn't believe that the big decisions could be made other than by government. He really had enormous faith in government and he enjoyed the power of it."[116] As Muldoon himself claimed, he had little faith in abstract economic theories, whatever their ideological provenance. For him, economics was a matter of pragmatic steering based on the kind of idiosyncratic, intuitive feel for economic management that he believed he alone possessed:

I have said time and time again that people are the essence of economics. Unless you understand the people of the country, their hopes, their fears and their responses ... to adversity, you will never be able to understand the economy of that country or indeed have any flair for economic management. ... [E]conomics is not money or figures on a piece of paper or even in a computer, but *people*, and anyone who can understand the people of a country has taken the first and most important step towards understanding its economy.[117]

In the end, Muldoon's own innate conservatism and pragmatism meant that, as in Australia, it was a succeeding Labour government that would set itself the task of fundamentally reversing the post-war economic paradigm.

To put it simply, New Zealand in the 1970s experienced severe economic difficulties.[118] From 1973 to 1979, the average real rate of GDP growth was 0.2 percent; on a per capita basis, the economy actually contracted an average of 0.7 percent a year over the period. As growth essentially stopped, inflation skyrocketed (hitting 17.1 percent in 1980), the balance of payments deficit mushroomed, and unemployment went from practically zero to 5.7 percent in 1984. In any number of categories, New Zealand was performing very badly, and in comparative terms, it was doing worse than and losing ground to virtually every other OECD economy. Believing that only a firm, controlling hand such as his could see New Zealand's economy through, Muldoon's solution was strong government intervention.[119] As both Prime Minister and Minister of Finance, he essentially set economic policy himself, by personal whim, often disregarding the advice of colleagues and officials.[120] Muldoon's economic policies reflected this essentially personalistic approach – they fluctuated frequently, with the only constant being Muldoon's personal belief in the virtue of intervention. His fiscal policies were largely Keynesian – expansionary when economic downturns appeared, followed by a certain restraint when the budget deficit seemed too high. The result in the context of the turbulent times was fiscal deficits of 4–8 percent of GDP throughout his tenure, with the deficit hitting a high of nearly 10 percent in 1984.[121]

Undoubtedly, Sir Robert will best be remembered for his ultimately unsuccessful attempt at government-led economic investment: the "Think Big" projects. In a word, Think Big was the product of Muldoon's belief that there were significant developmental opportunities for New Zealand that, in a period of economic downturn, private enterprise was unwilling to exploit. As a former high ranking Labour minister explained, "I think the failure of the [protectionist] paradigm, plus the impact of the two oil shocks, led the National government into a kind of *reductio ad absurdum* of the paradigm in the sense of moving to an extraordinarily high level of controls, of intervention, of a massive industrialization program, which was clearly unsuited to New Zealand's needs or potential."[122]

To Muldoon, it was the government's duty to step in and take control of large economic development schemes. For a country the size of New Zealand, the projects were massive. In all, Think Big approached a price tag of NZ$10 billion – in a country whose total government expenditure in 1983/84 was only NZ$14.3 billion. Moreover, the projects were economically unsound, even leaving aside their cost. For instance, for New Zealand's greatly expanded steel production capacity to have been economically worthwhile, half of its production would have had to be exported – at a time of world oversupply of steel.[123] Roger Douglas would later ridicule Muldoon's approach as typical of the sins of government regulation:

> In the case of the "Think Big" projects … we would have been better to take the NZ$10 billion that they cost on to the top of the harbour bridge and dropped it over the side. The return would have been better, for we would have had a few New Zealanders out there swimming, and they would have grabbed a bit of the money and they would never have invested in any of those projects. We would have been a lot better off. They are a write-off under all circumstances. The Motonui expansion was premised on the basis that oil would now be NZ$100 a barrel. We have a little way to go to get to that figure.[124]

By 1984, New Zealand was at the stage of fiscal crisis.[125] As Table 3 shows, public debt had leveled off toward the end of the 1970s, but with the advent of Think Big, total public debt rose from 49.1 percent of GDP to 70.6 percent over the period 1981 to 1984.

In short, Muldoon's attempt to jump start the New Zealand economy by means of classic policies of domestic defence had failed. As one National MP put it, "Controls begat further controls and at the end of the day it was Sir Robert versus the rest of the economy."[126] Once Muldoon and the National Party lost the election of July 1984, the way was open for the Labour Party and its new Minister of Finance, Roger Douglas, who had his neoliberal package ready to go from the start. As

Table 3. Total Public Debt, New Zealand (percentage of GDP)

Year	Pct.	Year	Pct.
1974–5	41.3	1980–1	47.5
1975–6	47.6	1981–2	49.1
1976–7	44.6	1982–3	58.1
1977–8	48.5	1983–4	63.5
1978–9	50.4	1984–5	70.6
1979–80	49.1		

Source: OECD (New Zealand) 1985, 9.

is discussed in the next chapter, this policy agenda was to prove among the most radical of any contemplated by democratic governments in the industrialized world. Thus, in New Zealand as in the other three cases, the perception that the old paradigm had failed (one consciously nurtured by norm entrepreneurs; see chapter four) helped the neoliberals discredit the old approach in the eyes of many and created an opportunity for them to promote its replacement by a new neoliberal imaginary.

3 The Neoliberal Revolution of the 1980s and Beyond

Having sketched the background to neoliberalism in chapter two – specifically, the dominant economic paradigm that obtained in the Anglo-American countries during the post-war period, as well as the economic difficulties faced by governments there in the late 1970s and early 1980s – we now turn to the actual period of neoliberal change that began in the 1980s and continued thereafter. What the neoliberal governments of the 1980s and 1990s actually did, and the ways in which they went about doing it, is the focus of this chapter. Here, we consider the actual policy revolutions that were initiated by one side of politics in these countries and later consolidated and entrenched by the other – the changes that succeeding chapters seek to explain and interpret.

Emphasizing, however, the often highly contingent, case-specific nature of ideational and policy change, this chapter seeks to show how the transition to the new neoliberal political-economic imaginary did not occur in a single, consistent way in the four Anglo-American countries. While, by the end of the 1980s, and certainly by the turn of the twenty-first century, neoliberal economics were firmly entrenched as the economic orthodoxy in all four countries, the path to that point was not a uniform one. Rather, reflecting the variety of institutional structures, economic challenges, and unique strategies of norm entrepreneurs in each country, it is evident that the pace of policy change, the scope of the policy revolution, the fervor with which neoliberalism was pursued, and even the tone of the political rhetoric surrounding each government's economic rationalist program differed in important ways. As this chapter illustrates, there were two identifiable patterns of neoliberal change in these cases: the first, a "revolutionary" model, in which norm entrepreneurs adopted the economically rationalist view with a fervor and commitment approaching that of religious dogma, implementing radical change with the explicit goal of thoroughly shifting their countries' basic economic paradigms; and the second, a relatively more gradual, less overtly doctrinaire transition away from the old consensus, implementing a neoliberal program in such a way that a new political-economic imaginary came to be instantiated, albeit in a significantly more incremental, even evolutionary way.

These differences point to the fact, discussed in chapter one, that there are multiple, diverse approaches and strategies to instantiating a new political-economic imaginary. Neoliberalism as a set of "first-order" ideas operating, as in Figure 1, at the level of the imaginary did not imply a uniform mode of implementation or policy actualization. Rather than implying the adoption of a single set of policy instruments across all four countries, neoliberalism admitted of multiple policy programs, functioned within a variety of political and economic structural contexts, and was implemented at various paces by norm entrepreneurs who differed in background, temperament, and partisan affiliation. For these reasons, neoliberalism in the Anglo-American democracies should not be viewed as a kind of general model, or even ideal type, of neoliberalism change applicable universally. Instead, neoliberalism in these cases can be seen as the case-specific, contingent application of a more general ideational construct to the unique circumstances of individual economies. The application of these ideas created, so to speak, British, Canadian, Australian, and New Zealand species of a larger, increasingly global, ideational genus – that is, these ideas and policies derived from a similar ideational source, but were adapted and applied in ways unique and allegedly appropriate to each national case. To paraphrase Finnemore's observation quoted in chapter one, isomorphism did not produce equifinality.[1]

We begin with the first, revolutionary model of change – that of the British Conservatives and New Zealand Labour – where the goal was explicitly to change the very basis of economic policy or, in the terms of this book, the underlying imaginary. The discussion then turns to Canada and Australia, where norm entrepreneurs – again, Conservative and Labor, respectively – shared a relatively more gradual, less overtly doctrinaire and confrontational approach to neoliberal change. In the end, however, while the methods, pace, and scope of neoliberal reform varied between the four cases, the final result of the 1980s in these countries was the same: the entrenchment of neoliberalism as the normative economic policy paradigm. The chapter concludes with an examination of the ways in which the governments that succeeded the initial norm entrepreneurs maintained intact nearly all of the key elements of the new economic paradigm, adopting a neoliberal orientation as their own. In so doing – by adopting a nearly identical underlying philosophical orientation and thus effectively removing neoliberalism as a key point of partisan political debate – these successor governments helped consolidate the new political-economic imaginary as an increasingly taken-for-granted part of the ideational and policy landscapes in their countries.

The "Crash Through or Crash" Approach to Norm Entrepreneurialism

The first two cases considered here constitute the pattern of revolutionary change aimed squarely at the post-war interventionist political-economic imaginary – those of Britain and New Zealand. In these countries, the governments – one Conservative, one Labour – instituted a program of radical economic change with the goal of fundamentally restructuring most aspects of their national economies and enshrining an economically rationalist, market-driven model of economic and social relations as the norm. Not content to introduce piecemeal changes that selectively addressed pressing problems at Figure 1's level of policy settings, but rather explicitly aiming to fundamentally reshape the philosophical basis of economic relations in their countries, the governments of Margaret Thatcher and David Lange adopted what could be labelled the "crash through or crash" approach: a radical ideational shift pursued as part of a deeply held ideological commitment to the alleged superiority of market outcomes, forcefully implemented with little heed for current economic conditions, political risk, or social opposition. Market liberalization was pursued by these governments with a zeal and depth of faith usually reserved for religious crusaders and zealots. Markets were to be freed from the warren of controls and regulations that allegedly sapped their vitality, the "dead hand" of the state and its pervasive economic intervention were to be eliminated, and individuals were to be liberated from the "nanny state" and its "socialist" pretensions of equality, redistribution, and social justice.

In this campaign, it is important to note, neither government came to power unprepared. Rather, in different ways, norm entrepreneurs had laid the groundwork for their radical economic programs before coming to power. In the case of Margaret Thatcher and the British

Conservatives, the development of the new Tory commitment to neo-liberalism had been clear. From her accession to the party leadership in 1975 to her arrival in Downing Street in 1979, Margaret Thatcher had led the party on a well-publicized shift away from the traditional, Butskellite consensus policies of the past to the new dogma of monetarism, entrepreneurialism, and "getting the state out" of the economy. The key event in the transformation of the party's economic policy was the 1977 publication of *The Right Approach to the Economy*. In it, the Conservative Party outlined the major elements of what would become the new economic faith and, in so doing, became one of the first parties in the world to systematically shift its economic philosophy to the newly emerging tenets of neoliberalism.

In the case of New Zealand Labour, the conversion to economic rationalism after it took office in 1984 came as a shock to many. The party had given virtually no public indication in the run-up to the 1984 election that it would be as radical as it proved to be once in office.[2] As a result, many in the party and beyond felt blindsided by the Fourth Labour Government's attempt at constructing an economic rationalist revolution.[3] As a member of that government recalled, "When we first got in [in 1984], there was no economic policy. It hadn't been written."[4] This was only partly true, however. The party manifesto had indeed given no hint of what was to come. Yet, the new Finance Minister, Roger Douglas, had not hidden his own conversion to neoliberal economics. His 1980 book, *There's Got to Be a Better Way!*, can be seen as his first blast against the old consensus, signalling that, as least as far as Douglas was concerned, the next Labour government should lead a dramatic turnabout in economic policy.[5] As the same Labour minister would put it, "If you looked at his book and look[ed] at what happened, he was really upfront and honest, and he did practically everything he said he'd do."[6]

The most defining aspect of the "crash through or crash approach," however, was the fundamentally doctrinaire way in which economically rationalist policies were pursued in Britain and New Zealand. Simply put, free market economics took on something of the status of religious dogma, with the goal being the replacement of the "consensus," interventionist political-economic imaginary with a neoliberal one. Deregulation, privatization, free markets, and the virtues of individual initiative and self-reliance were held to be ontologically correct and true, while the old policies of consensus, communitarian values, and a mixed economy were relegated to the status of economic delusion, either (at best) hopelessly irrelevant and antediluvian or (at worst) part of the Hydra-headed beast of "socialism."

Thatcher above all personified the dogmatic zeal of the neoliberals. A self-described "conviction politician," she made no attempt to hide the philosophical commitment underlying her approach: "The other side have got an ideology ... we must have one as well. ... There are dangers in consensus: it could be an attempt to satisfy people holding no particular views about anything. ... No great party can survive except on the basis of firm beliefs about what it wants to do."[7] One of her ministers added, "She was never happy unless she had a doctrinaire explanation of what she was going to do. ... It was very characteristic when she was considering a decision – she would go up to a bookshelf and she would try and find some reference which would justify it. She was always looking for the theoretical justification."[8] The same could be said of Roger Douglas in New Zealand. There, economic rationalism was adopted, not as an expedient, or a pragmatic experiment when all else had failed. Rather, it was promoted as a self-evidently necessary program of change to be forced through at maximum speed with "no room for reflection or an alternative analysis."[9]

We begin with Britain. No sooner had the dust settled on the selection of Margaret Thatcher as the new leader of the Conservative Party in 1975 than she set about reordering the party's fundamental approach to economic policy.[10] As mentioned previously, the key initial statement of the new approach was to be found in a Conservative economic policy manifesto, *The Right Approach to the Economy*. Issued in 1977, it definitively stated Thatcher's intention to break with the post-war consensus pattern of public policy and to set Britain on a path of economic reform that, it argued, would restore the market's potential for growth and lead to a reversal of the long-term decline of the British economy. To the Thatcherites, the enemy was the state and the goal of public policy must be national liberation from it.

> Our policies are designed to restore and defend individual freedom and responsibility. We mean to protect the individual from excessive interference from the State or by organisations licensed by the State, to stop the drift of power away from the people and their democratic institutions, and to give them more power as citizens, as owners and as consumers. We shall do this by better financial management, by reducing the proportion of the nation's wealth consumed by the State, by steadily easing the burden of Britain's debts, by lowering taxes where we can, by encouraging

home ownership, by taking the first steps towards making this country a nation of worker owners.[11]

Despite the campaign-style hyperbole, the message was clear: Britain was to see a government committed to a radical free market vision of state-society relations. Central to this program was an extreme economic individualism. Rejecting the traditional, paternalistic Conservative concern for social harmony and community, the Thatcherite dries emphasized the virtues of a healthy self-interest. Her famous remark, "There is no such thing as society," and her contemptuous dismissal of those who "drool and drivel" about caring for others, reflected with brutal clarity the deeply individualistic, anti-communitarian values informing the political-economic imaginary she envisioned for Britain.[12] In the words of one of her own ministers, "One of the things she was good at articulating was that your wants and needs are not all selfish. They are yours and they are probably right to be so. They are quite natural rights. You have nothing to be ashamed of."[13]

Once in office, Thatcher and her first Chancellor, Sir Geoffrey Howe, set about creating this new individualist Britain through the application of the Tories' key economic policy: monetarism.[14] To put it simply, monetarism in Britain was motivated by the single, overriding goal to stamp out inflation. All other considerations, including the social costs of her anti-inflation crusade, were ignored. Inflation was framed as the fundamental enemy to be defeated at all costs.[15] As Thatcher stated in 1975, "Inflation is a pernicious evil capable of destroying any society built on a value system where freedom is paramount. No democracy has survived a rate of inflation consistently higher than 20 per cent. When money can no longer be counted on to act as a store of value, savings and investment are undermined, the basis of contracts is distorted and the professional and middle-class citizens, the backbone of all societies, is disaffected."[16]

Encouraged by her in-house monetarist advocate, Sir Keith Joseph,[17] Thatcher had adopted the ideas of Milton Friedman and others[18] that the fundamental cause of – and cure for – inflation could be found in the size and rate of increase of the money supply. In the monetarists' view, Keynesian-inspired reflations of the economy simply produced momentary increases in output at the cost of higher long-term inflation and growing public debt. Once the reflation was over, output returned to a more natural level, but the injection of inflation into the economy remained. Therefore, according to this view, "growth without inflation was most likely to be obtained if the government adhered to rigid targets for monetary growth and maintained a low public sector borrowing requirement (PSBR) *whatever the state of the economy.*[19] This was a clear rejection of Keynesian, "that great engine of creeping socialism."[20] Instead of following the classic Keynesian route of acting to jump start an economy in the midst of an economic downturn through the application of expansionary fiscal and monetary policies, the monetarist view was that tight fiscal and monetary policies should be maintained at all times, regardless of current economic conditions, in order to keep inflation at bay.

In addition, "there was a nice sense of automatic justice to the operation of monetarism"[21] – in a restrictive monetary environment, "unreasonable" wage demands from "belligerent" trade unionists would simply cost them their jobs. In this sense, too, monetarism signalled the end of a key element in the consensus political-economic imaginary. The traditional emphasis placed on conciliation and compromise with workers was replaced with one in which workers – and, in particular, "unreasonable" ones – were framed as the enemy. The role of the state in this new paradigm was no longer constructed as ensuring social stability and harmony through the fair and equitable resolution of industrial conflict. Instead, it was to promote economic growth by "holding the line" against workers and their demands – the healthy "individualism" of the entrepreneur had to be defended against the destructive "selfishness" of the worker. The logic was explicitly spelled out by Howe: "If workers and their representatives take pay decisions which are unwise because they seek too much, they will find they have crippled their employers and gravely harmed themselves by destroying their own jobs."[22] It is important to emphasize the degree to which monetarism – in and of itself a policy setting – was rooted in the new neoliberal, free market political-economic imaginary. As one of Thatcher's ministers described it, she successfully, rhetorically coerced the skeptics in her cabinet this way:

We [had to] run the most rigorous monetary policy. In fact, it became an obsession ... that [was] ludicrously scientific. They went right over the top the other way. ... I remember Mrs. Thatcher lecturing the whole cabinet about how if the PSBR rose sort of one penny above (in those days) six billion, this would have some amazingly mechanical effect of automatically raising interest rates. And any member of the cabinet who wanted to spend a penny more – "Oh, so you want higher interest rates, do you?" So you were frozen by this alleged harness. Of course … none of these mechanical links really existed, except in the minds of the really dry monetary "scientists."[23]

In actual fact, Thatcher's self-declared "firm and unshakeable" resolve to adhere to tight monetary targets produced decidedly dubious results. While the policy failed to control the growth of the money supply to the extent the government wished, it undoubtedly contributed to levels of unemployment unseen in Britain since the Great Depression. According to the new program, dubbed the Medium Term Financial Strategy (MTFS), both monetary and fiscal policies were directed at eliminating inflation and restoring British competitiveness and growth.[24] The government's plan was to set specific targets for the yearly growth of the money supply, to be achieved primarily through the manipulation of interest rates and the control of government budget deficits. As it turned out, control of the money supply proved well beyond the government's capacity.[25] As Table 4 shows, year after year, the annual growth of the money supply exceeded the government's stated targets. Even with interest rates approaching 20 percent, the strategy did little to stem monetary expansion. However, despite this failure and notwithstanding the fact that a deep recession was underway – with unemployment in the double digits and real GDP declining – the government initially held firm to the dogma of strict monetary control.

In the years to come, the government was increasingly forced to abandon its single-minded approach to inflation, while never openly admitting that its monetarist strategy had failed. It initially tried targets on other monetary aggregates – M3 was joined by M0, M4, and M5[26] – while the targets themselves were increasingly relaxed (and usually exceeded in actual fact).[27] Five percent – not zero – "effectively became the 'target' inflation rate, with the government only tightening policy when inflation looked set to breach this ceiling."[28]

Whether the monetarist experiment in Britain contributed to the dramatically reduced rates of inflation by the end of the 1980s is debatable.[29] Two facts, however, are not in dispute. First, monetarism marked the end of Keynesianism as the dominant policy orientation of government: "Monetarism had become synonymous with Thatcherism (or Thatcherism with monetarism) and [the Prime Minister] remained wedded to her simple beliefs that governments had no business printing money and that markets must be allowed their play."[30] Second,

Table 4. Money Supply Targets and Actual Outturns, Britain

	Medium Term Financial Strategy Targets (percent per annum)										
	1980	1981	1982	1983	1984	1985	1986	1987	1988	1989	Actual
M3											
80/81	7–11										20.0
81/82	6–10	6–10									14.5
82/83	5–9	5–9	8–12								10.0
83/84	4–8	4–8	7–11	7–11							9.8
84/85			6–10	6–10	6–10						9.5
85/86			5–9	5–9	5–9	5–9					14.8
86/87					4–8	4–8	11–15	**			18.0
87/88					3–7	3–7					22.1
88/89					2–6	2–6					22.4
M1											
82/83			8–12								11.0
83/84			7–11	7–11							11.0
84/85			6–10	6–10	**						
85/86				5–9							
M5											
82/83			8–12								9.0
83/84			7–11	7–11							12.3
84/85			6–10	6–10	**						
85/86				5–9							
M0											
84/85					4–8						5.5
85/86					3–7	3–7					3.5
86/87					2–6	2–6	2–6				4.0
87/88					1–5	1–5	2–6	2–6			5.0
88/89					0–4	0–4	1–5	1–5	1–5		7.5
89/90						1–5	1–5	1–5	1–5		6.0
90/91									0–4	0–4	2.7

Source: Healey 1993, 138–9.
** Target range abandoned

monetarism marked the end of the commitment to full employment, the "Ark of the Covenant of all political parties,"[31] in the 1950s and 60s. The control of unemployment – that great and much feared enemy of the ordinary worker and a *sine qua non* of government policy for decades – ceased to be a prime goal of British government policy. Indeed, the active role of the state in combating unemployment would come to be largely excised from the national political-economic imaginary. In its place was a single-minded determination to control inflation. As unemployment climbed, the contrast between Thatcherite monetarism and old One Nation Toryism looked even starker. As a Thatcher minister put it, "Despite the reassurances of the monetary gurus that it wouldn't lead to high unemployment if we ran a very tight monetary policy, … it did. And the million [unemployed] that Ted Heath had regarded as a disaster in '72 rapidly became two million and so on."[32] Yet, the government was not to be moved – its only responsibility was to control inflation, regardless of the employment consequences. Nigel Lawson, a future Chancellor, enunciated the priority of inflation over unemployment quite clearly in 1982, at the height of recession:

> [For] so long it was believed that governments could always maintain full employment by accommodating fully, in monetary terms, whatever wage or price push happened to occur … By contrast, now that we have learned the hard way that [this] … leads not to full employment but to accelerating inflation, the political pressure is greatly weakened and the moral pressure reversed. Thus the important change in the economic framework is not that we happen to be passing through a particular stage in the trade cycle. It is that *the notion that governments can guarantee full employment is now recognised for the cloud-cuckoo-land it always was*; and the moral that management and unions alike cannot be protected from the consequences of their own actions has at last been drawn.[33]

Perhaps the Thatcherite attitude toward unemployment is best summed up in the following anecdote, reported by Jenkins: "Before the end of [1980] unemployment, at 1.3 million when [Thatcher] came in, had exceeded two million. 'How much responsibility do you feel for unemployment?' Sir Keith Joseph was asked in an interview. Sincere as ever, he replied, 'None. None'."[34]

The skyrocketing unemployment of the early 1980s contributed to another important element in Thatcher's policy program – the emasculation of the trade unions.[35] As described in chapter two, the 1970s, and particularly the latter years of the decade, had been a period of tremendous industrial upheaval. During the 1970s, an average of 12.9 million workdays a year were lost to industrial disputes, compared with an average of 3.6 million in the 1960s.[36] The Heath government had lost two major confrontations with the miners, in 1972 and 1974, and the Callaghan Labour government had been felled by the massive series of rows with public sector unions during the Winter of Discontent. On both sides of politics, and among the public at large, the mood was shifting toward one of hostility toward trade unions. Whereas in 1970, the *Economist* could claim that "now … a lot of people, ranging from Ford car workers to Tory schoolmistresses and farmers, regard strikes and demonstrations as exciting and fashionable things,"[37] by the end of the decade, even the attitudes of such committed consensus-era, "middle way" politicians as Lord Hailsham had hardened: "Of course Trade Unions were formed to defeat hard faced masters, Thomas Gradgrind and his kind. But if I may coin a phrase: who are the masters now? … It is one thing to picket Thomas Gradgrind's factory. It is another thing to picket a hospital, a school, or a magistrate's Court."[38] This rising sense of frustration and anger over the industrial warfare of the late 1970s helped provide an opportunity for Margaret Thatcher to directly take on trade union power. At the Conservative Party Conference in 1979 she signalled the tone her labour policies would take:

> What madness it is, that winter after winter we have these great set-piece battles, in which the powerful unions do so much damage to the industries on which their members' living standards depend. … The unions win awards their members have not earned; the company pays out increases it can't afford; the prices to the consumer go up; Government prints the money to make it all possible, and everyone congratulates it on its success as an honest broker, with or without the beer and sandwiches at Number Ten.[39]

The government was no longer to be the "honest broker" in semi-corporatist bargaining between employers and workers. Instead, it would now "stand up to the unions." As discussed previously, a large part of the government's strategy was to run such a tight monetary policy that the economy simply could not accommodate wage increases – workers could then easily find themselves priced out of their jobs if they insisted on "excessive" pay increases. In the public sector – the locus of most of the conflict during the Winter of Discontent – the government's new cash-limited budgets sought to enforce the same restrictions on ministers: if they granted overly generous pay awards to public employees, their departments' budgets would run short. Under no circumstances, however, would the government consider a return to the old strategy of incomes policies, attempting to either negotiate or enforce a predetermined rate of pay increase on workers.[40] The "free market" would determine what pay rises could be awarded – a market, that is, heavily constrained by the government's tight monetary regime.

This "conscious decision to allow unemployment to increase to record levels, thereby destabilizing union membership and weakening the bargaining position of organized labour"[41] was supplemented by legislative acts – the Employment Acts of 1980 and 1982 and the Trade Union Act of 1984. Here we see an attempt to effect change in the underlying imaginary through change in policy settings. Capitalizing on public distrust, even hostility, toward industrial action, Thatcher legislated to restrict union prerogatives severely. In what were clear instances of material coercion, her government legislated, inter alia, to outlaw flying pickets, remove unions' legal immunity from civil action, compensate those expelled from unions in closed shops, and strictly regulate workers' ability to declare closed shops, elect union officials, and call strikes. The biggest challenge to the government came, perhaps unsurprisingly, from the miners in 1984. Having backed down over the threat of a miners' strike in 1981, Thatcher had prepared for a second round. With coal stocks at high levels at power stations throughout the country and with police well-organized to confront picketers, the miners under the leadership of Arthur Scargill were unable to create the disruptions of 1972 and 1974. To make matters worse for the union, the miners were divided – Scargill had not polled miners prior to calling the strike, and as a result, many pits remained open, worked by dissident miners who created a new organization, the Union of Democratic Mineworkers. As Thatcher refused any talk of compromise and as more and more miners defied Scargill and returned to work, by March 1985 the strike was over, and Thatcher had succeeded in breaking the back of one of the formerly most powerful unions.[42] In effect this was not only the end of miners' militancy – reinforced in large measure by the collapse of the industry as a whole[43] – but of industrial conflict altogether. As Table 5 shows, by the 1990s, the number of workdays lost to industrial disputes was at a post-war low.

A third major element in Thatcher's program was one to be repeated with a vengeance in New Zealand: the wholesale privatization of state-owned enterprises.[44] At the heart of the emergent neoliberal imaginary was the notion that private individuals and corporations are inherently superior, more efficient economic managers than the state. In its most extreme form, this view left precious little as legitimate state economic activities. On the one hand, any arguably necessary and beneficial social function notwithstanding, loss-making public enterprises were seen as nothing more than massive drains on the public purse. On the other hand, profitable enterprises could self-evidently compete in the private

Table 5. Industrial Disputes and Working Days Lost, Britain, 1960–97

	1960–9	1970–9	1980–9	1990–7
Industrial Dispute (avg/yr)	2,446	2,598	1,123	295
Working Days Lost	3,555	12,870	7,213	607

Source: International Labour Office, various years.

sector and should be returned there. In keeping with the spirit of the neoliberal project, efficiency and profitability – not social benefit – were the acid tests of economic activity. As the Chancellor, Geoffrey Howe, put it, "All too often subsidies have been paid in order to maintain production in those industries which were failing to sell their output profitably to the public. ... [W]e have tended to subsidize the production of those goods the public wants least, produced by those processes which are relatively least efficient, manned by employees who are most highly paid relative to their productivity – not a recipe for improving living standards!"[45]

The public tendering of state-owned assets also served to advance a long-cherished goal of Mrs Thatcher – to turn Britain into her vision of a property-owning society of ordinary citizen-capitalists.[46] As *The Right Approach to the Economy* – in a clear appeal to "advantage" or material persuasion – articulated the view,

> The Conservative Party's commitment to a property-owning democracy is long-standing. We believe the time has come to extend it to ownership, not only of homes, but of wealth in other forms as well. For us a free society is a society in which property in all its forms is held by as many people as possible. This is the antithesis of the narrow State ownership in which Socialists believe. We would like to see the habit of personal capital accumulation, making vast numbers of people owners as well as earners, much more deeply ingrained in our society.[47]

By the time the Tories left office in 1997, the Thatcher-initiated privatization program had resulted in nearly 50 state-owned enterprises being privatized, for total proceeds of more than £60 billion, or in excess of 10 percent of 1994 GDP.[48] Whereas in 1979, "the state had a major stake in many of Britain's most important industries, namely steel, motor vehicles, aero engines, aerospace, coal, rail, road haulage, air travel, oil, telecommunications, electricity, gas and water," by 1997, none of these

Table 6. Nationalization and Privatization in Britain, 1945–97

Nationalized Industries, 1945–79	Privatization, 1979–97
Bank of England (1946)	British Petroleum (1979–87)
Civil aviation (1946)	British Aerospace (1981, 1985)
Cable and Wireless (1946)	British Sugar Corporation (1981)
Coal (1946)	Cable and Wireless (1981, 1983, 1985)
Road and rail transport (1946)	Amersham International (1982)
Road haulage denationalized (1953)	National Freight Consortium (1982)
Land development rights (1947)	Britoil (1982, 1985)
Electricity (1947)	Associated British Ports (1985)
Gas (1948)	Enterprise Oil (1984)
Iron and Steel (1959)	Sealink (1984)
Denationalized (1953)	Jaguar (1984)
Renationalized (1967)	British Telecom (1984–94)
Rolls-Royce (1971)	British Gas (1986)
British Leyland (1975)	British Airways (1987)
British National Oil Corp. (1976)	Royal Ordnance (1987)
British Aerospace (1977)	Rolls-Royce (1987)
British Shipbuilders (1977)	British Airports Authority (1987)
	Rover Group (1988)
	British Steel (1988)
	Water companies, 10 (1989)
	Electricity companies, 12 (1990)
	National Power/Powergen (1991)
	Scottish Electricity Companies (1991)
	British Coal (1994)
	Railtrack (1995)
	British Energy (1996)
	Rail passenger franchises (1996–7)

Source: Coxall and Robins 1998, 62.

industries remained in public hands.[49] (See Table 6.) As a result of "selling the family silver,"[50] the share of British industry in public hands fell by 60 percent from 1979 to 1991, and the number of private citizens owning shares – and thus at least potentially with a personal stake in the new pro-market policies – grew substantially,[51] from 3 million in 1979 to 11 million in 1990.[52]

In short, the monetarist attack on Keynesianism, the unemployment it helped produce, the significant weakening of the trade unions, and the wholesale sell-off of public enterprises radically transformed the nature of the British economy throughout the 1980s. If one includes such policies as council home sales,[53] the reform of local government and its finances,[54] as well as shakeups in health and education,[55] the magnitude of the changes becomes even more apparent. In many important respects, the "frontiers of the state" were well and truly "rolled back." Over time – as high unemployment persisted, the number of trade unionists plummeted, and former state-owned firms remained in private hands – the neoliberal shift became naturalized into the British political-economic imaginary as a relatively unremarkable state of affairs.

This same crusading zeal to reshape a country's dominant economic paradigm was characteristic of the other "crash through or crash" neoliberal government of the 1980s, that of the Labour Party of New Zealand. There, Roger Douglas and a small coterie of fellow ministers – David Caygill and Richard Prebble, backed, for a time, by the Prime Minister, David Lange – drove the revolutionary pace of change. As mentioned previously, Douglas in the late 1970s and early 1980s had experienced a gradual conversion to neoliberal ideas. Despite being the scion of an old Labour family, he came to believe that New Zealand's economic troubles, and especially its lack of growth, stemmed from overregulation and a lack of private initiative and enterprise. In many ways, this was a personal conversion – largely on his own and certainly not shared by most in the Labour Party. Once Labour acceded to power in 1984, however, Douglas and his views came to dominate the making of economic policy. Given the sense of immediate crisis that pervaded both government and public opinion, the perceived failure of the Muldoon government's interventionist approach, and the new prime minister's admitted uncertainties about economic policy, Douglas took over the Finance portfolio in a position to effect significant change.[56] As David Lange himself put it, "when the crisis hit in July 1984 it was Roger Douglas who, above all, had thought through the economic issues – so, when the Cabinet needed to fall back on an economic philosophy, it was Douglas who had one."[57] Moreover, following the election of 1984, Labour had a solid majority – 56 of 95 seats in New Zealand's unicameral parliament – and thus faced virtually no institutional or constitutional obstacles to their emerging neoliberal program.[58] Once in power,

> [Douglas and his colleagues] began moving as far and as fast as the few institutional constraints allowed. Easton has called this the "blitzkrieg" approach: "In each case the lightning strike involved a policy goal radically different from the existing configuration, to be attained in a short period, following a surprise announcement and very rapid implementation."[59]

Critics and opponents were always on the defensive and left debating last week's reforms. The major decisions had already been taken; any consultation was left to details.[60]

Or, as the "blitzkrieg" approach was summarized by a disgruntled member of that government, "Instead of saying, 'We've got to change this. ... The water in the bath is a bit too hot and we've got to cool it down a bit' or something like that, ... they pulled the plug out just like that. It happened so fast that it's almost breathtaking now, when you think about it. We weren't coping with one change here and one change there. We were coping with thirty major changes all at once."[61] With striking similarity to Thatcher's neoliberal agenda, the program of economic, ideational, and structural change carried out in New Zealand centred on three key areas: the liberalization of markets and trade, a reduction in the size and scope of the state sector, and a monetary policy whose overriding goal was price stability.

As previously discussed, New Zealand, throughout most of the post-war period and certainly after Muldoon's large-scale "Think Big" interventions, was perhaps the most regulated economy in the Western industrialized world. With a political-economic imaginary that undergirded belief in both the appropriateness and necessity of state economic intervention, a wide range of government regulations, controls, subsidies, and restrictions affected virtually every aspect of the economy. New Zealand was, as David Lange framed it, "run like a Polish shipyard."[62] It was this elaborate system of controls that first felt the brunt of the Douglas steamroller.

The financial system was the first to be deregulated. As Massey puts it, "[w]ithin nine months of Labour's election victory in July 1984 the financial system went from being the most to possibly the least regulated within the OECD."[63] In July 1984, interest rate controls were abolished. In December, exchange controls were eliminated, allowing for virtually free capital flows in and out of the country. Then, in March 1985, the New Zealand dollar was floated. Foreign banks were allowed to operate in New Zealand, and a whole host of regulations strictly limiting the activities of financial institutions were eliminated.[64]

Deregulation was extensive in other sectors as well. In agriculture – traditionally the most protected and subsidized sector in a country once dubbed "England's overseas farm" – the government dismantled virtually all subsidies, controls, and supports. In fact, as Table 7 indicates, the effective rates of assistance to agriculture over the course of

Table 7. Effective Rates of Assistance to Agriculture, New Zealand

	1980/81	1983/84	1986/87	1988/89
Sheepmeat	11	100+	45	−3
Wool	−2	25	−7	−13
Milk	16	100+	3	−6

Source: OECD (New Zealand) 1989, 37; 1991, 63.
Note: Effective rates of assistance measure the degree to which an industry's value added is artificially inflated by government assistance. Thus, a rate of 100 percent indicates that for every dollar of value added, the state provides a dollar of assistance. A figure in excess of 100 percent indicates that the value of output was actually less than the value of inputs, when calculated at world market prices. Negative amounts exist when the "cost excess" – the cost due to higher rates of input prices caused by assistance to other sectors – is greater than the assistance to this industry.

the decade declined dramatically. By 1988, they were actually negative. The deregulation of agriculture was matched by the liberalization of transport. Previously, in support of the railroads, it had been unlawful for goods to be transported more than 150 kilometers by road. Similar protective controls existed for air transport, shipping, and ports. The government moved to deregulate these markets as well, including opening these traditionally well-protected sectors to foreign investment and control.[65]

Finally, in a move to significantly liberalize foreign trade, New Zealand's complex set of industry protections, tariffs, and import restrictions was drastically reduced.[66] The old system of protection had relied on high tariffs, strict import licensing rules, and New Zealand content requirements. The effect of these barriers was that, for all intents and purposes, most finished goods had to be produced in New Zealand itself, rather than imported. Seeking to expose its traditionally sheltered market to the allegedly invigorating rigors of international competition, the government implemented across-the-board tariff reductions in 1986 and 1987 and abolished most import quotas altogether in 1989 (Table 8). In addition, the Closer Economic Relations (CER) agreement, which Muldoon had signed with Australia, became fully operational in 1990 and thus essentially created a free trade zone across the Tasman. In short, the government's trade policies constituted a thoroughgoing reversal of the protectionist creed of domestic defence. While a few isolated sectors retained a higher degree of protection into the 1990s – notably textiles, clothing, and footwear – the effect of the

Table 8. Effective Rates of Assistance to Industry, New Zealand

	1981/82	1985/86	1987/88	1989/90
Pastoral agriculture	49	34	15	–6
Manufacturing	39	37	26	19
Food, beverages, tobacco	20	14	9	7
Textiles, apparel, footwear	90	160	69	59
Wood and wood products	51	28	21	16
Paper, printing, publishing	24	17	13	9
Chemicals, petroleum, rubber	37	38	34	23
Non-metallic mineral products	19	19	17	13
Basic metal industries	12	12	11	5
Metal products	69	58	51	34
Other	56	53	41	27

Source: OECD (New Zealand) 1991, 63.
Note: See Table 7.

Labour government's trade policies was that New Zealand companies now sank or swam based in large part on how well they were able to cope with the pressures of global competition.

A second key characteristic of New Zealand Labour's program was its approach to monetary policy. Paradoxically for a putatively social democratic government, it shared the Thatcherite determination to stamp out inflation as its first priority, regardless of the costs in higher unemployment. Retreating from the long-standing bipartisan commitment to full employment – one essentially pioneered by social democratic parties and that had become a cornerstone of the post-war political-economic imaginary in New Zealand[67] – the government pursued a near textbook program of the monetarist theology. In its post-election briefing to the new Labour government in 1984, the Treasury had stated its view that "ideally policy should be directed at achieving, in the medium term, a zero rate of inflation."[68] This, of course, was a maximalist statement of the driest possible neoliberal policy. Zero inflation could only be had (if indeed it were even feasible in a non-recessionary economy) by running a remarkably restrictive monetary regime – one unconcerned with unemployment and unwilling to consider reflation in times of economic downturn. Yet, the new Labour government quickly adopted this most doctrinaire of all anti-inflation policies as its own – price stability, not job protection, became the central economic goal.

However,. while pursuing the same anti-inflation objective as the Thatcher government, New Zealand Labour took a somewhat different tack. Rather than establishing precise targets for various monetary aggregates, Douglas and his colleagues instead relied upon the Reserve Bank of New Zealand to keep the lid tight on inflation through an increasingly aggressive monetary policy. The real test, however, would come with the 1987 stock market crash. With increasing calls for monetary relaxation to prevent recession, the government moved to strengthen the role of the Reserve Bank as the ultimate weapon against inflation. Its 1989 Reserve Bank Act codified the anti-inflation objective by establishing price stability as the *overriding* goal of monetary policy and instituted a mechanism whereby the Governor of the Bank could be dismissed if inflation exceeded the government's targets.[69] This, then, was an anti-inflation policy with teeth. Whereas the Conservative Thatcher government toyed with monetary aggregates (and never moved to make the Bank of England fully independent of the government), New Zealand's Labour government codified into law an anti-inflation objective. In section eight of the 1989 Reserve Bank Act, the government reduced the Bank's statutory charge from including "social welfare" and "full employment" to only one objective: "The primary function of the Bank is to formulate and implement monetary policy directed to the economic objective of achieving and maintaining stability in the general level of prices."[70] In one fell swoop, "[a]ll references to the social welfare of New Zealand, and to production, trade and employment, [had] been removed from the statutory objectives." From then on, despite the fact that New Zealand was experiencing levels of unemployment unprecedented in the post-war period, the government stuck to the neoliberal line that "the sole focus [should be] on the economic objective of price stability."[71] In this respect, perhaps, the New Zealand government proved to be the most radical of the four neoliberal governments considered here. By codifying the anti-inflation objective into law, this putatively social democratic party completely eliminated, by statute, the old consensus commitment to full employment. The social democratic vision in New Zealand had essentially been laid to rest by a Labour government.

Finally, the Labour Party imitated the British government's large-scale sell-off of state-run entities. Douglas's argument in New Zealand was that of Thatcher in Britain: the public sector was said to be bloated with inefficient, poorly-managed, usually loss-making enterprises that, rather than representing a net asset to the nation, constituted a drain on the public purse. In the mid-1980s in New Zealand, this sector of the economy was reasonably large – approximately 12 percent of GDP – in a variety of areas, including banking, mining, engineering, transport, and tourism.[72]

Initially, the government announced its intention to simply "corporatize" a number of state-controlled activities. That is, these commercial state operations would be converted into state-owned enterprises (SOEs) – public corporations that would have profit as their primary objective and that would in most respects resemble private sector corporations in their operation. In December 1986, the government established nine new government-owned corporations along these lines: corporations in land, forestry, electricity, telecommunications, coal, airways, the Post Office Bank, New Zealand Post, and Government Property Services were established. The pace of the reforms was remarkable. As Kelsey describes it, "the early corporatisation policy was implemented virtually without debate. The public service was widely perceived as inefficient, privileged and in need of a good shake-up, and no alternative models were being promoted. ... Critics ... were deliberately marginalised by the speed and secrecy of the reforms."[73]

Shortly thereafter, however, the government proceeded to shake up the public sector yet again, this time by initiating a large-scale privatization of government assets.[74] Whereas the SOEs were companies whose shares were ultimately held by the state, the privatized companies were to be completely placed in the hands of the private sector, severing the government link entirely. The sell-off began in Douglas's 1988 budget, but would continue well into the 1990s, even after Labour had lost power to the conservative National Party. The Labour privatization program was "breathtaking in its scope, speed and disregard for public opinion," becoming the largest sell-off (as a proportion of GDP) among OECD countries.[75] The government's goal seemed to be to simply rid the state of enterprises as quickly as possible – assets were sold to the highest bidder and, lacking Thatcher's personal interest in producing a property-owning society of "ordinary" capitalists, shares in New Zealand were not offered directly for public sale.[76] Traditional concerns about foreign ownership of key public assets were brushed aside. For instance, in the most significant case of foreign ownership, the largest single asset sale, that of Telecom, was to the US phone giants Bell Atlantic and Ameritech. Table 9 gives an accounting of the privatization program, both under Labour and National. To summarize the scope of the sell-off, between 1988 and 1990, 19 asset sales took place

Table 9. Privatization in New Zealand, 1988–94

	Year	Sale Price (NZ$ million)
New Zealand Steel	1988	327
Petrocorp	1988	801
Health Computing Service	1988	4
Development Finance Corporation	1988	111
Post Office Bank	1988	678
Air New Zealand	1989	660
Landcorp financial instruments	1989–90	77
Rural Bank	1989–92	688
Communicate New Zealand	1989	0
Government Printing Office	1989–93	39
Shipping Corporation of New Zealand	1990	32
National Film Unit	1990	3
State Insurance Office	1990	735
Tourist Hotel Corporation	1990	72
New Zealand Liquid Fuel Investment	1990	(203)
Maui Gas	1990	254
Synfuels stocks and current assets	1990–5	206
Telecom Corporation	1990	4250
Forestry cutting rights	1990	1027
Export Guarantee Limited	1990–3	20
Housing Corporation mortgages	1991–5	1316
Government Supply Brokerage	1992	3
Taranaki Petroleum mining licenses	1992–3	118
New Zealand Timberlands Limited	1992	366
Bank of New Zealand	1992	850
New Zealand Rail	1993	328
Fletcher Challenge shares	1993	418
Government Computing Services	1994	47

Source: OECD (New Zealand) 1996, 98.

with total proceeds exceeding NZ$9 billion, or nearly 14 percent of 1990 GDP.

As discussed previously, throughout the Fourth Labour Government's program of radical change, the strategy was to force through such a flurry of reforms that no real political opposition could materialize to what an Australian Labor prime minister dubbed the "coldturkeying" of New Zealand.[77] As a minister in the New Zealand Labour government put it,

Douglas said that you've got to hit [the people] before they know what has happened to them. Otherwise, they'll object. You've got to give them so many things to object to that they don't know which one to concentrate on. So they did it all at once. … Normally, if you had suggested privatizing one government department, then they would have created a furore and you would have had problems. But if you could contemplate privatizing the lot, and at the same time you're introducing GST, and at the same time you're pulling the plug on the farming sector, you've deregulated the finance industry and interest rates have soared to twenty-two percent, … which fire do you put out? If you concentrate here, they get you over there. If you do that one, there's this one, and there's always one in here that you haven't even looked at yet.[78]

In short, through a frenetic program of radical neoliberal change, Roger Douglas and his Labour colleagues dramatically altered the nature of economic policy and, in the end, the dominant political-economic imaginary in New Zealand. Just as in Britain the old "middle way" consensus in which economic efficiency interests were balanced by concerns for social cohesion was rejected, so in New Zealand the dominant political-economic imaginary of domestic defence was replaced by a pro-market imaginary. Reflecting the degree to which the British Conservatives and New Zealand Labour were successful in recasting their countries' respective political-economic imaginaries, a sea change in attitudes occurred. As is discussed later in this chapter, these neoliberal governments were succeeded by parties – "New Labour" in Britain and National in New Zealand – committed to consolidating and, in significant ways, even extending the reach of the neoliberal programs begun in the 1980s. This fundamental philosophical shift, even more than the specific policies each 1980s government enacted, was perhaps the real legacy of the 1980s.

Gradualism and Ideational Change

At first glance, it seems paradoxical, even erroneous, to speak of a more gradual pace of change in Canada and Australia. Taken in isolation, without comparisons to other cases, the changes witnessed in the 1980s in both countries were, by any standard, dramatic reversals of very long–standing public policy traditions and resulted in important shifts in each country's political-economic imaginary. In Canada, North American free trade essentially overturned more than a century's worth of National Policy–style protectionism. In Australia, deregulation and the liberalization of major markets virtually reversed its own version of domestic defence. To assert that these changes were anything less than groundbreaking misstates the significance of the 1980s in reordering the philosophical basis of economic policy in both countries.

However, when these two cases are compared to those of Britain and New Zealand, the different pace and scope of change in Canada and Australia becomes more clear. As discussed at the beginning of this chapter, these differences point to the variety of ways in which ideational change can occur. Even when the end result is similar – in this case, a neoliberal imaginary – the ways in which this can occur are both varied and highly case-specific. Thus, while the Canadian and Australian governments were definitely neoliberal in orientation – radically so, in some ways – the ways in which they set about pursuing economic change were not as overtly confrontational as they often were in Britain and New Zealand. Whereas the "crash through" governments pursued their policies seemingly irrespective of public opinion, and often counter to it, the market liberalizing governments in Canada and Australia were in a sense more circumspect. Brian Mulroney, for example, shied away from the overtly confrontational, dogmatic tone identified with Thatcher and Douglas. As a former trade union chief who also enjoyed close personal and political relationships with the economic and cultural elite, Bob Hawke consciously cultivated an image as a leader committed to consultation and cooperation with all sectors of society – what Goldfinch has called the "bargained consensus" model.[79]

Moreover, the approach to policy transformation as practiced in Canada and Australia was less explicitly focused on an overt shift in the political-economic imaginary than it was in Britain and New Zealand. In the latter, the Thatcher and Lange governments attempted what was, with few exceptions, a comprehensive restructuring of the entire economy based on the explicitly stated goal of radically reorienting their country's fundamental economic philosophy. In Canada and Australia, however, neoliberalism emerged first as a shift at the policy settings level. While the central neoliberal notions of growth, efficiency, and international competitiveness unquestionably underlay these policy shifts, in Canada and Australia there was far less of the explicitly doctrinaire, crusading zeal to radically reform the national political-economic imaginary.

Having said that, however, the end result over the longer-term in Canada and Australia was not qualitatively different than that in Britain and New Zealand: the emergence and entrenchment of a neoliberal political-economic imaginary. In these countries, the shift that eventually took place at the level of the imaginary did so primarily as the result of many relatively more incremental changes at the level of policy settings. As a consequence, the 1980s saw the firm establishment of such basic neoliberal nostrums as the priority of economic efficiency over social justice, the inherent superiority of market provision, and a deep suspicion of the role of the state in the economy, particularly in the service of non-economic, "social" goals. As shown in the concluding section of this chapter, what succeeded the neoliberal governments of the 1980s in all four countries were governments of both the left and right committed to extending the reach of neoliberal policies.

In Canada, the story of the 1980s can largely be summed up in one phrase – the throwing open of the country to foreign economic penetration. In that sense, the most significant legacies left by the Mulroney government were its deregulation of the energy market, the reversal of Canada's traditionally wary attitude toward inward foreign investment, and, most of all, the Free Trade Agreement with the United States. While the government also pushed through other neoliberal changes – attempts to tighten fiscal policy and improve Canada's budget balance; tax reform, including the introduction of a Goods and Services Tax (GST);[80] and the privatization of a number of Crown Corporations, including Air Canada and a minority share of Petro-Canada[81] – it was in the government's effective removal of barriers to foreign economic penetration where the most dramatic effects could be seen. Chapter two points out that, from the time of Macdonald's National Policy to Trudeau's inauguration of the National Energy Program (NEP), the prevailing policy theme had been to shield Canada from the potentially destructive impact of economic penetration from beyond, particularly from the United States. It was the major legacy of the Mulroney period to definitively reverse this approach.

The first major structural change undertaken by the Mulroney government was to abolish the NEP and to transform the Foreign Investment Review Agency (FIRA) into Investment Canada.[82] The abolition of the NEP was in keeping with Mulroney's basic market liberalizing approach. As he put it before his accession to the premiership,

It is absolutely clear that the private sector is and must continue to be the driving force in the economy. It is not a matter of whether government or the private sector should take the lead in rejuvenating the economy. In this context of intensifying competition, the role and purpose of government policy will relate primarily to how we can nurture and stimulate the Canadian private sector. A Progressive Conservative government [should] create an overall economic environment which provides exactly this kind of support.[83]

The abolition of the NEP also made good political sense – the move received a great deal of support from within his party, whose parliamentary benches were drawn disproportionately from Western provinces that hated the NEP, seeing it as yet another heavy-handed intervention by Ottawa at the behest of Pierre Trudeau. Worse still for Westerners, the NEP's provisions controlling the price of domestic energy meant that, when world energy prices were high, the large energy consuming provinces of Ontario and Québec in the east benefited from lower prices, while the energy producing provinces of the West suffered. Finally, the NEP's "back-in provision," allowing the federal government to claim a 25 percent share of all energy finds on federal lands, was deeply resented by oil explorers and producers in both the Canadian West and the United States.[84]

In March 1985, Mulroney moved to eliminate the NEP altogether through the Western Accord, an agreement with the provincial governments of Alberta, Saskatchewan, and British Columbia. The agreement essentially transformed Canada into a free internal market for energy – prices, outputs, and imports were to be determined by market forces; restrictions on exports were lifted; and a wide range of special energy taxes were abolished.[85] This was followed in October by the Agreement on Natural Gas Prices and Markets – which did for natural gas what the Western Accord had done for oil – and by the abolition of the 25 percent back-in provision. Over the course of 1985, Canada went from having a highly centralized, federally controlled energy regime to one essentially deregulated and open to market forces.

Virtually contemporaneous with the government's liberalization of the energy sector was the abolition of FIRA. In an important shift in both rhetoric and policy, the government made it clear that it did not intend to continue reviewing foreign investment in Canada with a skeptical eye. Instead, Canada would be thrown open to foreign investors. They would now be welcomed instead of suspiciously "reviewed." This policy shift represented a decisive change in attitudes toward the United States, particularly when compared to the Trudeau years of the 1970s and its "Third Option" attempt at distancing Canada from the United States. FIRA had traditionally been despised by many in the United States as typical of the old, protectionist Canadian attitude. When Trudeau renewed FIRA's mandate in 1981 and seemed likely to extend its review powers into additional sectors of the economy, "the howls of outrage from the American business establishment turned the guns of the Reagan administration on Canada."[86] The government quickly backtracked and declined to extend FIRA's reach, but "the memory of the NEP and FIRA would linger" and would be a prime impetus in the American push for free trade with Canada.[87]

In December 1984, the Mulroney government introduced legislation to transform FIRA into Investment Canada. Instead of seeking to limit Canadian exposure to foreign investment, the new approach would rather invite such investment, encourage Canadian entrepreneurs to seek capital abroad, and only limit investments that seemed particularly threatening to vital national economic or cultural interests. As a Tory minister put it in the House of Commons,

> By changing the name of the agency, we will be sending a positive signal, changing from that hostile-sounding terminology of Foreign Investment Review Agency, to one of: We are open for business again. I suggest that in changing the mandate from one of foreign investment review to Investment Canada we will demonstrate that indeed there is a strong, positive signal once again coming from Canada, with respect to our investment potential, and that those who have money to invest, be they Canadian or non-Canadian, are once again welcome in this country.[88]

This move toward deregulation, and particularly toward allowing increased foreign economic intervention, was part of the general neoliberal trend internationally but, in Canada, also the result of a growing belief that the time was ripe for a shift away from economically nationalist policies as typified by the NEP and FIRA toward those more conducive to foreign investment. As LeDuc and Murray show, a gradual shift in attitudes took place within the Canadian general public toward greater approval of US economic involvement in Canada. In 1974, only 18 percent of Canadians favoured closer ties with the United States, compared to 30 percent wanting closer links with Europe and Asia. By 1985, the attitudes had reversed – 45 percent now supported closer American relations, while those favouring Europe and Asia had dropped to 19 percent.[89] A similar shift in elite attitudes also occurred. The balance between economic nationalists and those more favourable to the United States had frequently shifted in the Trudeau cabinet and in the Liberal party as a whole. But, by the early 1980s, with a recession in full force and free market ideas gaining currency worldwide, there was a swing away from nationalist positions. The more centrist Marc Lalonde replaced the economic nationalist Allan MacEachen in the finance portfolio in 1982, and the government began to soften the harder-line attitudes toward the United States that were characteristic of the 1970s.[90]

It was not long before this generally more positive attitude toward the United States became an explicit call for a comprehensive regime of free trade between the two countries.[91] Initially, Brian Mulroney had been openly opposed to the idea, one first floated by Ronald Reagan during his 1980 presidential campaign. In the 1983 Tory leadership contest, Mulroney had scoffed at the free trade position of challenger John Crosbie:

> There's a real beauty for you. Now there's a real honey – free trade with the Americans. Free trade with the United States is like sleeping with an elephant. It's terrific until the elephant twitches, and if the elephant rolls over, you're a dead man. ... I'll tell you when he's going to roll over. He's going to roll over in times of economic depression and they're going to crank up the plants in Georgia and North Carolina and Ohio and they're going to be shutting them down here. ... That's why free trade was decided on in an election in 1911. ... It affects Canadian sovereignty, and we'll have none of it, not during leadership campaigns, not at any other time.[92]

But the tide was turning – neoliberalism was quickly becoming entrenched in Britain and the United States, and about to take off in the Antipodes. Mulroney's position was clearly out of step in this regard. Barely two years later, in September 1985, Mulroney told the Commons that Canada needed "freer trade" with the United States, a term that quickly became simply "free trade." As the new convert put it, "We need a better, a fairer, and more predictable trade relationship with the United States. At stake are more than two million jobs which depend entirely on Canadian access to the U.S. market."[93]

Key to the success of the free trade argument in Canada was fear of rising protectionist sentiment in the US Congress and the damage such protectionism could do to Canada. In this sense, free trade, not disengagement, increasingly seemed to many to be the safest way to prevent the American elephant from rolling over and crushing Canada. Mulroney himself made the link clear. During a Question Period session in 1986, he addressed rising protectionism in the United States:

As my hon. friend knows, I have tried to place Canadian-American relations on a friendly footing and I will tell my hon. friend that ... [it is]
extremely difficult for anyone, including Canadians, to be friends with the
Americans from time to time. ... My hon. friend is aware of the debilita-
ting protectionist initiatives in droves, by the dozens down there, many
of them designed to hit other countries but specifically impacting upon
Canada and Canadian jobs. It is because this kind of action can have such
a damaging effect in British Columbia and elsewhere that we have initiated a broader scope negotiation designed to free both countries from these
kinds of incidents which impact so unfavorably on both of us.[94]

One of Mulroney's cabinet ministers elaborated on this view:

Our experience with the Americans is that they love competition, with
only one caveat: as long as they win. If they don't win, there's something
wrong with the rules. We would get Senators standing up in Congress
introducing a bill to eliminate any timber coming into the States from
Canada. ... I think there was a feeling that we could do much better trading with the Americans if there were rules that [were] defined, ... so that
Senators trying to curry favor with their constituents could not wield the
cudgel as they [did].[95]

Playing a critical role in reinforcing this change in attitudes was the
publication in 1984 of a landmark report by the Macdonald Commission,
set up in 1982 by Pierre Trudeau and headed by former Liberal finance
minister Donald Macdonald. Charged with investigating and making
recommendations on the "economic union and development prospects
for Canada," its November 1984 report was something of a bombshell.
It was nothing less than an official call for a break with the old interventionist, economically nationalist consensus and a shift to neoliberal
policies, with free trade with the United States as its cornerstone.[96]
Macdonald called for a "leap of faith" – to abandon the old ways and
adopt free trade as the best way to spur competition, innovation, and
long-term economic growth in Canada:

We support the pursuit and eventual implementation of a Canada-U.S.
free trade agreement to encompass both tariff and non-tariff barriers. ...
Free trade is the main instrument in this Commission's approach to industrial policy. It is based on the same intellectual thrust which governs

Commissioners' approach to domestic economic policy: that the role of government is not to retard economic forces, but to complement them by positive adjustment measures. ... We Canadians are at a turning point in our history. The National Policy of 1879 has played itself out. The Commission is convinced of the general superiority of market forces to the attempts of governments in Canada to pick "winners" and "losers." Protectionism is counterproductive and self-defeating.[97]

This was a critical push for the Mulroney government to move toward free trade. Macdonald had clearly articulated the basic neoliberal philosophy shared by many at that point in the Tory party, among "business Liberals," by Bay Street and ultimately by Mulroney himself. Overthrowing a century of National Policy tradition might not be easy, but it was the obvious trade policy for neoliberal believers. Once Mulroney set free trade as his ultimate goal, he never looked back. Negotiations that began in May 1986 were completed two years later, and the Free Trade Agreement (FTA) was enacted into law in December 1988. Reflecting the magnitude of the shift it represented to Canadian public policy, however, free trade proved to be a divisive political issue. The election held in November 1988 was run almost entirely on this issue, with Liberal leader John Turner accusing the Tories of selling out Canadian sovereignty, while Mulroney and the Progressive Conservatives claimed the deal was necessary to ward off American protectionism and ensure continued access to the US market. In what essentially became a referendum on free trade, the Tories won 169 of 295 seats in the new House of Commons, and the issue was resolved. The Liberal Party continued for a time to oppose the agreement and its successor, the North American Free Trade Agreement (NAFTA), which was expanded to include Mexico. Turner's successor as Liberal leader, Jean Chrétien, even threatened to "tear up" the agreement if he felt it endangered Canadian's health and environmental well-being. Yet, almost immediately once in office, and with only the most minor of revisions, Chrétien approved the official proclamation of NAFTA in 1994, and the Grits settled on a free trade position virtually indistinguishable from that of the Tories, with Chrétien leading "Team Canada" trade missions overseas to tout the benefits of foreign direct investment and international trade. In Canada, then, as in the other three cases, the ground was decisively shifted by the events of the 1980s.

In Australia, the main story of the 1980s was also a general neoliberal program of deregulation and the pursuit of freer markets. As chapter two sought to demonstrate, the previous pattern of Australian public policy was domestic defence – a set of policies of regulation, protection, and government intervention calculated to shield Australia from the vagaries and shocks of the external environment. Until the 1980s, this pattern was essentially unassailable. Only in the late 1970s, under Malcolm Fraser's conservative Coalition government, did a minority of Liberal MPs begin making the case for change along neoliberal lines. They, however, were still a minority in the party, and Fraser himself largely resisted their calls and refused to countenance any significant policy reorientation. As a minister in that government recalled with some frustration, "The so-called dry movement within the Fraser government was just outnumbered. The government was at least two-thirds protectionist. ... We realized that we couldn't win the [liberalization] battle within the Fraser cabinet or even within the party room ... Within the cabinet, there was a rock solid protectionist majority."[98] With the conservative Coalition divided and the Prime Minister opposed to major neoliberal change, it was left, paradoxically enough, to Fraser's Labor successors to pursue significant market liberalization.

Almost immediately upon its election in 1983, the Hawke government set out on its first and possibly most important change to the structure of the Australian economy – the deregulation of the financial sector.[99] This sector had become in some ways the quintessential exemplar of domestic defence economics. A wide variety of government regulations controlled virtually every major aspect of finance in Australia: the activities in which banks and other financial institutions could engage, the kinds of deposits they could receive, the interest they could pay, the sorts of loans that could be made, and the rates of interest that could be charged. Furthermore, domestic access to the banking sector was highly controlled – with not a single new entrant to the market between 1946 and 1982[100] – and foreign entry to the Australian market was nearly impossible. Finally, the flow of capital into and out of the country was strictly limited, and exchange rates were government-controlled.

All of this changed quite quickly upon the new government's accession to power. Abandoning a key element in national economic sovereignty and a cornerstone of domestic defence, the government moved to completely float the dollar in December 1983. In addition to the dollar's floatation, a large number of foreign exchange licenses were granted, virtually all foreign exchange controls were lifted, and the heretofore strict limits on Australians investing overseas were eliminated. This abrupt opening of Australia to world markets quickly became the precursor to the opening of Australia's domestic financial sector. The following year, the banking and financial services industry was sub-stantially deregulated – controls over deposits, loans, and interest rates were removed, and, in 1985, 16 foreign-owned financial corporations were selected to receive licenses to do business in Australia.

The government also undertook a program of systematic tariff reduc-tion.[101] By the mid-1990s, a series of gradual reductions over a broad range of products had been implemented, bringing the duty on most goods from as high as 40 percent to as low as 5 percent.[102] As Australia's agricultural sector was highly efficient and relatively unprotected, these tariff reductions were aimed primarily at the manufacturing industry in an attempt to strip it of its traditional protections and force Australian firms to compete more effectively in world markets. Here, as in the other three cases, we see the clear reversal of previous policies.[103] In a direct criticism of policies of domestic defence, Hawke stated,

> Tariffs have been one of the abiding features of the Australian economy since Federation. Tariffs protected Australian industry by making foreign goods more expensive here; and the supposed virtues of this protection became deeply entrenched in the psyche of the nation. But what in fact was the result? inefficient industries that could not compete overseas; and higher prices for consumers and higher costs for our efficient primary producers. Worse still, tariffs are a regressive burden – that is, the poo-rest Australians are hurt more than the richest. ... We live in a world of unprecedented, indeed breathtaking, change. Our own region is a crucible of change. We can no longer afford the easy simplicities, the costly com-placencies of the fifties and sixties and seventies.[104]

At the same time the government was deregulating the financial industry, it also pursued a model of government-labour relations unique among the Anglo-American democracies considered here. Throughout its tenure in office, the government pursued a policy of corporatist bar-gaining and negotiation with trade unions.[105] The goal of these negotia-tions – resulting in regular agreements called the Accord – was to allow the government to trade off higher wage demands in exchange for a "social wage" of improved social welfare benefits and tax concessions. The government was thus freed to pursue an expansion of spending, particularly on social benefits enjoyed by workers, and, in exchange, the union movement agreed to cooperate with the governments' efforts to moderate wage demands, thereby controlling inflation and making Australian manufacturing more competitive in world markets.

Table 10. Changes in Real Hourly Earnings in Manufacturing, 1980–94

	1980	1982	1984	1986	1988	1990	1992	1994	1979–89
Britain	−0.7	2.4	3.6	4.1	3.4	−0.1	2.7	2.2	2.6
Canada	−0.1	1.1	2.2	−1.2	−0.1	0.0	2.0	1.4	−0.2
Australia	0.6	3.0	3.5	−3.7	−1.2	−0.9	1.5	−0.5	−0.6
New Zealand	1.5	−3.5	−3.7	3.6	1.1	−1.7	−0.1	−0.4	−1.8

Source: OECD Historical Statistics, various years.

The adoption of such a strategy is, in some ways, not surprising. The Australian Labor Party, like British and New Zealand Labour, had close links with the trade union movement, and Hawke himself had been its head, as president of the Australian Council of Trade Unions (ACTU), prior to his entry into parliament in 1980. In addition, as discussed in chapter two, Australia had a centralized system of wage fixation virtually unique among industrialized democracies. Given these facts, the government's adoption of a corporatist approach did not seem incongruous.

What is remarkable, however, is not the government's consensual approach, but the success it had in dampening down wage pressures. As Table 10 shows, real hourly wages in manufacturing in Britain actually grew during the 1980s, despite the Thatcher government's attempts to force wage restraint on unions even at the cost of lost jobs. But in Australia, the government achieved wage restraint in active coalition with the trade unions. From 1985 to 1990, average real manufacturing wages in Australia fell more than 2 percent. Or, put differently, in the March quarter of 1983, when the Labor government was elected, the average male worker earned A$394.70 a week. By the time Hawke left the premiership in 1991, that same worker earned in real terms A$395.[106] Every single year wages came in at or below the government's targets. Hawke himself justified the stagnant wages in this way:

The trade unions have been prepared to forego the industrial capacities that undoubtedly they've had to extract higher wages. They have tolerated, in the interests of economic growth, some reductions in real wages. They have seen and recognised, to their ever-lasting credit, that it was better, rather than to push for unacceptably high levels of wage increase, it was better to have moderate increases and to push properly for improvements in the social wage, in a way which would mean that more of their fellow Australians would be employed.[107]

In reality, the compensation for lower wages in the form of a higher social wage was quite limited. From 1983 to 1994, average household income only rose from A$164.40 a week to A$176.70, an increase of somewhat more than one-half of 1 percent per year. Despite this, however, the government remained committed to its policy of active wage restraint achieved in annual Accords with labour.

The government also began taking the first steps toward the privatization of a number of key Australian state-owned assets.[108] Initially, the government was firmly opposed to this seemingly radical idea coming from the dogmatic neoliberal governments in Britain and New Zealand. For example, in 1985, Hawke asked, "What, in the name of reason, is the justification for breaking up and selling off the great and efficient national assets, like the Commonwealth Bank, Telecom, TAA, Qantas?" Privatization, he declared, was a "recipe for disaster" and the "height of irrationality."[109] But, paralleling Mulroney's eventual conversion to Canadian free trade with the United States, Australian Labor's attitude toward privatization gradually changed. As expressed by a former Labor prime minister and quoted in chapter one, "Through time, you had positions that people have adopted ... which they regard as fundamental, which to me seem absolutely irrelevant. ... For example, your government must run the airline of the country. This is a fundamental tenet of faith that the government must run a bloody airline. Bullshit. That's got nothing to do with reality – and has nothing to do with optimizing opportunities for growth." [110] In a similar course of events to that in New Zealand, the government first sought to corporatize a number of state-owned enterprises, putting them on a competitive, profit-oriented footing. But, in time, corporatization gave way to privatization. Of the state-owned enterprises partially privatized by the federal government – which, in any case, only held a minority of Australia's publicly owned assets[111] – the two largest and most symbolic were those traditional Australian icons, Qantas and the Commonwealth Bank of Australia (CBA).

However, reflecting the less frenetic pace of neoliberal change in Australia, the scale of privatization there differed dramatically from that in New Zealand or Britain. In contrast to the massive sell-offs in those two countries, privatization was fairly limited in Australia, as indeed it was in Canada. Qantas was gradually privatized, with a majority stake going public only in 1995, and the Commonwealth Bank was not fully privatized until the accession to power of the conservative Coalition in 1996. Table 11 nicely illustrates the difference between the

Table 11. Privatization in the Anglo-American Democracies, 1979–92

	% of GDP*
Britain	12.0
New Zealand	14.1
Canada	0.6
Australia	< 1.0

Source: Boix 1997, 475.
*Accumulated privatization proceeds as a percentage of average annual GDP over the privatization period.

"crash through" and the more "pragmatic" approaches to neoliberal policy change, and privatization in particular. Whereas in Britain and New Zealand total privatization proceeds from 1979 to 1992 exceeded 10 percent of average 1980s GDP, in Australia and Canada, the figure was less than 1 percent.

In short, then, the Australian Labor governments of the 1980s and 1990s saw a definitive break and, in many ways, a reversal of traditional forms of domestic defence economic policies. Important sectors of the economy were deregulated, tariffs were nearly eliminated for a wide swathe of goods, state-owned enterprises were privatized, and the government effectively held down wages through a series of high-level corporatist-style agreements. On the one hand, the ALP did not attack the issue of economic reform as aggressively and comprehensively as did its counterpart in New Zealand. Yet, as in the other three cases, when one compares what came after the 1980s to what came before, the transformation is obvious. A set of new economic policies, founded on radically different philosophical bases, replaced the policies of the old consensus. Perhaps there is no stronger evidence of the degree to which key elements in each country's political-economic imaginary had indeed shifted than the record of the governments that succeeded the initial wave of neoliberalism. Reflecting the normalization – the "taken-for-grantedness" – of neoliberalism in the new political-economic imaginaries is the fact that what followed was no reversion to the policies of the past, but rather "more of the same" – at times, radically more.

The Entrenchment of Neoliberalism Beyond the 1980s

Had the experience of the 1980s been a singular event, a passing fancy of both right- and left-wing parties with a faddish economic doctrine, it would perhaps have been remembered as little more than an interesting, but ultimately unimportant, deviation from more traditional policies. Such is not the case. The lasting significance of the programs of neoliberal change outlined in this chapter lies in the fact that the 1980s heralded long-term shifts in each country's political-economic imaginary. Far from being an odd, isolated deviation, the experience of the 1980s in the Anglo-American democracies signalled that a deep, long-lasting shift in the dominant policy paradigm was underway. Indeed, one of the most significant effects of neoliberalism in the 1980s was to lay the philosophical bases for governments to follow in the 1990s and beyond.

The impact of the neoliberal political-economic imaginary shift is most strongly evidenced by the fact that, in all four countries considered here, the governments that succeeded the neoliberal governments of the 1980s adopted the basic neoliberal perspective as their own. While policy specifics naturally varied to some degree, the fundamental pro-market, deregulatory, privatizing, anti-state biases of neoliberalism were enthusiastically adopted by the successor governments. In Canada and Britain, the Tory governments of the 1980s were replaced, in 1993 and 1997 respectively, by centre-left governments that had bitterly opposed neoliberal change while in opposition. Yet, by the time they took office, the Canadian Liberal and British Labour parties had come to accept neoliberalism as their basic policy orientation. In the Antipodes as well, Australian and New Zealand Labor gave way to conservative oppositions even more dogmatically committed to neoliberalism than they had been. The Coalition in Australia and National in New Zealand not only had been won to the neoliberal side in the 1980s, but also set about applying the neoliberal medicine with even more vigor – and to sectors Labour had balked at reforming. In all four cases, the ground had been well and truly shifted. Neoliberal Tories had been replaced by neoliberal Labour/Liberals, and neoliberal Labor had been replaced by neoliberal conservatives. I briefly consider each case in turn.

The transformation of the British Labour Party has been one of the most thoroughly dissected and analysed events in recent political history.[112] Reeling from its landslide defeat to Thatcher in 1983, the party set itself on a path of internal reform and policy change that would ultimately lead to its own landslide victory in 1997. Through three successive leaders – Neil Kinnock, who took over in the wake of the 1983 election debacle; John Smith, whose leadership was cut short by his untimely death in 1994; and Tony Blair, who completed the rightward shift of the party and its ideology and led the party to victory in 1997, 2001, and 2005 – the Labour Party underwent a protracted and painful transformation. Its 1983 manifesto had been a classic statement of everything the old Labour left held dear. Dubbed by the Labour right "the longest suicide note in history,"[113] it would be the last real Labour riposte to neoliberalism. Over the course of the next decade and a half, Labour was transformed into a party praising the virtues of the free market and boasting of its new-found support from leading corporate executives.

In fact, the Labour Party had shifted to the point that its 1997 manifesto explicitly committed itself to maintaining the most important policies of the long Tory period – something it consistently did once in office. So complete was the transformation that such analysts as Colin Hay began to speak of a "new bipartisan consensus" in British politics – a consensus around neoliberalism.[114] To counter the image of Labour as a high tax, high spending party, it promised to stay within Tory spending plans for the first two years in government and, over the same period, pledged not to increase the basic or top rates of tax. Not only did it keep these promises, but the Blair government would later move to cut income, corporate, and capital gains tax rates. In monetary policy, the government not only adopted the neoliberal line on the priority of controlling inflation – adopting a 2.5 percent or less target – but went even farther than the Conservatives had been willing to go by, in one of its first (surprise) acts in government in 1997, granting independence to the Bank of England.[115]

Moreover, in contrast to previous Labour governments, Blair not only refused to countenance any renationalization of privatized industries, but adopted the same pro-private sector position of the Tories. For instance, his Public–Private Partnerships scheme – whereby private capital is encouraged to undertake what would otherwise be state sector investments[116] – further extended the reach of the private sector into such traditional state activities as the building and operation of roads, hospitals, prisons, schools, and, most contentiously, the London Underground. The contrast to Clause IV of the pre-1995 Labour constitution – which committed the party to "the common ownership of the means of production, distribution, and exchange" – could not be more clear.

Finally, New Labour left intact all significant elements of the Conservatives' industrial relations policies.[117] Blair made clear that he had no interest in revisiting those policies, and, aside from relatively minor adjustments, Tory policies born of Thatcher's anti-union stridency remained in place. Thus, laws once bitterly opposed by Labour – for example, regulating union registration and strike balloting, outlawing secondary strikes and flying pickets, and, most significantly, banning compulsory unionism and the closed shop – were openly embraced by the Blair and subsequent Brown governments. Once again, the contrast with the past, the irony for a party calling itself "Labour," is clear.

Much the same could be said about the government that succeeded the Tory government in Canada. There the Liberals under Jean Chrétien and Paul Martin broke decisively with previous Liberal policies and worked to extend the neoliberal program begun under Mulroney. It must be said that there are important differences separating the British Labour and Canadian Liberal parties – the Canadian Liberals never had the institutional ties to unions that Labour did, they never had as strong a left-wing faction within the party, and, as more of a centrist coalition, the party did not suffer anything like Labour's mammoth intraparty turmoil as it moved right. Yet, having said that, the fact remains that the Canadian Liberals did move dramatically toward neoliberalism once in office. Taking over from a decimated Progressive Conservative Party in 1993, the Liberals adopted the Conservatives' most important policies – whether they be fiscal restraint, privatization, or free trade – as their own.

Throughout the 1990s, Finance Minister (and later Prime Minister) Paul Martin explicitly cultivated the image of himself as a fiscally responsible, prudent economic manager whom the markets could trust. His first budget set the tone, with a public sector wage freeze and significant spending cuts. The remaining years of the decade would see the government balance sheet, driven by spending cuts and an economic boom, recover from the deficits of the late Mulroney years and enter the new century in significant surplus. This drive for fiscal "responsibility" also manifested itself in the government's 1996 shake-up of the unemployment insurance system. Its Employment Insurance Act tightened eligibility requirements, made replacement rates less generous, shortened the maximum period recipients could receive benefits, and provided a sliding scale whereby benefits would be reduced for "repeat users" of the unemployment insurance system.[118]

The government also remained committed to privatization, as initiated under the Tories. Its Programme Review, commissioned shortly upon taking office, outlined a set of scalebacks and cost savings to be achieved in the public sector. It led, in 1995, to two of the biggest privatizations ever undertaken by any government in Canada, as the Chrétien government reduced the government's share of Petro-Canada stock to less than 20 percent and sold off that venerable national institution, the Canadian National Railway.

Finally, the Chrétien government did a dramatic about-face and adopted a vigorous free trade position. As discussed previously, this was a particularly abrupt reversal of Liberal policy – from Trudeau's economic nationalism, to Turner's 1988 campaign against the Canada–US Free Trade Agreement, to Chrétien's own threat to "tear up" the NAFTA agreement should he become prime minister. Once in office, however, the Liberals not only presided over the implementation of NAFTA – an agreement negotiated largely by the Tories but officially proclaimed by Chrétien – but also sought to extend it. It vigorously pursued bilateral trade deals with various countries (including Israel and the EFTA countries) and, in 1996, signed a free trade agreement with Chile. This extension of the principles of NAFTA to South America was part of the government's goal – one shared in Washington – to use free trade with Chile as a launching pad for a Free Trade Area of the Americas (FTAA). Thus, in only a few years, the Liberal Party in Canada had gone from officially opposing free trade with the United States[119] to advocating free trade throughout the western hemisphere. In this respect, perhaps more than in any other, we see how neoliberalism had taken hold as the basic paradigm underlying Canadian economic policy.

In the Antipodes, economic rationalism was, of course, largely introduced by Labor governments. Given our standard expectations about philosophical and policy differences between parties of the right and left,[120] it is perhaps not surprising that, once in office, the Coalition parties in Australia and the National Party in New Zealand not only continued the pace of neoliberal change, but actually worked to accelerate it, pushing more-market ideas into policy areas left "unreformed" by Labor. The transition to this policy position, while unsurprising, was not an immediate one for conservatives in either country, however. In both countries, the right-of-centre parties were initially surprised and wrong-footed by the incongruous sight of purportedly left-wing parties pushing a neoliberal program of change.[121] Much of what would have logically been their ideological space had been occupied by Labor. They thus found themselves initially outmaneuvered by Labor parties advocating for freer markets. Before long, however, conservatives in each country regained their footing and attempted to position themselves not only as the "natural" neoliberals, but ones who could manage and implement neoliberal change better than Labor.

In Australia, Paul Keating's Labor government was defeated in the general election of March 1996. By then, the Coalition parties had transformed themselves into neoliberal true believers. In 1993, for instance, Liberal party leader John Hewson had fought the election campaign on a radical neoliberal program titled *Fightback!* The document called for, inter alia, thoroughgoing privatization of the public sector, deep spending cuts focused on social services, an end to Australia's centralized wage fixation system, and the introduction of a goods and services tax (GST).[122] While the Liberals lost that election, they would return to power in 1996 under John Howard with a remarkably similar economic policy agenda.

Put simply, the Coalition in Australia saw its job as being to push economic rationalism farther and faster than Labor had been willing to go. The Hawke and Keating reforms were seen as necessary changes, but ones that had been unnecessarily limited. The Howard government, then, moved to push the economically rationalist agenda further. The government continued the privatization program begun under Labor – for instance, selling its majority stake in the Commonwealth Bank of Australia in 1996, initiating the controversial and politically charged sale of Telstra in 1997, and finally completing its privatization in 2006. It also acted to create a competitive market for electricity supply and distribution, virtually eliminated any remaining review of foreign investment, and continued a policy of deep tariff cuts.

However, as discussed in chapter five, perhaps the Coalition's most significant extension of neoliberalism beyond that implemented by Labor had to do with labour market liberalization. Put simply, the Coalition rejected the Labor governments' yearly semi-corporatist Accord process, arguing for a drastic liberalization of the industrial relations system to allow for enterprise-level bargaining between employers and individual employees. Some moves toward enterprise-level bargaining had been made under Labor. The goal of the Coalition's neoliberals, however, was a fully "free" labour market – one in which employers and employees could bargain as "equals," without the interposition of troublesome trade unions.

So, barely six months into their first term of office, the Howard government enacted the Workplace Relations Act 1996. This legislation heralded a radical reshaping of the traditional pattern of Australian labour relations. Australian Workplace Agreements (AWAs) – individual contracts between employers and individual employees largely outside the award system – were introduced as a major step toward a deregulated labour market as the role of unions in organizing and collectively bargaining was more tightly restricted. When such agreements were in effect, industrial action became illegal, penalties for unlawful actions were strengthened, and the old awards system was reduced from mandating uniform, centrally-determined awards to simply providing a baseline, "safety net" of pay and working conditions – the 20 "allowable matters" – *below* which contracts could not be made.[123] In 2005, this legislation was followed by a program of further deregulation, dubbed *WorkChoices* by the Howard government. It continued to promote AWAs as an alternative to collective agreements, tightened workers' rights to claim unfair dismissal, and significantly limited the basic legal minimum conditions required in employment contracts (the "allowable matters").[124] While the newly-elected Labor government of Kevin Rudd moved in 2008 to eliminate the Coalition's AWAs and move Australia back toward collective bargaining as an industrial relations norm, the transformative effect of labour market deregulation begun by Labor under Hawke and Keating, and continued with fervor under John Howard's Coalition governments, is unmistakable. As a result of labour market deregulation begun under Labor and pursued with ideological vigor by the Coalition, Australia's industrial relations environment today is far removed from the highly structured, state-run system characteristic of the heyday of domestic defence.

In New Zealand, the storyline of the 1990s was remarkably similar to that of the 1980s: a government doing much the same thing as its Australian counterpart, but doing so in an even more radical way. There the conservatives had taken over from Labour much earlier. Unlike Australia, where Paul Keating managed to keep Labor in power until 1996, New Zealand Labour was defeated in 1990. Coming hot off the heels of six years of radical neoliberal change under Labour, the National Party was determined to keep the revolution going – like the Australian Coalition parties, pushing these policies farther than Labour had been willing to do.

The early years of the National government, particularly under Finance Minister Ruth Richardson, seemed calculated to rival Roger Douglas's frantic neoliberal agenda of change. The government moved across a wide field – cutting government expenditure, reducing taxes, introducing deep cuts and stringent means tests for social benefits, moving to eliminate tariffs altogether, extending the contracting out of government services, and privatizing what state-owned assets remained. In fact, National's neoliberal program was so dogmatic and thoroughgoing, so deeply unpopular with a country still reeling from the experience of Rogernomics, that the success of the 1992 and 1993 referendums to introduce a mixed member proportional (MMP) electoral system is seen by many as the result of a crisis of legitimacy of the political system itself, brought on by the withering pace of drastic and unpopular policy change.[125]

Most significantly, however, the National Party initiated a deregulation of the labour market unparalleled within the OECD. Its Employment Contracts Act 1991 marked the radical deregulation of industrial relations in New Zealand. Collective bargaining was no longer compulsory, enterprise bargaining with individual employer–employee contracts was introduced as the preferred norm, and any special bargaining rights of unions were removed. The role of the state was to be reduced to little more than that ideal libertarian minimum – the enforcement of contracts agreed between individual economic actors. As Bray and Neilson put it, the Act "heralded the final step in the establishment of the New Right paradigm in practice and probably represents the most radical withdrawal of the state from labour market regulation in the developed world."[126]

One final word remains to be said about New Zealand in this chapter. The country is remarkable not only for the scope of its Labour-led neoliberal program and the zeal of the conservatives who followed after. It is also significant in that it has seen the reelection and an extended period in office of the party responsible for the initial tranche of neoliberal change. Thus, the policies of the Labour-led coalition governments of 1999 to 2008 provide us an interesting test of the degree to which neoliberalism has truly become entrenched there.

A cursory look at the policies of prime minister Helen Clark's governments – first in coalition with the Alliance, then with the Progressive Party – indicates that New Zealand Labour, while repenting of what it now views as neoliberalism's most egregious excesses, was fundamentally changed by the experience of the 1980s. While rejecting the overt dogmatism of Roger Douglas (or Ruth Richardson), Labour's fundamental acceptance of the major elements of the neoliberal revolution is clear.

As Labour leader, Clark spoke of her government in Blairite terms: "ours is a classic Third Way government – committed to a market economy, but not to a market society."[127] Along those lines, Labour raised the top rate of income tax, reestablished income-linked rents in the public housing market, and increased spending on health and social welfare. However, its most significant step away from pure neoliberalism was its Employment Relations Act, which came into force in October 2000. The Act modified the industrial relations structure implemented by National's Employment Contracts Act. It strengthened the requirement that parties bargain in "good faith," reestablished statutory recognition of unions as collective bargaining agents, liberalized somewhat the right to strike, and established a streamlined procedure for state-sanctioned mediation.[128]

However, the scope of this backsliding from pure economic rationalism has to be kept in perspective. Despite the significant change in rhetoric and tone, and despite Clark's claim to lead a government free of the radicalism of the past two decades, actual policy changes were limited in scope. Virtually every important element of the neoliberal revolution remained in place. As Clark herself pointed out in the aforementioned speech, Labour committed itself to controlling government spending in line with National's Fiscal Responsibility Act, made no move to modify the Reserve Bank Act's sole mandate to control inflation, and was an enthusiastic supporter of trade liberalization. Moreover, even its modifications to the labour market discussed previously, while moderating some of the most extreme elements, kept intact the most important elements of the deregulated regime instituted by National: the right of employees and workers to conclude individual contracts at the enterprise level and the ban on compulsory unionism and the closed shop.[129]

In short, the return of New Zealand Labour indeed heralded some changes. The kamikaze approach to change and the dogmatic rhetoric about neoliberalism were gone. In some respects, the most extreme aspects of economically rationalist policy were modified. But, these changes in no way threatened the fundamental structural changes implemented in New Zealand in the 1980s and 1990s. Ironically enough, while decrying the radicalism of dogmatic neoliberalism, the Fifth Labour Government, by leaving intact virtually all the policy transformations of the 1990s, actually worked within an economic policy regime significantly more neoliberal than that which existed at the end of the Fourth Labour Government in 1990. While the tone changed and the pace of any future change is likely to be slower – in part because so little on the neoliberal agenda remains to be accomplished in New Zealand – reforms once thought dangerously radical and right-wing have now been accepted largely intact. What led to such astonishing transformations in all four countries is the focus of chapter four.

4 The Strategic Construction of the Neoliberal Political-Economic Imaginary

In the preceding two chapters, the argument was made that a fundamental shift in the underlying political-economic imaginary in Britain, Canada, Australia, and New Zealand occurred in the 1980s and 1990s. As described in those chapters, a policy, structural, and ideational shift replaced the post-war interventionist "consensus" paradigm with one centred on the alleged superiority of deregulated, "free" markets. This chapter attempts to explain that shift, detailing key reasons why this shift occurred, and showing how, and in what ways, it was accomplished.

Specifically, this chapter makes the argument that the spread of neoliberalism in these countries was the result of committed norm entrepreneurs who, acting in strategic ways and in a social and political environment conducive to their aims, sought to effect a change in the fundamental bases of their countries' political-economic imaginaries. Thus, the neoliberal imaginary shift was not unintended, accidental, or the inevitable product of immutable market forces. Such an interpretation effectively removes the very real agency and strategy that the neoliberal norm entrepreneurs exercised in pursuing their policy agendas. This mechanistic view also has the effect of depoliticizing and "destrategizing" what was a deeply political – and, perhaps even more significantly, highly strategic – campaign of ideas. Rather, the new thinking was the result of committed norm entrepreneurs who sought – some more radically, some more incrementally – to reorient key foundational elements in their countries' political-economic imaginaries by strategically arguing that neoliberalism was the only rational, plausible economic policy orientation.

This chapter thus seeks to outline both why and how these neoliberal shifts occurred. It does so first by focusing on the norm entrepreneurs themselves and the role they played in ideational and policy change. I argue that a defining feature of this normative change was the role played by determined political leaders who consciously and strategically worked to transform prevailing attitudes about state intervention and involvement in the economy. I thus attempt to show that the neoliberal imaginary shift happened in these countries not due to accidental or inevitable "forces of nature," but rather as a result of elites' strategic actions to effect ideational change.

However, these norm entrepreneurs did not operate in a political, social, or institutional vacuum. The shift to neoliberalism in the Anglo-American democracies was not simply an ideational shift, occurring without reference to the material or institutional environment. Rather, norm entrepreneurs' efforts to achieve ideational change took place within discrete political, social, and bureaucratic environments – that is, material and institutional factors that influenced, interacted with, limited, and also facilitated the ideational shift to neoliberalism. The second part of this chapter thus seeks to complicate a more straightforward ideational account by introducing key material and institutional factors that, in these cases, proved to be an important part of the construction of a new political-economic imaginary. Specifically, it focuses on the environment and structures within which norm entrepreneurs in these countries operated, arguing that leaders were able to capitalize on the experience of national economic crisis, were bolstered by bureaucratic institutions advocating for neoliberal reform, and had the benefit of operating in political systems that offered little in the way of institutional resistance to their plans. The chapter thus seeks to show, in a preliminary way, a number of ways in which material and institutional structures and forces can bring their influence to bear on processes of ideational change.

Having considered the role of norm entrepreneurs and the material environments in which they acted – that is, why the neoliberal shift took place – the chapter then moves to an examination of how these norm entrepreneurs effectively crafted a set of arguments in order to attain maximum rhetorical force. Focusing specifically on the construction of neoliberalism as forms of both persuasion and coercion, as discussed in chapter one, it argues that political leaders in these countries linked the argument that their countries were in a state of crisis and national decline to the assertion that there was "no alternative" to the new policy paradigm. By arguing that neoliberalism was appropriate (rhetorical persuasion), desirable and advantageous (material persuasion), and, most importantly, the only rational option available (rhetorical coercion), these norm entrepreneurs worked to shut off other policy options and construct their policy and ideational goals as the only path to economic recovery and prosperity. Before we consider how these arguments were constructed, however, we turn first to the norm entrepreneurs themselves and the political, economic, and institutional environments within which they worked.

Norm Entrepreneurs and Ideational Change

Normative shifts do not generally emerge sui generis. In most cases – as indeed in the cases of neoliberalism discussed in this book – significant ideational change does not occur randomly, haphazardly, or still less automatically. Rather, as discussed in chapter one, the literature on norm entrepreneurs has convincingly shown that purposive, politically strategic agents often play key roles in planning, organizing, and mobilizing for fundamental normative change. As Abdelal, Blyth, and Parsons put it with respect to economic crises, "[w]ho gets to interpret the crisis, to speak what it is, and to specify what models can legitimately be brought to bear to tame it is worth attending to."[1] In the cases considered here, that role was primarily played by political elites. Such leaders, it bears noting, are generally unable to effect change solely by fiat. As is discussed later, the political, social, economic, and institutional environments in which norm entrepreneurs find themselves bear directly on their ability to effect the change they desire. However, should they find those political and structural environments conducive to change – or are able to make them so – their role in promoting normative change can be fundamentally important.

A transformative impact by political leaders is not automatic or preordained, however. While one could argue that an important role for political elites is obvious and their influence a given, I argue that the Anglo-American cases of neoliberalism actually point to the highly variable, contingent role that leaders might (or might not) play. That is, leaders can choose a wide variety of positions vis-à-vis political change. They can, for instance, seek to maintain the status quo, opposing or seeking to limit change. They can also work to make marginal changes to policy settings or institutional structures, leaving intact their underlying ideational bases. Or they can seek to be more or less full-fledged norm entrepreneurs of the kind described in this book. While these are certainly not the only choices leaders make with respect to change, the point is that the role of leaders in effecting change – indeed, the extent to which they seek to effect or retard change in the first place – is not at all a given, but rather is variable and contingent. Indeed, in the very countries considered here, we have several examples of leaders who proved unwilling to go down the neoliberal path that others later took. Prior to the accession to power of the neoliberal governments of the 1980s, these political elites were openly in opposition to, or only weakly in support of, the novel freer-market policies beginning to gain public attention in the 1970s. As discussed in chapter two, Ted Heath in Britain spoke of less government, then presided over the famous 1972 U-turn. Conservative leader Robert Stanfield in Canada was a believer in the traditional notion that government intervention was necessary to ensure social fairness and cohesion. In Australia, Malcolm Fraser resisted calls from within the Liberal Party for thoroughgoing deregulation in the early 1980s, and in New Zealand, Robert Muldoon was not averse to dramatic government intervention. What makes their successors – the norm entrepreneurs discussed here – different is that, in just a few years' time, they would take up the banner of neoliberal change and use the political capital available to them to enact dramatically different policies from those of their predecessors. For this reason, their roles are worth considering in some detail.

As discussed in chapter three, in Britain and New Zealand, the goal was a thoroughgoing shift in the country's political-economic imaginary; in Canada and Australia, the initial goals were more moderate and gradual, but the end result for the political-economic imaginary was similar. But in each case, neoliberal change was driven by one or more committed norm entrepreneurs – Thatcher in Britain, Mulroney in Canada, both Hawke and Keating in Australia, and Douglas in New Zealand. Each was complemented by a supporting cast of true believers: Geoffrey Howe and Nigel Lawson in Britain, Michael Wilson in Canada, Peter Walsh in Australia, and Richard Prebble and David Caygill in New Zealand. Central to the political-economic imaginary shifts discussed here is the fact that each government's neoliberal program was tirelessly promoted by a key point-man (or woman) – one committed to his or her own particular brand of deregulation and determined to see it enacted.

In Britain, the case of Margaret Thatcher is the stuff of legend – and in many ways the very model of, in her words, a "conviction politician."[2] In a way paralleled in these four countries only by Roger Douglas in New Zealand, she had an ideology that shaped every aspect of her government's program, economic or otherwise. It was this fundamentally doctrinaire approach – this single worldview – that fundamentally motivated her drive for thoroughgoing change. Using the language of political psychology, Stephen Benedict Dyson argues that Thatcher evinced "behavior consistent with a lower complexity cognitive style," in which "black-and-white thinking" led her into inevitable conflict with colleagues with opposing, often more nuanced views.[3] Even when ideologically inspired policies – monetarism being a key example – did not work as successfully as envisioned, her doctrinal commitments usually prevailed over more pragmatic considerations. As one of her ministers described her approach,

> She certainly was doctrinaire. She was there to be doctrinaire. And in her view and in Keith Joseph's and in quite a few others', what Britain needed above everything else was somebody who had the guts to be doctrinaire and not to listen to people who said you can't have prescriptions charges and you can't tie the teachers to the cost of living and you can't do all these other things. ... She didn't want anyone, she didn't need anyone, to say, "Don't do it," or "It's dangerous." She felt it had to be done.[4]

One of her Chancellors, Nigel Lawson, stated,"The indisputable element of the revolution which so astonished Whitehall was Margaret Thatcher herself. She had set out from the very beginning as a Prime Minister who knew her own mind, and led from the front from the word go. ... She considered the Treasury to be *her* department."[5]

In the other three cases as well, very strong leaders were able, largely through the force of personality, persuasion, and adroit political manoeuvring, to bring their parties and traditional supporters into line with their own policy preferences. Mulroney did this with the deeply divisive issue of free trade, initially opposing it, but then adopting it as his own personal crusade. According to Doern and Tomlin, the free trade issue in Canada was largely the product of one man's decision and support – Brian Mulroney's:

> It was [he] alone who ultimately decided that the risks of pursuing the free trade initiative were worth the political candle. Although he consulted his colleagues, there was no serious discussion of the issue in cabinet prior to ... August 1985, when Mulroney had already made his decision to leap. ... [T]he Conservative cabinet received the [free trade] decision as a *fait accompli*, already judged and decided to be worth the risk by the prime

minister and his advisers. ... Ministers knew without any doubt that this was Brian Mulroney's show.[6]

This personalistic assumption of the neoliberal cause – what became at times a quasi-messianic "sense of destiny" or Weberian "mission"[7] – was clearly present, not just in Thatcher and Mulroney, but among the Antipodean leadership as well. In Australia, the leadership tandem of Hawke and Keating was an effective team pushing for policy change. Hawke was the more human face of economic rationalism, a person committed to deregulation but able to present himself as a likeable larrikin, a man of the people who understood the lives of ordinary Australian battlers and would ultimately protect their interests. Keating, meanwhile, was imperious, hard-nosed, and razor-tongued.[8] Supremely confident of his own abilities and the government's new policies, Keating gleefully derided all those who preceded him – even those of his own party – as hopelessly antediluvian in economic policy terms. The message was clear: we are the economic experts, and our policies are the only ones a government could rationally pursue in the modern world. The policies of the past – particularly those of the previous Labor government of Gough Whitlam, from which Hawke and Keating studiously distanced themselves – were antiquated, naïve, and hopelessly anachronistic. Keating drew the self-congratulatory distinction between the current government and those of the past: "In terms of the Labor agenda, this government has left every other Labor government before it bare-arsed. No other Labor government even gets within a cooee of it. We have a Cabinet which has a degree of economic sophistication which puts the Whitlam government into the caveman class in economic terms."[9] Keating's approach was perhaps extreme in its personalism. As he gained experience in economic issues and as his confidence grew, he increasingly began to project himself as the only person able to lead Australia out of the economic wilderness. As he famously declared in 1990,[10]

> I say this seriously: I walk around with the world financial markets as much in my pocket as any finance minister in the world. I walk around with organised labour, I walk around with the central bank and the most committed bureaucracy in the history of the country, an interested press and a conscientious electorate. But what would [opposition Treasury spokesman Peter] Reith walk around with? Would he walk around with the financial markets? With organised labour? Would he walk around with

the confidence of the central bank? Would he have the confidence of the Treasury and the other major control departments of the Commonwealth? It will all fall apart very quickly indeed, because to hold it together is a full-time job and you have to build those confidences.[11]

In New Zealand, Roger Douglas took a less openly abrasive approach. Yet while the style was somewhat different, the substance – and particularly the pace – of change was even more radical. Douglas's aim was to achieve an overpowering public policy victory in as short a time as possible. As illustrated in chapter three, he made no secret that he felt the only way to achieve significant political-economic imaginary change in New Zealand was to personally bombard the country with large numbers of dramatic changes and to give effect to them so quickly that the opposition was continually wrong-footed and unable to respond effectively. The normal push and pull of democratic politics was, in his view, lethal to radical change. The longer a proposed change was debated and considered, the more time the opposition had to organize and mount a challenge to it. As he described his strategy,

> Do not try to advance a step at a time. Define your objectives clearly and move towards them in quantum leaps. Otherwise the interest groups will have time to mobilise and drag you down. ... Speed is essential. It is almost impossible to go too fast. ... Once the program begins to be implemented, don't stop until you have completed it. The fire of opponents is much less accurate if they have to shoot at a rapidly moving target. ... Don't blink. Public confidence rests on your composure.[12]

In a statement reminiscent of Thatcher's conviction politics, Douglas said that "compromised policies lead to voter dissatisfaction; letting things drift is political suicide."[13] Former National prime minister Jim Bolger described Douglas's personal one-man "crash through or crash" approach in this way: "The Douglas approach was novel, to say the least. Aware that the democratic system could only respond to a certain amount of change at any one time, he determined to move so fast that the system's checks and balances couldn't keep up. No sooner had he infuriated his opponents with one action, then they would discover that he had done something considered even more outrageous somewhere else."[14] And in the words of a National Party minister,

> I think all credit must go to Roger Douglas. .... Roger Douglas really was the driving force. He got a small group around him that decided, "Yes,

we've got to do something. It's got to be radical. It's got to be spectacular. Otherwise, we will continue to be a one-term government" – which is
what they had been. ... So that small team that he surrounded himself with
said, "Realistically, if we want a second term, we've got to do something
dramatic. It's got to be something that people will buy into eventually."[15]

In fact, Douglas and his colleagues were so successful in overwhelming the normal deliberative capacity of the democratic system with
rapid-fire change that many observers credit him with creating a crisis
of majoritarian democracy in the country, one that contributed to the
adoption of the mixed-member proportional (MMP) electoral system
in New Zealand in 1993.[16]

In short, that fact that neoliberalism "happened" in the 1980s, and
took the form that it did, is in large measure a reflection of the ideologies, perceptions, and political and economic goals of the norm
entrepreneurs at the centre of the campaign for normative change.
That is not to say that free market change in these countries can simply
be explained by the single variable of voluntaristic leader effects. As
Leonard Seabrooke argues, the process of ideational and institutional
change is not "auto-legitimating" – leaders are not able to unilaterally
implement change and simply command public support and legitimacy.[17] If personal influence was all that mattered, Paul Keating would
have succeeded with his 1984 proposal for a goods and services tax,
Roger Douglas would have implemented his preferred flat rate income
tax, Brian Mulroney would have been able to remove the full indexation of pensions to inflation in 1985, and Margaret Thatcher would
have been able to continue her reign ad infinitum. Despite these policy
failures, however, the leadership variable was a critically important
one. In fact, as with most examples of dramatic ideational change, political elites in these four countries proved fundamental to the process of
neoliberal policy change.

Norm Entrepreneurs and the Political-Economic Environment

As just discussed, norm entrepreneurs rarely enjoy the untrammeled ability to implement their desired changes wholesale, particularly as their policy goals extend over time and multiple issue areas.
Particularly in open, pluralist, democratic societies and polities, elites
do not generally have carte blanche to mandate the implementation
of their preferred policies; they must contend with a variety of social,
political, economic, and institutional factors that directly affect their

chances of success. These factors interact with, and influence, the more purely ideational factors at work – ideational change does not occur in isolation from, or immune to, the "surrounding" material environment, what Bob Jessop calls the "materiality of social relations."[18] Should these environmental factors prove propitious to the ideational goals of norm entrepreneurs, success is more likely. Should they work against these goals, ideational shifts are much less ensured. Thus, a key consideration in assessing how neoliberalism was made possible is the material political-economic context within which the neoliberal norm entrepreneurs operated.

In all four Anglo-American countries considered here, the drive for neoliberal change was greatly assisted by a number of these environmental factors. One might even say that the political and institutional stars were aligned in such a way that they, while by no means ensuring the success of the neoliberal norm entrepreneurs, worked to assist them in critically important ways. Specifically, three critical factors stood out: (1) national economic crisis, (2) the encouragement of key bureaucrats in the economic ministries, and (3) the majoritarian political-institutional structure in each country. All three combined to assist and make more possible the normative shifts advocated by political elites.

National Economic Crisis

A great deal of work on policy change has emphasized the important role that economic or political crises can play in setting the stage for significant policy shifts.[19] In such crises – or even when such crises are only perceived to exist[20] – "the politics of ideas becomes increasingly important,"[21] and openings emerge for entrepreneurial elites to critique past policies as the cause of the crisis and to present their arguments for a dramatic policy shift as the only solution to it. A crisis in and of itself does not specify a single solution: "crisis is never a purely objective process or moment that automatically produces a particular response or outcome."[22] Instead, crises can provide the opportunity for norm entrepreneurs to create a discourse in which the new policy agenda is the only right and obvious solution.[23] Ideas that in "normal" times might have seemed inappropriate, undesirable, or even radically dangerous can be effectively presented at a time of crisis as the very answer to the country's problems. In such circumstances, opponents of new approaches are often hampered in their ability to counter them effectively, especially if norm entrepreneurs are successful in framing their opponents as out-of-touch, antiquated, and as advocates of little more than the obviously failing status quo. Thus, to the extent that aspiring norm entrepreneurs can successfully frame the current crisis as a direct result of past failed policies, the way is opened for them to discredit their rivals and argue that their own policies are an attractive alternative – perhaps the *only* alternative.

This is precisely the situation that existed when the four neoliberal governments came to power. Interview respondents in this study agreed that the key element allowing these governments to effect radical, neoliberal change was the atmosphere of economic turmoil and crisis in which they came to power. As discussed in detail in chapter two, the 1970s had been, in these countries as in most of the world, a period of economic upheaval that produced a profound sense that the days of prosperity had given way to a distinctly uncertain and frightening future. The twin oil shocks of 1973 and 1979 had effectively laid to rest the notion that the long post-war boom would continue indefinitely. Runaway inflation joined rising unemployment – a direct challenge to the Phillips curve theory, which holds that inflation and unemployment are largely antithetical, mutually exclusive phenomena. The emergence of this "stagflation" – inflation during a period of stagnant growth – shook the confidence of policy-makers that the old Keynesian methods were useful in managing the economic cycle. The "misery index," a composite of inflation and unemployment rates, clearly paints the picture of crisis (Table 12). In all four countries, the 1970s had seen the emergence of both rising prices and growing joblessness.[24] Coupled with growing budget deficits, increasingly hostile confrontations with trade unions, and worsening terms of trade, to name but a few, the 1970s marked a clear departure from the growth periods of the 1950s and 1960s. In this atmosphere, governments found themselves struggling to make sense of the new economic environment and attempting to stave off what seemed to be an inexorable slide in overall living standards.

Each reforming government, then, took office in an atmosphere of economic anxiety, one in which the argument for change could more easily be made: in Britain, the Winter of Discontent seemed the disastrously fitting denouement to a decade of turmoil and decline;[25] in Canada, recession, a sharply deteriorating state fiscal position, and growing protectionist sentiment in the United States loomed as economic threats; in Australia, drought and depressed agricultural prices were throttling the terms of trade and threatening the country's primary

Table 12. The "Misery Index": Combined Rates of Inflation and Unemployment

Year	Britain	Canada	Australia	New Zealand	OECD Avg.
1970	8.6	9.0	5.5	6.7	8.9
1971	12.2	8.9	8.0	10.5	8.8
1972	10.2	11.0	8.4	7.3	8.6
1973	11.4	13.1	11.4	8.4	11.3
1974	18.1	16.2	17.7	11.2	17.3
1975	27.4	17.7	19.9	14.9	16.7
1976	21.3	14.6	18.2	17.3	14.1
1977	21.0	16.0	17.9	16.2	14.4
1978	13.4	17.2	14.3	13.7	13.3
1979	18.1	16.6	15.2	15.7	15.2
1980	23.6	17.6	16.2	19.3	18.9
1981	20.9	20.0	15.4	19.1	17.5
1982	19.0	21.7	18.2	19.6	18.4
1983	15.8	17.6	19.9	13.0	19.3
1984	16.2	15.5	12.8	11.8	16.6

Source: OECD Historical Statistics, various years.

industry-based economy; and in New Zealand, government spending and, in particular, Muldoon's Think Big development schemes had brought the country close to default. While details varied from country to country, the perception that change was necessary was common to all. As is discussed in detail later, this sense of economic crisis was directly used by the neoliberal norm entrepreneurs to make their case for policy change. Current economic problems were, in the hands of the norm entrepreneurs, magnified and directly attributed to the policies of the past. Without radical freer market change, they argued, their countries would continue to falter and continue what some argued was a secular slide in wealth and prosperity relative to other countries.

The Role of Economic Bureaucrats

A second key environmental factor was the support and encouragement that came from the key economic ministries in each country. It is clear that, whatever policy predilections they may have brought to office, governments in these countries were, in important ways, influenced and supported in their reform plans by the leading officials in the civil service – ones who were in this period increasingly economic rationalists or free marketeers. In many ways the influences were complex and synergistic. No government was by any means a cipher for the views of its leading public servants, nor was the impact of the economic bureaucracy uniform across all four cases. For instance, the British Conservatives and New Zealand Labour governments came to power with their reform packages largely in hand, while the Canadian Tory and Australian Labor governments showed greater signs of evolution once in office. Yet, the influence of economic advice coming from "true believer" free market government officials was significant. No government was the captive of its Treasury; however, neither is it possible to divorce the actions of these governments from official bureaucratic approval and support for their neoliberal programs.

Perhaps unsurprisingly, given the contradictions seemingly posed by Labor parties pursuing economic goals so counter to their own party traditions, the bureaucratic influence was particularly important in the cases of Australia and New Zealand.[26] There, what had been fairly typical social democratic Labor parties were strongly encouraged to move away from their traditional policies by committed free marketeers within their respective economic bureaucracies.

In Australia, the senior levels of the economic bureaucracy had, by the 1980s, come to be dominated by economic rationalists. Beginning in the mid-1960s, ideologically committed free-market advocates – led in particular by a young John Stone, who would serve as Secretary to the Treasury from 1979 to 1984 – began to position themselves to eventually "dominate Treasury thought and its advice to government," as Treasury became "the leading edge of a change taking place throughout the Canberra public service."[27] In the process, which Michael Pusey describes in detail, the "real problem-solvers in the public service" – those whose approach was fundamentally flexible and pragmatic – were "demoralized, colonized, and in many cases driven out" by the neoliberal ideologues.[28] Thus, over time, economic advice coming from the Treasury came to be controlled by a "neoclassical economic rationalism that [was] anti-statist, anti-union, and either asocial or anti-social in its basic orientation to policy."[29] When this advice combined with a Labor government eager to carry out neoliberal reforms, the result was a political-bureaucratic nexus committed to economic rationalism. Paul Keating, in particular, was pushed by Treasury to become a strong advocate for the neoliberal line. As a former Secretary to the Treasury described the influence of Treasury on Keating, who came to office largely an economic neophyte, "I think for the first few years in his time as Treasurer, Keating … was a kind of tabula rasa, a

totally blank sheet of paper, really, on which the Treasury wrote assiduously for the first eighteen months or so. ... [Then] he became a kind of
apostle, almost, burning with zeal for deregulation and all the things
which would, I think, quite rightly be dear to the Treasury's heart."[30]
And as an Australian Liberal member saw it, "I'm sure Treasury was on
his back every day. ... I think they influenced him heavily. Keating was
a great admirer of people intelligent, qualified, artistic. I don't think he
was any of them himself, you know, but he was greatly influenced by
them. I think once he got amongst the boffins of Treasury – let's face it,
Treasury had all its reform policies carefully bound up in ribbons just
awaiting a new Treasurer, and away they go."[31]

In New Zealand as well, "the role of the Treasury was pivotal."[32] In
a way largely paralleling that in Australia, by the late 1970s, the New
Zealand Treasury (and Reserve Bank) had come to be dominated by
economic rationalists committed to radically reshaping the country's
fundamental economic practices and institutions. Taking what was
then perceived as cutting-edge economic thinking and attempting to
move politicians in that ideational direction, these economic bureaucrats effectively positioned themselves to actively support like-minded
politicians once they came to power. Roderick Deane, the former
Deputy Governor of the Reserve Bank of New Zealand and himself
an economic rationalist, stated, "The only reason the Treasury and the
Reserve Bank were ready and willing to implement the reforms of the
past decade was because the leadership of those organisations, although
handcuffed by the Muldoon Government policies of the 70s and early
80s, nonetheless tolerated or created environments within which the
staff were able to discuss and develop the analysis which subsequently
was utilised during the reform process."[33]

The Treasury's effect in New Zealand, however, was somewhat different from that of Australia. Unlike Paul Keating, Roger Douglas was
not an economic tabula rasa. Rather than introducing Douglas to free
market ideas, the New Zealand Treasury served the crucial role of con-
firming, deepening, and providing theoretical justification for his budding neoliberal views. According to Goldfinch and Roper, "the fourth
Labour Government ... consistently implemented the monetarist economic strategy, market liberalization and redesign of the Welfare State
advocated by Treasury." The Treasury's economic agenda was nearly
pure neoclassical economics:

> [T]he ideal world as portrayed by the Treasury ... would be one inhabited
> by rugged entrepreneurs, where markets were allowed free reign largely

unencumbered by consumer and environmental laws, and free from the influence of unions and other interest groups. Social services would be provided by the market, and access to them would be through direct income transfers or private charity. The functions of government would be limited to controlling the money supply in order to maintain price-level stability, distributing limited income transfers, guaranteeing the legislative and institutional framework for the efficient operation of markets and defending the "free enterprise system" against internal and external threats (maintaining "law and order" and "national security").[34]

The influence of this consistent neoliberal line was attested to by prime minister David Lange himself, who "described Treasury as being 'almost like a religious cult' when its competence, discipline, and persistence were combined with a 'zealous, cohesive commitment' to free-market economic doctrine."[35]

In the cases of Antipodean Labor, the influence of the economic bureaucracy was clearly to convince – and critically reinforce – free market-leaning politicians that their reversal of long-standing national policy traditions and their own parties' ideological heritage was both necessary and desirable. In Britain and Canada, under Conservative parties that, in many ways, had more natural affinities to freer-market ideas and policies, the role of the bureaucracy was more additive and complementary. Certain parts of their neoliberal programs were supported by the public services in these countries. Yet, this support was not unequivocal or uniform. Unlike the dominant economically rationalist "Treasury line" the Labor governments of Australia and New Zealand received, the public service in Britain and Canada was more divided. Its support was not in and of itself decisive, and, especially in their early years in government, Conservative ministers were suspicious of the public service as being too closely linked to the policy traditions of the past. This was true in both countries: Thatcher felt the British bureaucracy was still too tied to "One Nation" consensus policies,[36] while Mulroney initially distrusted the Canadian public service, suspecting it of being too closely linked to Pierre Trudeau and the long reign of the Liberal Party.[37]

In Britain, the Treasury's support for the Thatcher program was initially mixed. In his memoirs, Nigel Lawson discusses the general Treasury attitude to the initial program of Thatcherite change:

[I]t was clear that our policies did not commend themselves to more than a small number of Treasury officials. The official Treasury recognized that the old policies had failed. ... However, they had little faith in any alternative. They welcomed our determination to curb public expenditure ... But monetarism was seen by most of them, not least by the Permanent Secretary, Douglas Wass, as at best an intellectually interesting variety of mumbo-jumbo to which lip service probably had to be paid to appease the financial markets.[38]

However, monetarism did have a strong bureaucratic supporter in the Bank of England. Whereas the nearly sole focus of the Treasury was the control of public expenditure,[39] the Bank of England took a different view. Thanks to its closeness and sensitivity to the predilections of the City, the Bank was a very early convert to monetarism. Its governor claimed that monetarism appealed even to "the layman's apparently intuitive perception of the broad relationship between monetary growth and inflation – perhaps clearer to him than to the professional who knows all the necessary qualifications."[40] Throughout the period, then, the Bank of England was generally quite supportive of the government's monetarist anti-inflation campaign (though its influence was undoubtedly constrained by its lack of statutory independence and the firm political control of the Thatcher government).[41] However, unlike the unstintingly neoliberal bureaucratic line in Australia and New Zealand, in Britain, Thatcher and her government played the decisive role, with the civil service – the Bank of England excepted – in varying degrees of support.

With respect to the single most important transformation of the Canadian economy in the 1980s – the advent of free trade – the economic bureaucracy there was similarly divided. Initially, important elements of the public service were quite hesitant, concerned about the potential effects likely to stem from continental free trade. Free trade threatened to overwhelm Canada with the economic and cultural power of the United States – from heavy industry and finance to movies and television programs.[42] Sectoral free trade was nearly always the bureaucrats' preferred option, and it was only after consistent government prodding that their view increasingly began to shift to one of comprehensive free trade. Despite this overall tepidity toward free trade, however, there was one particular bureaucratic "true believer" who spearheaded the cause of free trade within the public service: Derek Burney, the under-secretary at the Department of External Affairs, later to become Mulroney's chief of staff and ambassador to the United States. Doern and Tomlin write of his influence:

[O]ne of the surprising features of the agenda-setting phase of the free trade story is that the initiative was kept on the agenda despite opposition from most of Ottawa's senior mandarins. And here the role of Derek Burney was pivotal. … [He] was virtually the long ranger of free trade in the External Affairs bureaucracy. He kept nudging the issue forward, ensuring that it was not pushed aside, insisting that ministers be presented with a full array of alternatives, including comprehensive free trade, over the opposition of other senior External Affairs officials. … A personal rapport and trust developed between Mulroney and Burney, serving Tory desires to reach below the top level of official Ottawa to find sympathetic allies in the bureaucracy. … As one senior official put it, "Burney *was* the prime minister on trade issues."[43]

Thus, in the case of the economic bureaucracy, we have what is a supporting player – a player, but a supporting one nonetheless. It is clear that, in the Anglo-American cases, elected politicians took the lead in promoting the neoliberal policy program. It was not forced on them unwillingly – even in Australia and New Zealand where the radical influence of the Treasury was particularly strong. Yet, while the role of politicians remained decisive, their programs received crucial support from those charged with executing the policy shift.

The Structure of Political Institutions

A third important, but often overlooked, environmental factor that helped make possible the neoliberal shift in these countries was the political-institutional structure of each system.[44] Specifically, in all four countries, neoliberal politicians operated within an institutional and partisan framework that presented virtually no barriers to their policy plans.

As George Tsebelis points out, these barriers – or "veto players" – can be a significant obstacle to rapid or dramatic policy change.[45] The more consensual, consultative, and deliberative a political structure is, the more opportunities exist for opponents of change to inhibit or derail policy agendas. Conversely, majoritarian political systems dominated by a relatively closed group of powerful elites often offer little in the way of such barriers, and their institutional structures can often be mobilized effectively in the service of dramatic policy shifts.[46] As Blyth puts it, "more hierarchic state structures that concentrate decision-making power essentially institutionalize ideas very quickly, and because of this such states are more likely to exhibit cognitive locking."[47] Moreover, within such majoritarian systems, parties' governing power may be enhanced by their mobilization of significant parliamentary majorities, by the ineffectiveness of opposition parties, and by the added influence often afforded newly-elected governments in their "honeymoon" period.[48]

To put it simply, all of the neoliberal reforming parties considered here enjoyed the relative absence of significant opposition from either "institutional" or "partisan" veto players – they faced a "thin set of political institutions," as Alan Bollard has characterized the New Zealand system.[49] In fact, one could more properly say that these governments were actually empowered, rather than obstructed, by the political and partisan structures in which they acted. Operating in classic Westminster parliamentary systems, these entrepreneurs were never in any doubt as to their ability to marshal their governing parties behind their programs. All four parties had workable – and in some cases, substantial – majorities in their respective lower houses of parliament.[50] Moreover, given the fact that three of the governments – in Canada, Australia, and New Zealand – came to power after having spent large parts of the post-war period in opposition, their members of parliament were even more willing to extend a "honeymoon" period to their leaders, giving them a wide berth for policy change.[51]

Enhancing government's powers further, these significant parliamentary majorities operated essentially untrammeled by veto players in upper houses of parliament.[52] In three instances – Britain, Canada, and New Zealand – the influence of upper houses was largely negligible. The British House of Lords and the Canadian Senate have only limited powers of legislative delay, and, given their rather undemocratic composition – the Lords was, in this period, dominated by Conservative hereditary peers, while the Senate was, and is, an appointed chamber with little democratic mandate – neither proved an obstacle to neoliberal change. In New Zealand, there is no upper house at all. Since the abolition of the Legislative Council in 1951, the country's parliament has been unicameral, allowing the government of the day – in the 1980s elected under a majoritarian first-past-the-post electoral system – full sway in the legislative process.[53] Only in Australia do we encounter a powerful upper house. However, the Labor Party, though without a Senate majority, was generally able to secure the support of the centrist Australian Democrats or the conservative Coalition parties to ensure passage of its neoliberal program.[54]

In short, these three underlying environmental factors – the experience of national economic crisis, the role of bureaucratic institutions, and the empowering political-institutional structures of these democracies in this period – all made neoliberalism possible. While neither necessary nor sufficient in and of themselves, each go a long way toward answering the classic "How possible?" question posed by constructivists. However, the underlying environmental conditions experienced by each neoliberal government were, in a sense, simply the stage on which the larger drama played out. Of critical importance were the norm entrepreneurs in each country and how they strategically constructed the argument – how they employed the tools of persuasion and coercion discussed in chapter one – that change in a neoliberal direction was not only appropriate and desirable, but eminently necessary. How these norm entrepreneurs rhetorically constructed neoliberalism as a necessary policy shift – one ultimately implicating the very nature of the dominant political-economic imaginaries in their countries – is the question to which we now turn.

Constructing the Neoliberal Necessity

In constructing the "need" for neoliberal transformation, the norm entrepreneurs of Britain, Canada, Australia, and New Zealand made four basic arguments – ones that mixed appeals to appropriateness (rhetorical persuasion) and advantage (material persuasion) with the claim of no alternative (rhetorical coercion). Specifically, these four arguments involved the following: (1) the conscious cultivation of a sense of economic crisis, to which neoliberalism was said to be the most appropriate response; (2) the strategic linkage of that sense of crisis to the perception of long-term national decline, one that was directly attributed to the purported failure of the old, consensus policies; (3) the use of international comparisons and examples to argue that, in an age of economic liberalization worldwide, countries must adapt to the new neoliberal realities or find themselves marginalized and uncompetitive; and (4) the construction of what I term the "TINA meta-argument," that is, the rhetorically coercive strategy of positing that "there is no alternative" to the new policy orientation. Building on – and consciously contributing to – the sense of economic crisis discussed previously, these norm entrepreneurs sought to convince their audiences of the need for and appropriateness of substantial change, to promote the supposed benefits that would accrue from such changes, and to coerce hostile opponents or reluctant observers into accepting that no other alternative to their plans existed. It was through this conscious, strategic interweaving of these arguments that opponents to neoliberalism were largely marginalized and wrongfooted in public debate, ultimately coming to accept many of the underlying principles of free market economics as inevitable and necessary.

The Economic Crisis Argument

As discussed in detail in chapter two, each country in the late 1970s and early 1980s went through a period of difficult economic circumstances that many observers – of all political stripes – argued was tantamount to full-blown economic crisis. This sense of pessimism and fear was perhaps the most potent weapon in the rhetorical arsenal of the neoliberals, allowing them to present the crisis as the consequence of failed consensus policies, to which the only solution was a turn to the "free market." That is, the sense of crisis allowed norm entrepreneurs to employ both rhetorical persuasion – arguing that the policies of the past had been proved to be failures – as well as, more implicitly, material persuasion – holding out the claim that only with the new economic approach would prosperity return. The appeal was thus to norms of appropriateness (the right economic policy) as well as to material advantage (what will end the crisis and bring about economic recovery).

This sense of crisis was perhaps felt first, and most acutely, in Britain. The persistent trade union conflicts of the 1970s, seemingly uncontrollable inflation, the humiliation of Britain's 1976 application for an IMF loan, and, finally, the Winter of Discontent all served to produce the perception that "something has to be done." This growing sense of anxiety – even panic – helped make the case for radical neoliberal change.

In the hands of the Thatcherites, the economic tumult of the 1970s became the best argument – and the golden strategic opportunity – to pursue an economic policy revolution. A former Conservative minister recalled the following:

> I think there was a fairly broad realization that the country was due [for change] after the 1970s, which were pretty awful years for Britain. ... There was the feeling that the mood was right for some tougher action and [Thatcher] was brave enough to take it on. I think the prices and incomes policy is a case in point in that Mrs. Thatcher was prepared to let rip with

no control over prices and incomes, and allow unemployment to rise very rapidly. And she got away with it – whereas, in the early 70s, you wouldn't have gotten away with it.[55]

Thus, economic crisis was presented as ultimate proof of the failure of "socialism" and the only evidence needed that radical free market change was required. Promoters of neoliberalism in all four countries used this sense of crisis to rhetorically persuade their national publics that the old ways were broken and to advance their own brand of economic medicine. For instance, Roger Douglas, several years before the start of his policy blitzkrieg in New Zealand, sounded an apocalyptic warning – one that would become a common refrain among neoliberals everywhere: "As at no other time in its history, New Zealand stands a divided, confused, dispirited nation. ... Its standard of living has dropped and continues to drop visibly. It stands on the brink of economic ruin. It has stifled innovation for mediocrity. ... How much further will New Zealand sink before we start to fight back?"[56] Perhaps the most famous example, however, of the use of such dire rhetoric to promote the neoliberal agenda was Australian Treasurer Paul Keating's "banana republic" declaration. When the Hawke government first took office in 1983, it had engaged in an immediate expansion of the economy through increased government spending. However, as the fiscal cost of this boost became clear, and with the Australian dollar under enormous pressure on world markets,[57] the government backtracked from its first – and in many ways, last – "old style" economic policy. By 1986, Keating announced that only radical "adjustment" would turn the situation around. Conjuring up the worst specters of decline should the country not follow the reform path, he declared,

> I get the very clear feeling that we must let Australians know truthfully, honestly, earnestly, just what sort of an international hole Australia is in. It's the prices of commodities – they are as bad in real terms since the Depression. That's a fact of Australian life now – it's got nothing to do with the government. It's the prices of commodities on world markets but it means an internal economic adjustment. And if we don't make it this time we will never make it. If this government cannot get the adjustment, get manufacturing going again, and keep moderate wage outcomes, and a sensible economic policy, then Australia is basically done for. We will just end up being a third-rate economy. ... If in the final analysis Australia is so undisciplined, so uninterested in its salvation and its economic

wellbeing ... the only thing to do is to slow the growth down to a canter. Once you slow the growth under 3 per cent, unemployment starts to rise again. ... Then you [are] gone. You are a banana republic.[58]

When asked in an interview about this statement, a former top economic bureaucrat remarked that Keating's comment may well have been unplanned. However, Keating quickly saw how it could be used strategically to promote his economic program: "I think, frankly, that Keating just blurted that out. ... I actually do believe that those words just came out ... Then people put the spin on it and said, 'Well, you've done all this in order to put the fear of God into people and really wake the Labor Party up' ... and he himself, I think, then [thought], 'Well, this would have this useful advantage.' So he could never deny it and he went on from there."[59] Whether this interpretation of this particular incident is accurate, perhaps only Paul Keating knows. What is undoubtedly true is that the economic policy choice, as portrayed by the neoliberals, was stark: the patient could either take the bitter medicine or continue on to inevitable doom. Across all four countries, and across the political spectrum, interview respondents attested to the impact of perceptions of economic crisis in justifying the case for policy change. A minister in the New Zealand Labour government stated the following:

> We came into office against the short-term background of a total crisis. ... Against that sort of background [of] crisis, the need to take dramatic action to address the fiscal situation, the fact that there are all of these Think Big debts and stuff coming on board – it created an atmosphere of crisis which fed into the Douglas/Prebble agenda in that regard. And so bit by bit, I think you said, "Oh, yes, ... we've got to free up the financial markets, we've got to float the exchange rate, we can't go back to all this nonsense again."[60]

Thus, a perception of crisis, urgency, and impending economic doom was extremely significant in the shift to neoliberal economic policies. The notion that past policies – that is, the consensus policies of the past – had led to the current crisis was explicitly promoted by each of the neoliberal governments. The interventionist norms of the old political-economic imaginary were said to have failed miserably. There was no option to return to "all the nonsense" of the past. As a minister in the Mulroney government put it, "When we came in in '84, it was clear that change had to occur because everything heretofore had failed in terms of addressing what it was intended to address – job creation, regional disparities, economic growth, productivity. We were lagging in a whole range of economic indicators. … I knew we were going to have to do things differently."[61] What the crisis situation demanded, according to the neoliberals, was a concerted, innovative way to bring the country out of economic difficulties. Complacency and the policies of the past were insufficient. Only the market medicine could hope to revive each country's economic malaise.

The Long-Term Decline Argument

Very closely related to this sense of imminent crisis was the perception of long-term national economic decline. The 1970s were not only a period of economic crisis and distress, they were also the decade in which, in the eyes of both government elites and ordinary citizens, their countries were declining in relation to the rest of the world. In every case, the sense of national economic weakness and poor performance vis-à-vis other countries was both a sense of embarrassment and concern.[62] From the years of economic prosperity each country had enjoyed in the past, the decline was perceived as tangible and real. Advocates for neoliberal change were thus able to buttress their arguments about the failure of past policies with the warning of national economic decline. The persuasive strategy was the same: argue that "we are slipping" because of failed policies (rhetorical persuasion) that only the new policies can rectify and reverse (material persuasion). A Thatcher minister described how this feeling of decline fed into the agenda of neoliberal change in Britain:

> We were manifestly falling in world league tables. We appeared to be a country in the process of inevitable decline, not just relative, but in some respects absolute. There was a great awareness and a great feeling that "we can't go on like this." … This was creating a sense of national malaise so that when, as it were, the gospel according to Friedman or Hayek or any of [the others] … found voice in this country in ways which appeared to relate very clearly to our own scene, there was a recognition that perhaps this is the way we ought to go.[63]

Interviews in all four countries revealed the extent to which neoliberal politicians used specific international comparisons to highlight the severity of their country's relative decline. As Brian Mulroney argued in 1983, shortly before becoming the prime minister of Canada,

> In per-capita production, we used to be Number Two in the world, second only to the United States. Now we have dropped to Number Twelve among the twenty-four countries that make up the Organization for Economic Co-operation and Development. ... *Euromoney*, the leading economic journal from London, rates the performance of countries according to an accepted set of economic criteria. ... And where was Canada? Second? Tenth? Fourteenth in the world? On the basis of our economic performance between 1974 and 1982, Canada landed in fortieth place. Our great weakness was poor economic growth. We ranked fiftieth in economic growth in the last eight or so years. How the mighty and generously endowed have fallen![64]

Sir Geoffrey Howe made much the same case for Britain in his first speech as Chancellor:

> It is important for the whole House and, indeed, for the country to understand the gravity of our condition. ... If we look back to 1950, we find that even at that time Britain was still one of the world's great commercial and industrial nations. We accounted at that time for one-quarter of the world's trade. Our standard of living then was almost the highest in the world – almost twice as high as that in Germany or in France. ... It is during the last 15 years that the deterioration has become serious. Our share of world trade has fallen to less than 10 per cent. This has been accompanied by a steady decline of some of our major industries. We produced no more iron and steel last year than in 1957. Last year we produced no more cars than we did in 1960. In the past 15 years, our share of the world market for cars, ships and steel has been halved. Over the same period, more than 1 million jobs have been lost in manufacturing.[65]

In New Zealand, too, the decline in relative prosperity was the centrepiece of the Fourth Labour Government's argument for radical change. As Roger Douglas maintained,

> It was true that New Zealand had enjoyed the third highest living standard in the world, but that was 30 years before. By 1980 we had dropped to about twentieth place and were still falling. If that rate of relative decline continued, by the end of the century, we would be running sixtieth or

seventieth, behind Malaysia and Taiwan. The country was in a downward slide that could not be arrested by tinkering, or reversed by faith, hope and nostalgia. To set the country moving forwards would take a serious commitment to making some hard policy decisions.[66]

And as he put it just before taking office in 1984, "[We have had] the slowest 9 years of economic growth in New Zealand history. ... [T]he average growth rate in gross domestic product for each person during the past 9 years has been virtually nil – one-third of 1 percent a year. The equivalent rates are 4 percent for Japan and 1.5 percent for Australia. New Zealand is usually at the bottom of the heap for the 24 OECD countries; it is not always at the bottom – sometimes it comes twenty-third – it just manages to beat Turkey."[67] This link of relative decline to failed policies was an explicit one. In 1984, the Australian Treasury put it bluntly:

[E]ven in the 1950s and 1960s, when macroeconomic policies were conducted considerably more successfully than in the 1970s and, to date, the 1980s, Australia's growth rates generally lagged behind the OECD average. At the risk of some over-simplification, it can be said that, in the main, this was the result of inappropriate macroeconomic policies – excessive regulation ... and protection in many guises. ... [Ultimately] structural change cannot be avoided. ... Attempts to *resist the inevitable* put at risk the beneficial effects that can and do flow from structural adjustment.[68]

Thus, as these quotes illustrate, there was a clear rhetorical strategy among economic policy-makers to argue that change was necessary. The reality, it must be said, was somewhat more complex than the neoliberals would admit in their calls for radical change. The extent of the purported decline has been challenged by some recent work and, even when it can be said to have existed, it was more precisely a relative, not an absolute, decline.[69] What McAllister and Vowles argue for the Antipodes was true of all four countries: ordinary citizens "in the late 1980s remained substantially more prosperous than their counterparts twenty years earlier."[70]

However, perceptions often count for more in public opinion than actual material reality. As a result, the immediate 1970s experience of economic crisis and the oft-repeated claim of longer-term economic decline each nation was said to be experiencing both contributed to and buttressed the argument that neoliberal change was necessary.

Neoliberal norm entrepreneurs argued that, if radical changes were not made, history would most likely repeat itself: the crises and upheavals of the 1970s and early 1980s would return, and the supposed secular decline of each country relative to the rest of the world would become entrenched and irreversible.

The International Argument

The comparison the neoliberals made to other countries' economic fortunes tied directly into what, in more recent times, would be called the globalization argument. Policy-makers regularly referred to the international environment as a prime argument for the supposed necessity of neoliberal policies. This was thus an appeal both to appropriateness and to advantage – that is, rhetorical and material persuasion. The argument to appropriateness rested on the claim that "everyone is doing it, so it must be right," while the claim to advantage was that the only way to success and prosperity was to compete internationally. Specifically, in a world of ever-increasing globalization, the claim was that states have the choice to either get on board to a rapidly changing world economy or be left behind. Because this globalization process was seen as essentially an inevitable free market phenomenon, "getting on board" meant adopting neoliberal economics. Neoliberalism, whether one liked it or not, was said to be the way the globalizing world economy increasingly operated. To be a successful, competitive member of the international economy, then, states had to "adjust" and "restructure" their domestic economies accordingly. In a world of burgeoning capital mobility, one in which investors freely seek out the most attractive (that is, deregulated and open) markets, state subsidies and regulations had to be cut, taxes reduced, state-owned enterprises privatized, and barriers to trade and foreign investment brought down.[71] In the brave new world of globalization, the argument went, state policy autonomy was more apparent than real – the key questions were how and in what ways the state would deregulate, not whether the deregulation itself should take place.[72]

Moreover, according to neoliberals, the new free market project transcended old left–right partisan divisions. Its alleged universal acceptance was proof that what matters in the globalizing world was not partisan ideology, but one's willingness to adapt to the new, immutable realities. Its "truth" – its appropriateness – was verified by its supposed universal, global support by both sides of politics. As Roger Douglas argued, the old left-right dichotomy was anachronistic:

> There are new groupings, new divisions. What we have now are interna-
> tionalists – *the realists* – and the isolationists or protectionists. The former
> understand that the world is more and more becoming a single market
> and want to be a part of it. The second group hanker for the past. They
> want to put up barriers and pretend that they can operate outside the glo-
> bal market. Both groups are represented in the main political parties of the
> world, whether they are labeled "left" or "right."[73]

Not surprisingly, perhaps, the influence of external factors was most strongly emphasized in the three, much smaller, trade dependent economies: Canada, Australia, and New Zealand. In Canada, as discussed in previous chapters, the problem was the overwhelming economic might of the United States coupled with Canada's deep trade dependence on it. In such a vulnerable state, the Conservative push to open up markets and conclude a free trade agreement with the United States was presented as the only way to impose some order and predictability on the Canadian-American economic relationship. Throughout the early 1980s, members of the US Congress had become increasingly vocal in their calls for protectionism. Spurred on by the 1982 recession, they argued for stiffer protectionist measures as a means of protecting threatened American jobs.[74] Such efforts were viewed with great trepidation in Canada. Making a clear appeal to advantage, advocates of the free trade agreement explicitly invoked the disaster that loss of access to the American market would bring as their prime argument for free trade. As the MacDonald Commission argued in its 1985 report recommending free trade,

> Whether our association with our neighbour is easy or not, we "need"
> the United States. It buys about a fifth of what we produce, and it sells us
> many of the products which make our own lives rich and varied. We watch
> American television, drive American cars, eat American vegetables, drink
> American orange juice, and wear American clothes. The United States,
> however, also needs us. It needs our iron ore to make cars, our paper to
> print newspapers, our subway cars to travel to work, and our lumber to
> build homes. We are not only their best customer, but also their principal
> supplier. The extent of our links is demonstrated by the fact that every day
> of the year, thousands of cars, planes, trains, trucks, people and ideas flow

back and forth across the Canada-U.S. border: More traffic than between any other two nations on earth. The closeness of this relationship offers both tremendous benefit and risk of harm. We Canadians are wealthier because of the Americans, but we are also vulnerable to changes in their fortunes. ... Canadian business has reached a stage where our domestic market can no longer assure our continued growth, and where our access to foreign markets is no longer perceived to be secure enough to stimulate long-term, job-creating investment.[75]

Thus, the argument was one from international economic vulnerability. Canada had little choice but to sleep with the American elephant – hopefully, on mutually agreeable terms.

In Australia, Bob Hawke made a similar argument based on the economic challenges faced by a small, vulnerable trading nation: "The first [challenge to Australia] is for us to realize that this tough, increasingly competitive world of five and a half billion people does not owe, and will not give, seventeen million Australians an easy prosperity. The days of our being able to hitch a free ride on a world clamouring, and prepared to pay high prices, for our rural and mineral products are behind us. *From this fact flows everything else.*"[76] In a similar vein, a former National minister argued that New Zealand was simply unable to resist the dictates of international capital. Rather than resist international economic forces, he argued, countries could only embrace them as a given. "[B]eing realistic, we have to accept that there's an international world. We have to accept that people like Soros and others are going to move money all around the world and one day we'll find that something's happened to our share market because he's just moved a whole bundle of dough in here and then he might move it out the next day. That's the life we live now. So you can't insulate yourself. If we had tried to do it the old way, we would have been in deep [trouble] now."[77] The supposed inevitability of adaptation to this neoliberal world was emphasized by reference to events elsewhere in the world. As neoliberal respondents in all four countries pointed out, the obvious failure of Soviet-style communism was proof of what the neoliberals claimed to "know" all along – that policies of state intervention and regulations were fatally flawed. As a minister in the Thatcher government argued, "There was a worldwide swing to the more radical policies on the right and a recognition that the world had gone far too far down the road of social dependency, state control, state financing. It was becoming apparent that centralized markets wouldn't work. The

Soviet Union was in the process of collapsing. So these tides of opinion [went] together."[78] A Hawke government minister made quite the same argument with reference to France: "The way I would view it is that the world economy was undergoing a structural sea change and it was illusory to imagine that we could somehow isolate ourselves from it. The French socialists tried to do that in the early 1980s and then, within a couple of years, [had] to undertake a policy reversal and austerity program that makes anything the Labor government ever did look pretty mild by comparison."[79]

In short, allegedly irresistible pressures posed by a globalizing, neoliberal world economy played a central role in making the argument for radical change. While not explicitly controlling the nature, scope, and pace of reform, international influences nonetheless provided a continual backdrop to neoliberalism as the motivation and justification for change. In this way, it interacted with and reinforced politicians' own personal perceptions that neoliberal change was appropriate and necessary in the first place. It was a complex balance – international pressures reinforced elites' preconceptions about the need for change, while at the same time often providing the critical "proof" that only neoliberal change could succeed. Perhaps the best summation of this interaction came from a minister in the Australian Labor government. In his own assessment,

> The international environment was absolutely decisive. But certain individuals picked up that ball and ran with it very strongly – Keating being the prime example. It's no accident that governments, social democratic governments, socialist governments, all around the world [had] to confront similar problems. We're just simply not unique. There's a school of thought on the left that views all this as some peculiar sellout by a Labor bloke with political figures. But what gives the lie to that is the fact that the left can't explain why all over the world a similar phenomenon is occurring. Clearly, major international developments were driving all of this. But that doesn't mean that individuals can't play a key role in either retarding or accelerating what might be seen as a necessary or inevitable adjustment.[80]

In this formulation, then, governments are essential players, moving about on a stage set by international economic forces. The international market and its capitalist basis are assumed, unchallenged. States no longer – if they ever could – seek to transform, resist, or alter that structure in significant ways. It is a given. States and state policies must, in this view, largely accept and adapt to that ultimate reality. Put simply, in the words of the aforementioned Labor minister, the international forces are the ones "driving all of this." Politicians, then, are said to be able only to "retard" or "accelerate" the "necessary" and "inevitable."

TINA: The Meta-Argument

To this point, we have considered three distinct arguments put forward by the neoliberalism norm entrepreneurs: that economic crisis, national economic decline, and a deregulating, globalizing world all demanded neoliberal change. Armed with these three arguments, these norm entrepreneurs attempted to both rhetorically and materially persuade their compatriots that neoliberalism was both appropriate and "true," but also the only option available for economic growth and prosperity. Yet, the impact of these three was magnified exponentially by what I call the "TINA meta-argument" – an overarching tool of rhetorical coercion that asserted that "there is no alternative" to neoliberal reform.[81] Simply put, neoliberals of both the left and the right in these four countries deployed the simple, yet powerful, argument that there simply was no alternative to the neoliberal economic medicine. No matter how painful, no matter how apparently contrary to previous policies or, in the case of Antipodean Labor, their long-standing social democratic tradition, neoliberalism had to be pursued as the only policy choice that made any sense in the new globalizing world economy. Put simply, the TINA argument was deployed in such a way that it served as a "cognitive lock"[82] that closed off argument, shut down debate, and narrowed the field of policy options to one, and only one – the neoliberal program. In this way the TINA argument served a twofold purpose: it served to justify neoliberalism in the minds of its own advocates, particularly the Labor politicians who might otherwise have been skeptical of it, and second, it served as a powerful rhetorical tool, working to rhetorically coerce other political elites and the general public into an acceptance of the notion that, as unpleasant as neoliberalism might be in practice, it was entirely necessary and unavoidable.

Key to the argument that there was no alternative to neoliberalism was the systematic discrediting of what went before. As discussed in chapter one, this fits the strategy of rhetorical coercion. By discrediting alternatives as irrational, unworkable – even "unthinkable" in current circumstances – these norm entrepreneurs sought to present their own views as uniquely correct. Thus, in Margaret Thatcher's parlance, the Keynesian consensus was "socialism," an obviously failed economic system. As she put it,

> No theory of government was ever given a fairer test or a more prolonged experiment in a democratic country than democratic socialism received in Britain. Yet it was a miserable failure in every respect. Far from reversing the slow relative decline of Britain *vis-à-vis* its main industrial competitors, it accelerated it. We fell further behind them, until by 1979 we were widely dismissed as "the sick man of Europe." ... To cure the British disease with socialism was like trying to cure leukaemia with leeches.[83]

Put simply, the efficiency and superiority of the market and capitalist economics were argued to be objective facts, not something open to partisan, ideological debate. The British Tories were the first proponents of this markets-as-objective-fact argument. As *The Right Approach* put it in 1976, "The facts of life invariably *do* turn out to be Tory"[84] – that is, our free market, neoliberal program is not fundamentally a matter of ideology. It is economic fact. Ergo, there is no alternative to it.

This was a theme Thatcher, Douglas, and the other neoliberals hammered home to their respective public audiences. There simply was no argument about the superiority of free markets and, hence, no alternative to them. Any other proposition was simply irrationality. The argument seemed effective on both fervent neoliberals and their wavering "wet" colleagues. As Hugo Young so aptly puts it, TINA "became a beautiful propaganda weapon. There Is No Alternative grew from a conventional piece of impudent bravado on the part of the monetarists into an assertion that mesmerised the anti-monetarists, terrorising them into spellbound if curmudgeonly acquiescence. They could think of alternatives, but no Alternative. They escaped, at best, into agnosticism."[85] Lord Carrington, a traditional One Nation Tory "wet," essentially echoes Young's claim:

> "There is no alternative" was [Thatcher's] reiterated maxim, and the phrase "TINA," was adopted and derided by her opponents as epitomizing a dogmatic and uncaring approach. I believed that there was, in fact, probably no alternative. ... Under the Conservatives other ways to salvation had in the past been tried and one had to admit that, at least in the particular circumstances of Britain, they hadn't worked. In all this

Margaret Thatcher had been more far-seeing than her critics and more so than the doubters among her colleagues, of whom I'd been one.[86]

And, as put by a committed "dry" in the Thatcher cabinet, "TINA – there is no alternative – became a term of abuse on the left. But it was a catchword which nobody could ever say, 'Well, if there is an alternative, what is it?' In the end we have discovered that there *isn't one*."[87]

The TINA theme was a staple in Canada, Australia, and New Zealand, as well. As a high-ranking minister in the Mulroney government explained, Soviet state intervention had failed. Framing the choice as between Soviet socialism and the free market – a clear tactic of rhetorical coercion – he argued that there was no alternative to the market.

> This whole century has been dedicated to the notion that governments are the most efficient, effective and fairest way in which to distribute resources. But in its extremes, the Soviet Union with its seventy years of [state control was], in fact, a dismal failure. So with all of that history, it's not altogether surprising that people have pretty well come to the view now that there are things government can do. But the notion that governments can do it better if there's an alternative in the private sector – that just doesn't have an audience. A few Marxists in a few universities, but that's about it.[88]

And as John Crosbie, a die-hard free trade proponent and the Minister of International Trade in Mulroney's cabinet argued, "Some day we're going to have a North American continent that's an economic union. ... *That's inevitable*. These economic forces are there, and government policy *can't stop them*. It's only a question of, 'How do you get into a more secure position?' They're next door and geography dictates. Whether we like it or not, we're going up or down with the U.S."[89]

All the aforementioned factors pushing these governments toward neoliberalism came together in the TINA argument. A globalizing world was said to brook no opposition. No alternatives to adjustment to that world – on its own neoliberal terms – existed. Countries that tried to find and implement alternatives would be ruined.[90] In fact, one member of the New Zealand Labour government put it in exactly those terms. When asked how an allegedly left-wing Labour government could pursue such a radical free market program, he answered, "TINA. There is no alternative. There *was* no alternative. We were, as they say, up the creek without a paddle. Roger Douglas made the observation to us that if we had been a Spanish-speaking country, it would be all over – the IMF and the others would have said, 'We're not interested. Call in the debts, fellows.' We were right up the creek."[91] The argument that no credible alternatives to neoliberalism exist was articulated most succinctly by a former Australian Labor prime minister: "[The market has] been with us for a long time. It's not operating perfectly by any means and it certainly has not always operated fairly. But it's there. … What is the other, obvious, outstandingly clearly relevant [thing] about markets? It is that the communist command system has been given an opportunity to work. What's the answer? Abject failure. It's finished. Where does it operate? Cuba? North Korea?"[92] Finally, a minister in the New Zealand Labour government summed up how the TINA argument worked: the past was discredited, credible alternatives were non-existent, and neoliberalism was the only way forward. His argument is worth quoting at length:

There was no substantial theoretical basis on which you could sustain opposition [to economic rationalism] because there had never been anything like it. They'd say, "There is no alternative." And you'd say, "Well, there is." [They would reply,] "Oh, that's the old [way]. We used to do that. You can't do that anymore."

And then when you looked at what they were doing, you had to actually devise a theory, according to them, to combat what they were actually doing now. "Forget about that we used to do it that way. That was all old cloth cap socialism. This is the new way and you've got to get with it and get real, and there is no alternative" and so on.

Now when you started to work your way through that, you found that the liberal Keynesian centre-left was ill-prepared for this assault. If you just went back and said, "Well we used to do it this way and what was wrong with that?," they'd say, "Well, everything's changed. It's a different world, da da da, globalization" and so on and so on.

So even though you might instinctively think that the theories that were there before were still sound, you were put in a box as being a Neanderthal. You almost couldn't use them. If you did, [they would say,] "That's old, that's all the old stuff, that never worked." And they just wiped the past like that. And you would say, "Well, hang on a second, it did work. We used to have full employment here. We used to have a decent health system, an education system and a decent housing system. We had a fair society and we were known as one of the most pleasant places in the world to live. What was wrong with that?" "Oh, that was the old days and you can't have that back now." So they just wiped the history of

New Zealand just like that. And if you tried to resurrect it, you were put in a Neanderthal category ...

They just completely drew a line in the sand. Everything that happened before, it was like Ground Zero, it was like Pol Pot. They called us ... Pol Pot-ists, because we wanted to go back. In fact, my view was that *they* were Pol Pot-ists. They just drew a line and said, "Everything in the future. We've got to forget all that, wipe the history of New Zealand, start from Day One."[93]

Conclusion

From the neoliberal perspective, all signs pointed to the need for a radical free market economic shake-up. Taking together the factors discussed in this chapter, we see that, piece by piece, using the strategies of rhetorical persuasion, material persuasion, and rhetorical coercion, the argument was assembled that radical economic policy change was necessary and that neoliberal economics were self-evidently the only rational, appropriate policy choice. Economic crisis and perceived national economic decline combined with determined leaders, ideologically committed bureaucrats, and a world economic environment following a seemingly irresistible path to produce the belief – and the public selling of the notion – that "there is no alternative." As the New Zealand minister quoted previously pointed out, the TINA argument had incredibly powerful effects of rhetorical coercion – ones that only magnified and threw into sharper relief the arguments based on appeals to appropriateness and advantage. By systematically discrediting previous approaches and policies as the causes of economic crisis and decline, by asserting the necessity and inevitability of neoliberalism, and by casting as hopelessly anachronistic all potential alternatives to neoliberalism, it effectively served to shut down debate. In so doing, it sought to narrow the range of policy options from many to one. Neoliberalism in its different forms became the only supposed choice, the only alternative. Despite important differences in the ways in which neoliberalism was implemented across the four countries – a focus of the next chapter – the basic policy paradigm was the same: the market was the reality to which governments had to adapt.

5 Labour Markets and the Power of Partisanship

To this point, we have seen that market deregulation was constructed in the 1980s and 1990s, not as a particular economic ideology characteristic of the political right, but as an ontological fact to which all rational and responsible governments must adapt and conform. In that sense, then, the Anglo-American democracies are remarkable for the similarities linking them. Despite varying greatly in geographic size, population, location, and economic structure, all four went down the neoliberal path in remarkably similar ways.

However, as discussed in chapter one, there is no reason to believe that changes in societies' central imaginaries need be uniform across countries – all moving toward a common end in ideational lockstep. Rather, such changes are likely to be influenced, guided, and transformed in various ways by the diversity of political, economic, and institutional contexts within which they occur. Norm entrepreneurs, in attempting to reshape important aspects of their societies' political-economic imaginaries, must contend with a wide array of political, economic, and social opportunities and barriers – including already extant imaginaries – all of which have the power to advance, inhibit, reshape, and transform their intended programs of ideational change. The consequence, as discussed previously, is that, even within specific ideational paradigms – neoliberalism, for instance – the actual policy programs that governments pursue are likely to vary considerably.

A key concern, then, is not whether ideational change occurs – it clearly can and does – but when, how, under what conditions, by whom, and to what extent. The analysis in the previous chapter attempted to address some of these key questions in the context of Anglo-American neoliberalism. In it, I argued that the project of neoliberal political-economic imaginary change in these countries was facilitated, inter alia, by a sense of crisis (the economic dilemmas of the 1970s giving apparent credence to the TINA argument), by conducive political arrangements (e.g., the power of governments in majoritarian parliamentary systems), and by dynamic, transformative leadership. In these respects, the Anglo-American neoliberal projects shared important similarities – though neoliberalism differed in its specific application, the political, economic, and contextual conditions that norm entrepreneurs faced in each country proved largely conducive to their plans for ideational change.

Yet, as this chapter illustrates, there is another important consideration potentially affecting the potential for successful transformation of political-economic imaginaries: the degree and extent to which the intended ideational shift challenges, or attempts to change, a society's fundamental structures, practices, and institutions. While all normative change – and especially change as significant as the replacement of one political-economic imaginary by another – implies important changes in basic structures and practices, not all such structures are equally fundamental to the nature and functioning of society itself. Consequently, those societal "building blocks" that are more fundamentally important will prove more resistant to change than less central ones. As a result, norm entrepreneurs will find that some aspects of their societies give way relatively more easily to their ideational goals, being reshaped to fit the expectations of the new imaginary, while others prove more stubbornly resistant.

Therefore, we should expect fundamental social building blocks – those that undergird the major systemic or structural characteristics of the society, polity, and economy – to be more resistant to the efforts of norm entrepreneurs than the more "epiphenomenal" features that populate those systems and structures. Thus, marginal tax rates – as a particular feature of a country's economy – should be more amenable to change than the entire system of accumulation itself. The interaction, then, between societal structures and the imaginary in which they are rooted, is yet another avenue for significant variation in the extent to which similar efforts at ideational change achieve similar (or divergent) results. The more thoroughgoing the entrepreneurial efforts at change in social or political imaginaries, the deeper their effects on society's basic structures are likely to be.

This is precisely what we see with respect to the neoliberal imaginary shift in the Anglo-American democracies. There, the application of neoliberalism interacted with the traditional structure of partisanship to create divergent policy outcomes in at least one key area: labour market policy. While parties of both the left and the right in these countries deregulated capital markets, liberalized their trade policies, privatized state-owned industries, and enshrined economic efficiency as the acid test of public policy, when it came to labour relations, a clear distinction emerged. Simply put, the Labor parties of Australia and New Zealand shrank from a rapid and radical deregulation of the labour market. While neoliberalism in the Anglo-American countries proceeded to cut a wide swathe through a large number of formerly sacrosanct policy areas, it also collided with a very substantial modifying factor: traditional partisan policy stances and political alliances. When this collision took place, neoliberalism – at least with respect to labour market policy – essentially bifurcated into two distinct paths, following a much more gradual and incremental course in Labor-governed Australia and New Zealand than it did in Thatcher's Conservative Britain.

This outcome should come as no surprise, however. Partisanship has long been recognized as a constitutive, necessary part of modern democratic political systems, and it is widely accepted that this competition – and the choice it provides voters – is at the heart of electoral democracy. Democracy is only meaningfully democratic when competing office-seekers present voters with a choice – policy programs that differ from each other in substantial ways and that would produce appreciably different public policy outcomes if implemented. As Klingemann et al. put it, "For democracy to mean all that it can ... there must be some policy consequence of elections."[1] Thus, whether "parties matter" is one of the "concerns that lie at the core of democratic theory. ... By changing the partisan hue of those who govern ... can voters reasonably expect policy to be changed in more or less predictable directions?"[2]

That parties not only should, but do, "matter" in the determination of economic and social policy has "stood the test of time and ever more technically elegant [empirical] inquiry."[3] As summarized by Manfred Schmidt, "Regarding policy outputs, there exists a law-like tendency of partisan differences in public policy: cross-national variation, and within-nations differences, in public policy are significantly associated with – and by inference, dependent upon – differences in the party composition of government. Furthermore, a change in the party composition of government is associated with – and by inference causally related to – changes in policy choices and policy outputs."[4]

Thus, what partisan theory leads us to believe is that partisan differences – as one of the prime structuring elements in modern democratic politics – should be durable and resilient, even in the face of economic crisis and significant ideological shifts. The actual nature or content of the partisan difference may, in fact, change – as it did in the Anglo-American democracies during the period in question. So may the degree of ideological distance between parties – which also narrowed dramatically in these countries. What should remain, however, is at least some degree of partisan differentiation. To put it differently, ideational change is likely to be influenced by strong partisan considerations. Such change may indeed take place, but much previous scholarship implies that basic partisan preferences and ideologies will likely prove to be a significant source of resistance and inertia – with change occurring not haphazardly or randomly, but in ways inevitably influenced by parties' histories, traditional ideologies, and bases of support.[5] It is that interaction between ideational change and partisanship with respect to labour market policy in Britain, Australia, and New Zealand that this chapter explores.

First, however, a word about Canada. Canada does not fit into this comparison, and labour relations under the Mulroney government will not be considered here. The reasons for this are straightforward. First, only about 10 percent of Canadian workers are covered by federal labour law, the Canada Labour Code. The rest are covered by a disparate set of provincial labour laws that vary significantly in their provisions.[6] Thus, the federal role in Canadian labour policy is quite narrow and limited. Second, Canada's labour market much more closely resembles the more liberal and open US industrial relations framework than that formerly in place in either Britain or the Antipodes.[7] In fact, Canada's basic labour market structure is closely modelled on that contained in the 1935 US National Labor Relations (or "Wagner") Act.[8] Taken together, this meant that the Mulroney government had little need or desire to radically reform Canadian labour law, and its neoliberal program included no significant statutory changes to its structure. In fact, the only significant area of labour market liberalization in Canada in the 1980s and 1990s – indeed, the only area of labour market deregulation urged on it by the OECD in its influential, and largely neoliberal, *Jobs Study* – was a series of reforms that restructured, and made less generous, the Canadian system of unemployment insurance.[9] In short, without a traditional regulated labour market to liberalize, Canada cannot be easily or appropriately compared to the other three Anglo-American cases in this respect.

Labour Market Policy: Variations on a Neoliberal Theme

The effects of partisan differences on public policy, though at first glance not obviously supported by the remarkably similar neoliberal revolutions in the countries considered here, nevertheless manifested themselves clearly. In the area of labour relations and labour market policy we see a clear divergence based on partisan political consider- ations in Britain, Australia, and New Zealand. Here, more than in any other aspect of policy, we see these countries dividing along traditional partisan lines. In many ways, labour market policy and industrial rela- tions constitute an important case study of the partisan hypothesis just discussed. Given the fact that left- and right-wing parties have traditionally drawn a core of support from class-based constituencies, we should expect to see policy differences emerging in those areas of greatest salience to each party's main support base. Thus, it is the close, institutionally-codified links between the Antipodean Labor Parties and trade unions that most distinguish them from their conser- vative counterparts. If, as traditional partisan theory would suggest,[10] we should look for policy differences arising from different bases of party support, then it follows that the close, institutionalized relations between Labor and trade unions should provide a particularly signifi- cant point of difference between Labor and Conservatives.

In fact, this is just what we shall see: the key point of policy distinc- tion between Conservative and Labor occurred precisely at the point of greatest difference between them in terms of history, organization, and electoral support, that is, in relations with and policy toward organized labour. In fact, the distinction is even more clear when the comparison is extended to the conservative successors of Antipodean Labor – in each case, the conservative parties that followed proved eager to reform the labour market in ways Labor was unwilling to do. Thus, while neo- liberalism spread to all four Anglo-American democracies in the 1980s, its influence was, in this central aspect of economic policy, conditioned by more traditional partisan considerations. The end result, then, was a narrowed, but still recognizable, field of political competition. The traditional left-right distinction continued to matter, but it did so within more tightly defined parameters – those set by neoliberalism. Catley sums it up well: "During this process it remained possible to discern a Left-Right axis of the kind classical to developed capitalist economies. But the whole axis moved broadly to the Right and came to resemble more the American political spectrum than that of European social democracy."[11] We now consider the cases in turn – one Conservative government's hostility to unions, and two Labor governments' gradual and cautious moves to introduce some measure of labour market deregulation.

Britain: The Unions as "Scapegoats of National Decline"

By the time the Thatcher government came to power in 1979, the view that "something has to be done" about the unions was widespread throughout Britain. The economic upheavals of the 1970s and, in particular, the massive series of strikes over the 1978–9 Winter of Discontent served to convince most people that trade union militancy was one of the problems at the heart of the "British disease." Unions were widely viewed as exercising a stranglehold on the British economy, pursuing narrow, sectoral interests at the expense of society as a whole. For instance, in September 1979, 80 percent of Britons expressed the belief that unions had become too powerful – including 69 percent of trade unionists themselves.[12] By the end of the decade, "[t]he lurid picture of obstructive and tyrannical trade unions as the bovine obstacles to the achievement of an economic miracle enjoyed ... the potency of a national myth and it coloured as well as polarized attitudes across the entire political spectrum."[13] The trade unions had well and truly become the "scapegoats of national decline."[14] A Tory minister echoed this view: "To appreciate Thatcher, really, you've got to understand what the position was in '79. The country was on the brink of ruin. It was disastersville."[15]

The full story of post-war British industrial relations is an interesting and complicated tale.[16] For our purposes, however, the roots of the Thatcher attack on the trade unions can be most proximately traced to the attempts of the Wilson and Heath governments to introduce changes to the legal status of the unions. Prior to the 1970s, the law governing most trade union activity was the 1906 Trades Disputes Act.[17] In it, the unions – which until the 1870s had been treated as illegal conspiracies – were provided the legal basis for what would become their considerable power and influence in succeeding decades. The law granted nearly comprehensive immunity from civil suits arising from their actions "in contemplation or furtherance of a trade dispute." The Act stated that "Any action against a trade union ... in respect of any tortious act alleged to have been committed by or on behalf of the trade union, shall not be entertained by any court."[18] Strictly speaking, the right to strike itself was not positively protected by British law. Instead, the legal protection granted by the 1906 Act was a negative one in that it simply provided for legal immunity for unions and their officials. Yet, in practice, this immunity meant that workers could legally undertake a wide range of industrial actions, even engaging other workers in picketing and secondary strikes so long as their activities were, in those all-important words, "in contemplation or furtherance of a trade dispute."[19]

In stark contrast to the Australian and New Zealand labour markets discussed later, British labour relations were characterized by "voluntarism" – the notion that workers and employers would make voluntary agreements between them, with as little state intervention or interference as possible. In fact, unless contracts specified otherwise, collective agreements between workers and employers were non-binding and not legally enforceable. Paradoxically perhaps, trade unions in particular valued this sense of legal independence. Their experience with state control in the late nineteenth century had often been that of coercion and repression, and they believed that their rights were best protected by direct bargaining with employers. Any special rights granted by the state, the thinking went, must inevitably come with coercive legal restrictions and obligations.[20]

By the late 1960s, however, both Tory and Labour governments had come to the view that the British state's traditional hands-off approach to labour relations needed to change. Governments of both political stripes became convinced that the state must take a more proactive role. In particular, governments' repeated, unsuccessful efforts in the 1960s to implement effective incomes policies and hold down inflation, coupled with a clear inability to limit industrial disputes, led to the belief that the state needed to take a more active role by more clearly defining the rights, privileges, and responsibilities of unions. Perhaps the main problem faced by governments was shop floor militancy and union leaders' inability to control unofficial strikes and other disruptions that, by the early 1970s, constituted 90 percent of work stoppages.[21] As a senior Heath cabinet minister recalled,

There used to be a tradition: Although they would have a lot of hard argument, in the end, the employers in most industries ... and the unions, when they had done their battle, came to conclusion that they had better make a settlement. And, on the whole, that settlement, when made, stuck. But then as militancy increased the official trade unions got in more and more difficulty because they found that what they had agreed to got increasingly disowned by the more militant ... members, either in a particular plant or sometimes in a whole industry. Therefore, it became more and more difficult to get a reasonable industry-wide agreement. ... What became clear was that the old capacity for managers and union representatives to make agreements was getting less and less, and shop floor militancy was getting greater and greater. The official union leadership was clearly losing control of the position, and shop floor militancy was becoming more and more of a problem.[22]

As it would turn out, two major efforts to address these problems were made prior to the accession to power of the Thatcher government – and both would fail.

The first was the product of the Wilson government's White Paper *In Place of Strife*, released in 1969. Convinced that British law needed to clearly recognize the special role unions played in the economic life of the nation, as well as to clearly define their rights and responsibilities as collective bargaining agents, the government proposed the first major shake-up of British industrial relations since 1906.[23] Wilson's Employment Secretary, Barbara Castle, took the lead in pressing for changes designed to strengthen the role of trade union officials and more clearly delineate their power. On the one hand, the proposed Industrial Relations Bill had provisions amenable to unions – it would have created a statutory right to belong to a union and provided for mandatory recognition of unions by employers when ordered to do so by the state. Also, as a result of strenuous union pressure, a provision to require secret ballots before strikes could be called was specifically excluded from the bill. Despite these provisions – which Castle argued made the bill a good deal for workers – the unions ultimately balked at two other "penal clauses," particularly one allowing the Employment Secretary to impose a 28-day "conciliation pause" before unofficial labour disputes could be called, the violation of which was punishable by hefty fines. Union leaders clearly recognized the problem of unofficial strikes and wished to find a way to exert more control over their more radical shop stewards. Yet, fearful of state control, they preferred to handle the problem as one of internal union administration and discipline rather than direct state intervention. When asked to explain the unions' opposition to Castle's White Paper, a former top union official explained it this way:

> I think firstly the belief that the trade union movement wanted to retain its independence without any government controls over cooling off periods, et cetera. And, secondly, because however much you tried to disguise it, it was a control on the trade union movement by the government. I think I would add one more thing. Had we realized that rejecting *In Place of Strife* meant opening the doors to an incoming Conservative government, which would be much more ruthless in its legislation, I think we may have looked more kindly on Barbara's proposals. But that's the gift of hindsight.[24]

In the end, the government was forced to backtrack in exchange for a "solemn and binding undertaking" that union officials would do all in their power to get unofficial strikes and work stoppages under control.[25] The succeeding decade, it turned out, would put paid to those hopes.

By the next year, the Conservatives had taken power under the premiership of Edward Heath. In their 1970 manifesto, the Tories had committed themselves to much the same task that the Wilson government had failed to accomplish: "We aim to strengthen the unions and their official leadership by providing some deterrent against irresponsible action by unofficial minorities."[26] The task fell largely to Heath's Employment (later Home) Secretary, Robert Carr. Essentially, Carr's Industrial Relations Act of 1971 was, like *In Place of Strife*, an attempt to strengthen the hand of top trade union officials, while at the same time increasing the state's regulatory control over industrial relations.[27] As a senior Heath minister expressed his view,

> People talked about union power getting unacceptable – that was how the public debate went. But those of us who were involved with it knew the real problem ... was that union power was almost zero. The tail was wagging the dog. And so more and more we began to think about how we could buttress the constitutional power of the unions. The main concept which [we focused on] ... was how did we provide a legal framework within which we could buttress the power of the official unions and reduce the power of the unofficial element. ... The whole purpose of that action was to buttress the trade unions and to weaken the militants.[28]

On the one hand, the Act held out to workers a new, more clearly delineated set of rights. The right to join a union was protected, union recognition by employers was mandated if workers voted for it in a secret ballot, rights of redress and appeal against unfair dismissal were strengthened, and, most significantly, the right to strike was legally enshrined.[29] On the other hand, these strengthened worker provisions were counterbalanced by new requirements on unions. In an attempt to limit the continual waves of unofficial strikes, the Act called for the official registration of "organizations of workers." Organizations that were not registered – and thus unofficial under law – were open to civil suits for damages brought by employers. In other words, the blanket immunity granted by the Trades Disputes Act in 1906 was henceforth limited to only those organizations on the state's official register. The Act did not make unofficial workers organizations or their activities illegal, but it did render them vulnerable to potentially lethal damage awards should they conduct industrial action. Moreover, a 28-day "conciliation pause" was resurrected from *In Place of Strife*, and provision was made to make all collective bargaining agreements legally enforceable, unless the contracting parties specifically agreed otherwise.

While the Act's provisions became law in 1971 and 1972, in the end, it proved to be largely a dead letter. The Trades Union Congress and its affiliated unions pursued a near-total boycott of the Act. Unions refused to register as official workers' organizations, and those that did were forced to deregister. Additionally, unions used the Act's loophole to insist on clauses in collective agreements exempting them from legal enforceability. The former head of a major trade union expressed the trade union movement's view:

> I think we have to recognize that there is a fundamental principle in trade union activities. I won't say it's unique in Britain, but it's almost unique – and that's the role of immunity, the fact that trade unions carrying out an industrial dispute will not be responsible for damages claims by employers. Now Robert Carr's measure was saying that we would lose that immunity unless we traded under a government license. That was coming close to dictatorial powers of the government over the trade union movement. And there, the trade union movement, at least on paper, was absolutely united in opposition to that Bill.[30]

Employers, for their part, largely acquiesced. Preferring to keep the peace with workers, most came to negotiated agreements with the unions and declined to avail themselves of the legal recourses offered in the Act. The Heath government's attempt to effect major change in industrial relations thus went the way of the Wilson government's.[31]

When compared with what was to follow, these governments' approaches to industrial relations reveal a critical similarity: both governments shared a fundamental conviction – one rooted in the post-war, consensus imaginary – that trade unions were a legitimate Estate of the Realm, a morally and economically central institution in modern society. Their efforts at change focused – as they themselves tried, rather unsuccessfully, to argue – on strengthening top union leaders, whom they viewed as more "responsible" and cooperative, rather than on undermining their position and that of trade unions in general. While both *In Place of Strife* and the Industrial Relations Act entailed restrictions on workers' latitude to take industrial action – especially unofficial action – neither the policies of the Wilson Labour government nor the Heath Conservative government remotely reflected the aggressive, anti-union philosophy that would become entrenched in government policy post-1979. No less a labour stalwart than Jack Jones, the General Secretary of the Transport and General Workers Union, would remember, "No Prime Minister, either before or since, could compare with Ted Heath in the efforts he made to establish a spirit of camaraderie with trade union leaders and to offer an attractive package which might satisfy large numbers of work-people."[32] Thus, what we see in these cases are very clear attempts at changing the legal, institutional structure of British industrial relations *within* the existing imaginary. In the conceptual terms of this book, these were attempted changes at the policy setting and structural levels without concomitant attempts at ideational change at the level of the imaginary – showing yet again that attempts at change can happen at multiple levels, or may be more restricted. The contrast with Heath's successor as head of the Conservative Party could not have been more stark.

The five-year Labour interlude before the accession to power of the Thatcher government can best be described as the last hurrah of old style British consensus policy – in labour market policy no less than in other areas.[33] Almost immediately upon taking office in 1974, the government repealed the Industrial Relations Act and replaced it with its own Trade Union and Labour Relations Act. This legislation, drafted with the direct participation of the Trades Union Congress, essentially returned British labour law to its pre-1971 status, including the full restoration of workers' traditional legal immunities. Moreover, in 1976, the

Labour Government amended its 1974 act to extend unions' immunities to include the breaking of commercial contracts as well as contracts of employment in the course of lawful industrial disputes.[34] This proved to be a prelude to the tremendous social upheaval and economic crisis of the late 1970s. As discussed in chapter two, the widespread industrial unrest of the 1978–9 Winter of Discontent in many ways served as the stage-setter to the Thatcher attack on the unions. A former minister in that Labour government expressed this view: "In 1979, when the Labour government lost power, it lost as a result of unrestrained trade union power. ... The unions cared about prices and were deaf to any wider considerations, and they were very unenthusiastic about any form of income [or] wage restraint. And so you had this massive series of industrial confrontations as a result. ... It demonstrated that although [the government was] negotiating with trade union leaders, in reality the trade union leaders had no control over their own members."[35] In another Labour minister's assessment, "The Winter of Discontent was what perhaps, more than anything, changed it. There was something that the radical right could get their teeth into: 'If we play this properly, we can swing the pendulum all the way back against the trade union leaders'."[36] Finally, a Thatcher minister argued that anger, frustration, and the feeling that "something has to be done" about the unions "got stronger and stronger throughout the seventies and reached its apotheosis with the Winter of Discontent and the rubbish in Leicester Square and the strikes. People just said, 'We have had enough of this. This era is over and we've got to liberate ourselves from these people'."[37]

With the Tory victory in May 1979 came a near complete break with the traditional pattern of state-labour relations and, over time, a very significant shift in this aspect of the underlying imaginary.[38] Mrs. Thatcher's position was clearly stated: the trade unions had established a position of dominance over the economic life of the nation. Such control, she argued, was abetted by the desire of previous post-war governments to achieve a peaceful, working relationship with organized labour – a willingness to compromise that, she claimed, was exploited to the unions' advantage by labour leaders bent on creating economic havoc in order to achieve unreasonable demands. Even a former Labour minister admitted some sympathy for this view: "This is against my Labour Party principles a bit, but I think there was a sense that the trade unions were adopting positions which were quite difficult for government as a whole – and that it took some party, it was going to take some government, to tackle this."[39]

In her memoirs, Thatcher paints herself as an early skeptic of trade union power, but one frustrated by the confines of the dominant paradigm of conciliation.

> Many of us on the right of the Party – and not just on the right – were becoming concerned about the abuse of trade union power … [and] I sought advice about whether I could introduce a Bill which would break or at least weaken the power of the closed shop. But here again there were difficulties. Although younger Tories and many backbenchers were restive on the issue, the prevailing ethos in the upper ranks of the Conservative Party was still one of accommodating and appeasing the unions. … The Whips made it clear to me that I would not have the Party's support.[40]

Once in power, though, Thatcher wasted little time mounting her attack on trade union power and privileges. Cognizant of the Wilson and Heath governments' failures to effect significant change through one comprehensive piece of legislation, Thatcher proposed to move one step at a time, gradually chipping away at union prerogatives. However, this effort was not seen as separate from the larger economic restructuring the government was attempting. Rather, the emasculation of trade union power was complementary to and in large measure the result of the government's other policies. That is, the policy was to coordinate other aspects of economic policy so that each contributed, in its own way, to the eventual emasculation of trade union power – and, of course, to a new paradigm of industrial relations. Nigel Lawson described the strategy as follows:

> [T]he transformation of the industrial relations scene in Britain depended just as much on the economic policy the Government pursued as it did on the reform of trade union law. In particular, the eschewing of pay policy, which conferred undue importance on trade union leaders while creating unnecessary grievances among their members, and the abandonment of the unfulfillable commitment to full employment, which had enabled the unions to hold previous governments to ransom, were both essential components of the new order – and of the "new realism" which the union leaders felt obliged to embrace. The privatization programme, too, which no previous Government had attempted, was important in this context: trade union leaders are least inclined to feel constrained by the economic facts of life when State ownership both politicizes the context and appears to provide a bottomless purse.[41]

More broadly, the government's tight monetary and fiscal policies were strategically intended to create an environment in which generous concessions to workers were impossible. Here we see clearly the operation of material coercion – that is, the formulation of policy so as to create conditions that forced workers into acquiescing to the new ideational and structural shift. Simply put, the Thatcher government sought to utilize for its own purposes the coercive threat of losing one's job. The reader will recall Geoffrey Howe's statement, quoted in chapter three: "If workers and their representatives take pay decisions which are unwise because they seek too much, they will find they have crippled their employers and gravely harmed themselves by destroying their own jobs."[42] This element of coercion in the government's overall strategy to weaken union power was made particularly salient by the spectacular rise in unemployment in the early 1980s. The skyrocketing jobless rates in the early years of the Thatcher government weakened the bargaining power of workers and precipitated a long, secular decline in trade union membership. Whereas full employment had been the "Ark of the Covenant"[43] of the consensus period, in the Thatcher years, unemployment became a particularly potent weapon of choice against the unions. It was "the acceptable cost necessary to ensure weaker unions and lower inflation."[44]

The contrast between the new paradigm and the old consensus imaginary was clear – there was no talk of conciliation; no commitment to full employment; no talk of moderate, consensual change; and certainly no Heathite references to the positive social contributions of strong trade unions.[45] The Butskellite acceptance of the trade unions as being legitimate social institutions had been replaced by an open hostility to organized labour and its leaders. As a leading member of the Heath government expressed his own unease at the passing of the old values,

I believed in the trade unions. I believed in trade unionism all my life. There was a wing of the Conservative Party which was rightly regarded as anti-[union]. Ted and I and Geoffrey Howe and people like us were not of that ilk. We believed that unions were the proper things and we welcomed strong trade unions ... as long as they're genuinely democratic and operate, as were the employers, within the framework of publicly enacted law. But very much *not* to weaken the trade unions. Now, I'm afraid that ... Margaret Thatcher's motivations were anti-trade unions – powerful trade unions are a menace. But in principle ... good, strong trade unions are a strength to society and to industry, not the reverse, providing they are democratic, operate within a framework of law, and providing individual people are neither forced to join or forced to stay out of joining. And ... we provided the individual with the right to join or not to join. ... One or two well-known [employers] refused to employ anybody who was a trade unionist at all. That, to me, was just as wrong as the reverse. Perhaps it's unfair to put words in Margaret's mouth, but I suspect Margaret rubbed her hands when she found that an employer wouldn't have a trade unionist. I'm exaggerating; but there's no doubt that her motivation was much more anti-trade union than Ted Heath's was or mine was. ... No prime minister tried so hard [as Heath] to understand the unions and to give them a chance to have a bigger say in government than they had ever had before or would ever have again.[46]

With this new attitude – this clear departure from traditional policies of conciliation and compromise – the Thatcher government moved in a series of legislative steps to dramatically reorder the industrial relations landscape in Britain. That is, the material coercion deriving from tight monetary and fiscal policies and high unemployment was made explicit in a program of legal changes to compel the deregulation of the labour market. With these changes, workers were to be compelled by force of law to be "free." When these legislative moves are combined with levels of unemployment not seen since the Great Depression, as well as Thatcher's nearly intransigent attitude toward strikers – particularly those in the 1984–5 miners' dispute – the cumulative coercive effect was revolutionary.

Specifically, the government passed four main pieces of industrial relations legislation – the Employment Acts of 1980, 1982, and 1990 and the Trade Union Act of 1984.[47] As mentioned previously, the strategy was intentionally deliberate and incremental, weakening union power gradually, but decisively. In 1980, the government mandated secret ballots for the introduction of new closed shops, made trade union officials liable for damages caused by secondary strikes, outlawed most secondary picketing, and provided public money to finance ballots on strike action and intra-union elections. In 1982, the government directly attacked the traditional immunities of unions – the element in British industrial law most highly prized by unions and so key to the exercise of industrial power.[48] In addition to requiring that existing closed shops be ratified by secret ballots every five years, the legislation strictly limited unions' legal immunity only to disputes directly concerned with terms of employment. Thus, any unlawful picketing, secondary strikes, or politically-oriented disruptions were exempted from the traditional immunity. The 1984 Trade Union Act went even farther toward circumscribing legal immunity. It mandated that immunity only applied to actions that had been approved by a majority of workers in a prior secret ballot. Thus, unofficial disputes, or actions called by union leaders without first polling their members (as the 1982 miners' strike), were liable to legal action. Finally, in 1988 and 1990, the government removed the last legal supports for the closed shop by making it illegal to deny employment to anyone on any grounds relating to membership in a union.[49] It also outlawed all forms of secondary strikes or actions and, in a near-total blow against immunity, made unions liable for the actions of all their officials, from the general secretary down to ordinary shop stewards.[50] In short, the legislation aimed at restricting the unions' scope of action by reducing their ability to conduct widespread, concerted industrial action, by subjecting them to possibly catastrophic legal action arising from strike activity, by making intraunion democracy legally necessary, and by protecting non-union workers wishing to work in formerly closed shops.

The cumulative result of these reforms cannot be overstated, especially when compared to the failure of the Wilson and Heath governments to enact much less sweeping industrial relations legislation. By the end of the decade, the Thatcher government had produced one of the most deregulated labour markets in the OECD. Moreover, the effect on trade union membership was remarkable. A decade of recession, high unemployment, and hostile government legislation helped reduce union membership from 56 percent of workers in 1980 to 40 percent, and falling, in 1990.[51] At the same time, workplace disputes fell to their lowest level since 1935 – another trend that would continue well into the 1990s (see Table 5).[52]

The former head of a major trade union summed up the Thatcher revolution in industrial relations as follows:

There was no doubt that Margaret Thatcher won the [1979] election on the basis that she would put the trade unions in their place. And let's not quibble about it, she succeeded beyond what anybody thought she could. From being relatively all-powerful, the [unions] became relatively impotent. This was achieved by a number of factors. Firstly, crippling legislation. Secondly, a substantial increase in the number of unemployed. And thirdly, the ... hostility of employers, with encouragement coming from the Thatcher government. Now in saying all these things to you, I'm not pretending that the trade union movement didn't make mistakes. I think it did. Whether it be governments, employers, or trade unions, all have the tendency to use the economic boot if [it] is on their foot. Governments use it, trade unions use it, and employers use it. [But] certainly since 1979, any question of liaison with the government of the day, or consensus, has been out of the question completely and absolutely.[53]

Thus, by the explicit application of material coercion – everything from subjecting unions to legal liability to banning the closed shop – the Thatcher government succeeded in breaking a key element of the old consensus. A former Labour minister summarized it this way: "If you say there was [formerly] a consensus on the place of trade unions as the third arm – employer, employee, and government – the answer was yes. Margaret Thatcher's period in history will go down as a period in which she broke the mould from the past."[54]

Australia and New Zealand: Maintaining the Unions' "Legislative Cocoon"

In comparing the case of industrial relations in Britain to the labour market policies pursued by the Labor Parties of Australia and New Zealand, the contrast could not be more stark. Instead of applying the deregulationist and liberalizing logic of neoliberalism to the labour market with the same enthusiasm with which they deregulated other aspects of their economies – and in the starkest contrast to the coercive strategy of the British Conservatives – these two Labor Parties actually sought to preserve critically important elements of their countries' traditionally highly-regulated labour markets. In both cases, the Labor governments in power reformed economic policy nearly across the board, but eschewed any significant labour market deregulation. As John Quiggin puts it, "The only major task they left to their successors was that of breaking the (already greatly reduced) power of the union movement through labour-market reform."[55]

This reticence to apply the neoliberal medicine to industrial relations should come as no surprise given the expectations of partisan theory. As with the British Labour Party, the Labor Parties of Australia and New Zealand grew out of the labour movements in their respective countries at the end of the nineteenth century and continue to maintain formal organizational links with trade unions.[56] Therefore, in these cases, we have an apparently obvious instance of partisan theory logic. Not only do trade unions and their members constitute a large part of the Labor Parties' electoral constituency, they also form an integral part of the party organizations themselves. Given this institutional position – to say nothing of traditional imaginaries in Australia and New Zealand (as in Britain) that held a robust trade union movement to be a necessary and appropriate part of a modern, democratic polity – the influence of trade unions should be apparent.[57] Indeed, in contrast to the British Conservative Party and its hostility to unions, the Antipodean Labor Parties sought, in various ways, to work with the unions to maintain their role in society and the economy. In doing so, they maintained a traditional "legislative cocoon" within which unions and their interests were relatively protected.[58]

As with all the neoliberal policy shifts discussed in this book, the course of industrial relations policy in these countries over the 1980s was not identical. Yet despite significant differences between the two, the one shared feature was that the pace of change with respect to labour market policy was significantly slower and more deliberate than it was with other aspects of the national economy. The contrast between gradual labour market change and rapid reform elsewhere was dramatic in both countries. As a former Liberal minister in Australia rather sarcastically put it, "So long as it didn't impinge on immediate, obvious trade union territory, then you could be a great reformer."[59] In contrast to the Thatcher approach in Britain, coercion was far less in evidence in the Antipodean cases – and really only made its appearance with the industrial relations shifts pursued by Labor's conservative successors. In Australia, the Hawke and Keating governments pursued neo-corporatist policies of negotiation and compromise with the Australian Council of Trade Unions (ACTU), largely securing trade union agreement to reform through appeals to appropriateness (rhetorical persuasion) and advantage (material persuasion). In New Zealand, the contrast was even more apparent. Compared to the blitzkrieg of reforms that Douglas and his associates undertook in virtually every other aspect of the economy, labour market reform was hesitating and remained largely incomplete until the accession of the conservative National Party in 1990. We consider each in turn.

Australian industrial relations were, of course, the product of the unique Antipodean system of centralized wage determination discussed in chapter two. Created at the federal level in 1904, the centralized system was conceived as a progressive way of promoting social peace and industrial growth, while at the same time ensuring that the rights of ordinary workers were protected. The hallmark of the system was the notion that workers had the right to a "fair and reasonable wage," defined in 1907 by Henry Bournes Higgins, the President of the Commonwealth Court of Conciliation and Arbitration, as "the normal needs of the average employee regarded as a human being living in a civilised community." The principle that workers were entitled, as a matter of law and morality, to a "living" wage "was established as an orthodoxy of the Australian public policy pattern"[60] and a key part of the domestic defence imaginary. In return for this living wage, workers and their unions had to submit to a system of state regulation and control governing everything from the size of unions to the legality of strikes and, most significantly, the size of their pay packets.

By the late 1960s and early 1970s, however, the centralized nature of the system was beginning to loosen. Workers increasingly discovered that, in conditions of tight employment, they could obtain better deals by directly negotiating with employers than they could by relying solely on the arbitration system. While the Conciliation and Arbitration Commission (as it became known) continued to hand down regular pay "awards," these awards became more and more a legal baseline for wages and working conditions – a statutory minimum that workers regularly were able to better in direct negotiations with employers outside the centralized system.[61] Thus, by 1973–4, national wage awards were contributing only 19 percent of the yearly increase in male wages – the rest came from "over-awards" that workers had negotiated on their own with employers.[62]

However, a series of events would soon prove to be a harbinger of the neo-corporatist policies pursued by the Labor governments of the 1980s and 1990s. Critical to this transition was the recentralization of wage setting, beginning in 1975. Attempting to hold the line on wage rises and inflation, the Commission reasserted its authority over wages with a decision granting full indexation of wages to the rate of inflation, but strictly limiting the grounds on which any additional wage increases could be granted.[63] This recentralization of wage fixing had an important effect on the labour movement in Australia in the late 1970s – one that would be central to the labour policy of future ALP governments – by encouraging trade union consolidation and cooperation under the leadership of the ACTU, led at that time by one Bob Hawke. This strengthening of the ACTU as Australia's peak labour organization coincided with a strengthening of its ties with the Labor Party itself, as high-level consultations between the two organizations began to plan for the return of the ALP to power. Thus, by the early 1980s, the groundwork for a close corporatist relationship between the ACTU and a Labor government had already been laid. In fact, when Hawke took over the leadership of the ALP in early 1983, the main components of the future Accord had already been agreed between the party and the ACTU.[64] As a minister in the Hawke government described the approach, "Hawke was one of a new generation of trade union leaders – he was the leading figure in it, I suppose you'd have to say – [who were] strongly committed to what you might describe as a corporatist model of how society should operate. You've got interests, you've got employers, you've got the labour movement, you've got the government. ... The model was to get everybody around a table and thrash it out and work out what needs to be done."[65]

In this way, the Accord – an agreement renewed annually throughout the course of the Labor government – would prove to be the fundamental basis of the Labor government's relations with the trade unions. This explicitly corporatist set of agreements between the ACTU and the Labor Party involved a commitment by the unions to work with and support the government's policy program. In what was an excellent example of the strategy of material persuasion – that is, an appeal to advantage – the government sought the unions' consent to limit wage demands in exchange for the commitment to steadily increase the quality of the "social wage" – that is, government spending on social services and programs of direct benefit to workers, such as health care, education, and pensions.[66] This, then, was an explicitly negotiated, non-coercive attempt to hold down wages.[67] The critical philosophical concept behind this approach was Hawke's belief that employment is dependent on a shift of national wealth from wages to profits. As he put it, the causal links run from "wages to profits to investment to jobs."[68] In the words of a former Labor prime minister,

> There could be circumstances in which you could justify wages that didn't fully maintain their real value if workers were getting income in another form. In other words, they didn't have to pay quite so much for health because it was being covered by national insurance. Or their children would be educated through scholarships provided by society as a whole. Then you could contemplate wages, some of the time, rising in money terms less than the amount that was necessary to maintain their real value – because the real position of workers was being improved in other ways. That was the essence of the Accord.[69]

As discussed in chapter three, this policy proved largely success-ful from the government's perspective: it succeeded in holding down real wage increases while at the same time it secured labour's support for the government's decidedly un-Labor like program of neoliberal change. The important philosophical shift underlying this corporat-ist enterprise – and one continually promoted by norm entrepreneurs within the government – was that more-market economic change did not have to be antithetical to the interests of workers. In fact, the reforms were said to be a necessary element in securing the future well-being of workers. Couching their arguments in the language of material advan-tage, Labor portrayed itself as playing a critical balancing act between labour interests and the "real world" of economic globalization, attempting to balance "historical tradition and contemporary loyalty against what seemed to be the weight of economic evidence"[70] – and, in so doing, lending credence, as only a centre-left party could, to the emerging neoliberal political-economic imaginary shift. Thus, despite the overall similarity, the contrast with the British Tory approach to labour relations is clear. To Margaret Thatcher, over-mighty unions were a central culprit in Britain's economic problems, and their weak-ening was a fundamental aspect of her (coercive) neoliberal agenda. For Bob Hawke – not unsurprisingly, given his trade union history – the labour movement was a critically important link in his reform effort, its voluntary support critical to the success of liberalization elsewhere in the economy.

This fundamental link between the support of trade unions and the success of Labor's program was attested to by a former Labor prime minister. When asked if the government's reform policies were depen-dent on labour support, he replied:

> To a very large extent they were. You couldn't have introduced such radi-cal changes as we did if you had a trade union movement which said, … "We're just going to go for it, grab what we can and push wages up." Then you wouldn't have had the noninflationary environment, and you wouldn't have had the nonconfrontational environment within which change had the best chance of operating. The Accord did keep money wage levels down. What it simply meant was that the community – via what we did in education, what we did in health, and so on – was meeting some of the cost bill of the employers. Essentially, if you put it in simple terms, instead of paying higher money wages so that people could buy health insurance and higher education, they paid lower money wages and

the community did more in these areas. And that provided a lower inflation rate.[71]

An additional important element was the close connection between the unions and the New South Wales Right, of which Keating was a member.[72] As a minister in that government recalled, "The Right was in the ascendancy throughout the party structure as a whole, mainly because it was in the ascendant position in the trade union movement. A majority of the unions, and therefore a majority of the delegates, were affiliated with the Right. ... [But] the unions as a whole, not just the right wing or the left wing of the unions but they, as a whole, were able to exercise influence in maintaining [the government's] commitments in industrial relations."[73]

For its part, the ACTU's willingness to work with the government, especially in holding down wages, can be explained by its belief that the Accord was the best way of ensuring workers' interests in a rapidly changing economic environment – that is, that the government's policies were the best way of securing the material advantage of workers. An important emerging idea in the 1980s was that of "strategic unionism" – the notion that unions in the modern economy must shift their focus away from a narrow struggle over wages and the distribution of the proceeds of production.[74] Recognizing that economic growth is essential to job preservation and expansion, they must, in this view, become full, "responsible" partners in the whole of the nation's economic health, focusing on increasing productivity and cutting labour costs as necessary parts of an overall growth strategy. A Labor minister and former trade union official described the unions' attitude well. His comments are worth quoting at some length. When asked what accounted for unions' willingness to work with the government to produce real wage restraint, he replied:

Unemployment and our inability to find a way through, I think. The problems with growing unemployment within the domestic Australian economy and a recognition that inevitably the levels of quality in the products that we made suffered, the efficiency of the economy suffered, and that protection delivered a poisoned chalice at the end of the day. This coincided with a [changing] view within the union movement. ... The ACTU – which then had about fifty-three percent union penetration of the workforce – discovered that by [conducting] a campaign over reduced hours and higher wages, we were able to succeed at winning higher wages and reduced hours. The trouble was that major unemployment followed, the profit share [of national output] declined, and the wages share rose. We weren't getting investment in industry and in development. ... [So] when we saw the devastation that was being incurred, we thought, "Well, look, this requires something else. This will achieve more leisure time and more disposable income for a shrinking number of workers. Is that what we're about? No." "No" was the unanimous view, right across all of the shades of political commitment or political view within the union structure. "No, that's not what we're about. So how do we go about it? We have to have a bigger say in the economy to deliver these outcomes." ...

[But] the opportunity to do it didn't occur until we were elected. What you had then was Ralph Willis, who had been Hawke's understudy at the ACTU, in parliament as the industrial relations minister and an economist, later a Treasurer, able to understand the economics of this from the government side. You had a government headed by an ex-president of the ACTU, who was an economist and who had ... gone through this theoretical debate and was for a free market. And you had somebody like [Bill] Kelty at the ACTU, with the support of a highly organized body, the ability to deliver it, and the guts to take on the challenge.

As a consequence, the ACTU made a trade-off, which was endorsed by our affiliates, that the priority would be for employment growth. If there was a casualty, it would be pushing wages further, faster. [So] they would try and do an Accord with the government to help manage that through. ... [Trade union leaders] preconditioned their members to accept the view that they should aim for high wage, high skilled jobs in high tech and medium tech manufacturing industries in Australia. That was their preeminent concern; wages were a secondary consideration. ... They never quite said it in these terms, but what underlay their view was if they could contribute to that industry type base, then their ability to negotiate higher wages would be sort of axiomatic. These companies could earn income which could afford good conditions for their members. [So] they saw a very strong role for themselves in helping create the right economic circumstances to bring that about.[75]

This trade union conversion to the goals of firm profitability and efficiency, of course, greatly facilitated a government set on neoliberal change. In fact, it represented unions' acceptance of the key neoliberal emphases on low inflation and "flexible" labour markets as the most important prerequisites for high employment. Thus, the Accord was a boon to the Hawke and Keating governments that – with both sides accepting a common ideological stance – served to create a positive working environment between government and labour. As Bramble and Heal point out, the Accord process – successful as it was in holding down real wages – failed in many ways to live up to its promise in terms of providing higher living standards and greater social equality. Yet, "in terms of the process it was a partial success – there was extensive consultation by the government with the peak union body, and union-busting was the exception, rather than the rule, as an employer strategy."[76] Consequently, Labor was able to carry out its reforms – and promote its general neoliberal ideational shift – in large part because of its close union ties. Arguments about low inflation, economic efficiency, wage restraint, and firm profitability were immeasurably more palatable coming from a Labor government run by a former trade union leader. From there, it was a short step for neoliberal policies to take on the "taken-for-grantedness" that is a hallmark of successful changes in political-economic imaginaries. As a former Liberal minister saw it, "[T]he trade union movement as a whole was frankly more likely to accept that sort of thing from a Labor government than from a non-Labor government. In the case of a non-Labor government, the automatic reaction would be, 'They're getting at us. They're at us again' and so on. Whereas, [under a Labor government, it is], 'Oh, it's our own people doing it. Perhaps it's not too bad after all'."[77]

Thus, it is not that the tide of neoliberalism somehow bypassed the labour markets of the Antipodes altogether, with Labor governments there refusing to countenance any moves to deregulation. Rather, the application of neoliberalism by the Labor governments of Australia and New Zealand was relatively more gradual and incomplete, with organized labour actively supporting – or at least acquiescing – to changes that their confreres in government argued were necessary.

In this "bargained" way, the Australian Labor government began to progressively move away from the highly-centralized industrial relations system in place at the beginning of its tenure. From 1987, wage awards began to be linked in part to productivity increases, which were negotiated at the enterprise level. Moreover, the 1988 Industrial Relations Act enabled firms and unions to hammer out agreements on wages and working conditions on their own, to be "certified" by the newly renamed Australian Industrial Relations Commission (AIRC), provided that they were not "contrary to the public interest."[78]

In the 1990s, this gradual shift to a more decentralized system picked up steam. Paul Keating, by then Prime Minister, declared in 1992 that while the old, centralized system had served Australia "quite well" in the past, it was now "finished." He foresaw further moves to a "much more flexible system, under which the vast majority of decisions over wages and working practices would be made at the workplace level."[79] In this vein, the 1992 Industrial Relations Act was amended to facilitate the certification process for enterprise-level agreements. The "public interest" test was replaced for many such agreements by a much looser "no disadvantage" test, allowing award conditions to be altered providing that, taken as a whole, the new terms did not disadvantage workers.[80] This trend continued with the Industrial Relations Reform Act in 1993, which further decentralized wage bargaining by encouraging both union and non-union workers alike to bypass the awards system and reach a wide range of agreements with employers at the enterprise level, again with the role of the AIRC being only to certify that agreements did not fall below a set of minimum "safety net" standards.[81]

However, as discussed previously, the most interesting aspect of this pattern of creeping deregulation of the Australian labour market is that the government sought and received union support throughout. Accepting the core elements of strategic unionism and enjoying the access to the policy-making process the Accord provided it, the union movement was an active and willing partner in the gradual decentralization of labour relations in Australia. For his part, ACTU Secretary Bill Kelty declared that workplace bargaining held out the opportunity for workers to be more involved in "all aspects of the way their industry and workplace operates, thereby driving enterprise reform and pushing up productivity levels"[82] – in other words, that there was the prospect of material advantage for all in deregulation. This marks a key point of distinction between neoliberalism as implemented by the Tories in Britain and the Australian Labor Party. In Britain, deregulation was confrontational, coercive, and combative, aiming for nothing less than the elimination of trade union power. In Australia, the process was gradual and negotiated, the unions ultimately buying into the government's neoliberal-inspired notions of workplace "efficiency" and "flexibility." There, the approach has been described as "a complex and sometimes contradictory combination of corporatism and economic rationalism."[83] In fact, a more accurate description might be "economic rationalism *through* corporatism" – that is, an economic rationalist government securing labour's acceptance of its program by means of corporatist consultation and negotiation. Union officials, then, were not blindsided by neoliberalism in Australia. By actively supporting the

ALP's reform program as one ultimately in workers' best interests, they served to silence the doubters and critics and thus became active agents of neoliberalism's spread.[84]

This consensual approach came to an end with the election of the Liberal/National Coalition in 1996. The Howard government's approach, while not as radical as that of its conservative counterparts in New Zealand, was to eschew Accord-style cooperation with the unions and move the country much more quickly down the road of labour market deregulation, particularly as envisioned by employer groups such as the Business Council of Australia.[85] Its 1996 Workplace Relations Act reduced the coverage of AIRC awards to only 20 "allowable matters" regarding working conditions – a limited baseline of minimum acceptable conditions with all else to be determined through private negotiations. This move essentially completed the transition of the Australian awards system from one of comprehensive wage setting and mandated working conditions to one based on a floor of acceptable pay and conditions below which agreements could not be made. Furthermore, the Act's introduction of Australian Workplace Agreements (AWAs) marked the first time it became possible for workers and employers to conclude purely individual agreements, opting out of the awards system altogether[86] – an option the government assiduously encouraged workers to take. This would be followed in 2005 by the Howard government's *WorkChoices* legislation. This further deregulation of the labour market promoted AWAs as the government's preferred model of individual employer–employee agreement, limited workers' ability to claim unfair dismissal – eliminating it entirely for workers in small businesses – and continued to reduce the minimal conditions (the "allowable matters") mandated in employment contracts.[87] While some elements of *WorkChoices* – AWAs in particular – would be gradually reversed by the newly-elected Labor government of Kevin Rudd beginning in 2008, significant parts of the legislation – particularly the limitations on unions' right of entry to the workplace and the mandate of secret strike ballots – were retained.[88] In this way, the basic pattern continued to hold: both parties moving toward a deregulated labour market, but the Labor Party doing so in a more moderate and gradualistic way than their conservative counterparts.

Numerous interview respondents echoed this basic conclusion, repeatedly identifying labour relations as a key point of difference between the neoliberalism of the right and left in Australia. As a former member of the Labor government described it,

There were a number of key areas of distinction where the ideology and the policies of this government could be differentiated from the full-bottle free market ideology. That's probably the case in regard to the labour market where, when we were elected to office, we were elected with a commitment to negotiate what was called an Accord with the trade union movement. ... [Thus,] the key area of ongoing distinction [between left and right] was the labour market. Initially, there was an Accord framework negotiated, with highly-centralized wage fixation, which changed over the life of the government towards a more limited role for the so-called awards system and an increasing emphasis on enterprise-level bargaining and a focus on productivity – linking productivity growth to wage increases. But that remained and still remains a major area of differentiation between the Labor Party and the current [conservative] government. ... [It's] partly driven and partly reflected by Labor's institutional link with the trade unions. The Labor Party originated in 1890 as the political arm of the labour movement.[89]

In an interview, a Liberal Party minister argued that the essential left–right difference is based precisely on the close association between Labor and trade unions. As he put it,

The Labor Party is a party that is very heavily based in the trade union movement. Structurally, you will find a very substantial majority of the decision-makers at all party organization conferences dominated by trade union members. You'd find its parliamentary representation heavily dominated by people from a trade union background. ... The policy of consensus which Hawke promoted was essentially an effort to elevate the role of the ACTU, of which he had been president, in the national policy scene, and he established an approach to policy-making ... which involved unions, government, and private enterprise working together. ... That tripartite approach gave the trade union movement a say in policy that it had never managed to achieve before. ... It meant that every area of policy was constrained by the institutional interests of the trade union movement. You couldn't move policy to any position that would damage the interests of the trade unions. And that meant, for example, that you couldn't deregulate the labour market because union power relied on a centralized industrial relations system. ... And you could go on in all of the policy areas, and you would find them dominant.[90]

In short, the Australian Labor Party initiated and carried through significant neoliberal change across a wide swathe of the economy, but stopped short of doing the same to the social and economic interests most closely linked to it. The extent – and limits – of Labor-led neoliberal change was described this way by a former Liberal minister: "There's no doubt that the Hawke government was the first genuinely liberal economic government in Australia's history. It broke the mold of Deakin, going right back to the early part of the century, but it did not break the mold of Henry Bournes Higgins, the Harvester judgment and all those sorts of things."[91] The breaking of that mould, while tentatively initiated by Labor, occurred at the hands of the conservatives who followed.

In New Zealand, the system of industrial relations throughout much of the twentieth century shared much in common with that of Australia. There, the structures set up by the Industrial Conciliation and Arbitration Act in 1894 served the same socially protective function as the Australian arbitration system. The goal of this then-radically prounion system was to eliminate "the 'sweating' of labour and other antisocial employment conditions by creating a floor of minimum labour standards in the labour market" and by providing "an institutional mechanism for resolving industrial disputes without resort to costly and sometimes disruptive strikes."[92]

However, the New Zealand arbitration system would over time lose its central place in the fixation of wages. In a similar way, but to a much greater degree than in Australia, the 1950s and 1960s saw the decline of centralized wage fixing and the emergence of direct bargaining and agreements between unions and employers as the most important aspect of wage setting. As labour shortages augmented the power of workers to gain increasingly generous concessions from employers in private agreements, the centralized system retreated in importance. National pay awards became more of a starting point onto which "second-tier" agreements between unions and employers were added.[93]

The role of the Arbitration Court in setting employment conditions was then decisively shaken by the events of 1968. That year, the Court issued a "nil" wage order, arguing that economic conditions did not allow any increase over the previous year's pay award. This decision incensed the unions and destroyed what little confidence they still had in the Court as an institution committed to fairly protecting their interests.[94] The result was that throughout the 1970s and early 1980s, unions in New Zealand rejected the centralized wage fixing system almost entirely, preferring to make their own deals with employers – ones that the government struggled to control through a variety of largely unsuccessful incomes policies.[95] The weakening of the centralized system played an important role in the structural weakness of the New Zealand labour movement. In contrast to the ACTU in Australia, which, in the 1970s under Hawke's leadership was consolidating its close neocorporatist links with the Labor Party, the Federation of Labour (FOL) in New Zealand remained weak and disunited. As a consequence – and again, in direct contrast to the Australian case – when the New Zealand Labour government took office with its radical neoliberal agenda, the FOL and the labour movement as a whole found itself marginalized and often unable to make its voice heard in opposition to the Douglas steamroller of neoliberal change.[96] The result was that nothing comparable to the Accord developed in New Zealand – that is, no highly institutionalized avenue was ever created through which the labour movement was regularly consulted and its support actively cultivated.[97]

Yet, despite the weakness of the New Zealand labour movement, the Fourth Labour Government did not duplicate its neoliberal blitzkrieg with respect to the labour market. In many ways, it proved nearly as unwilling as its Australian counterpart to effect comprehensive neoliberal restructuring of the labour market, especially reform perceived as counter to the interests of organized labour, and it certainly did not employ the coercive strategy it pursued elsewhere in the economy. This reticence is even more remarkable when viewed in the light of the thoroughgoing reform Labour brought to virtually every other aspect of the New Zealand economy. As Bray and Neilson aptly put it, "[i]n contrast to its approach in other areas, the New Zealand Labour Government's labour law strategy could be described as a medium-term approach of step-by-step cautious reform."[98] A former Australian Liberal minister and close observer of New Zealand's neoliberal revolution expressed it this way: "The Labour Party ... made some changes at the edges [in industrial relations]. But the fundamental changes that were made were actually not by Douglas, really – he found them difficult. It was [the National Party's] Bill Birch and the Employment Contracts Act."[99]

The Lange government, in fact, began its tenure in office with an act of labour market *re*-regulation by immediately enacting a return to compulsory unionism. The Muldoon government had legislated its end earlier in 1984, but, in keeping with traditional Labour policy predilections, the government reinstated it.[100] What then followed differed dramatically from the Australian case in that no neo-corporatist style agreement was reached with any peak union organizations, but also reflected an important similarity in that no dramatic efforts were made to scale back unionization or labour's (already relatively weak) influence. So while Labour introduced wholesale change to virtually every other sector of the economy, it shrank from doing the same to the labour market, leaving it to its National successors.

Labour's major labour market initiative was the 1987 Labour Relations Act.[101] Under the Act, unions could choose to opt out of the national award system and pursue an agreement at the industry or even enterprise level. This, of course, reflected the fundamental neoliberal principle of labour market "flexibility." Yet, the Act also reflected Labour's hesitance to implement radical change – the same opt-out clause was not available to employers, and those agreements could contain provisions for a closed shop.[102] In other words, the Act permitted enterprise-level contracts and, thus, represented a step toward labour market deregulation, but by making the opt-out of the award system available to unions but not employers, it effectively structured the new rules to ensure that labour would not be unwillingly disadvantaged by them. On the whole, then, the Act represented a gradual, incremental change, and in the end, the status quo ante was largely maintained.[103] In fact, the OECD reported in 1991 that, in its first few years of operation, the new industrial relations framework had only limited effects. Most awards continued to be made at the national level, and very few agreements had been concluded at the industry or enterprise level.[104] Put simply, Labour's rather incremental changes to the structure of industrial relations in New Zealand had only marginal effect.

It is possible to get a true sense of how marginal Labour's reforms of New Zealand's labour market were by comparing them to the near-total revolution of industrial relations implemented by the succeeding conservative National government. Its 1991 Employment Contracts Act was a veritable scorecard of neoliberal labour policies, an act that repealed the Labour Relations Act and, through the material coercion of legislative and legal fiat, deregulated virtually the entire labour market overnight. Among other things, it allowed employers and employees to select with whom they would associate or bargain, removed any preference or special position for unions or union members in negotiations, declared that individual workers were equal to "employee organizations" (the Act's telling euphemism for unions) in negotiations with employers, and outlawed secondary strikes. Moreover, the law did not require "good faith" bargaining; agreements for closed shops, or ones that give preference to union organizations, were made illegal; and there were no statutory requirements for minimum severance notice or severance pay.[105] Essentially, the Act created the neoliberals' ideal flexible, efficient labour market – one in which unions had no particular formal role in the workplace, agreements were "freely" contracted between employers and individual employees, and, whether they wanted to be or not, workers were legally coerced into being "free."

Such changes marked a critically important philosophical shift. As Dalziel and Lattimore point out, "Under previous legislation, the primary employment relationship was between the union (to which an employee was obliged to belong) and the employers' organisation (whose agreements bound all employers). Under the Employment Contracts Act, however, the primary relationship was between the individual employee and the individual employer, with neither party able to force a collective agreement on the other."[106] The ECA was thus the legislative enactment of a radically new ideational basis for the relationship between worker and employer. As Chaison aptly puts it, it rejected "a fundamental premise of the labor laws of industrialized nations, that is, the presumption of inequality of bargaining power between the employer and the individual employee, that employees are inherently in a weaker position, and that the law should ameliorate this imbalance."[107] As a result, New Zealand in the 1990s had a labour market that was the most deregulated of any in the OECD.[108]

It is here that we see the most significant differences between Labour and the conservatives in New Zealand. The Douglas reform package had cut a wide swathe through traditional economic policies and structures and reformed virtually all of them – except one. The country's traditional industrial relations structure largely remained, presenting a task to be taken up in the extreme by the conservative National government that followed. As a Labour Finance Minister put it, "National highlighted [the differences] almost immediately. … By the extremism of its changes in the industrial relations regime, it wasn't simply a move away from a highly protected labour market. It went right to the other end in terms of where the power lay."[109]

The reason for this divergence is clear: the special links between the Labour Party and the trade unions. As Jim Bolger, the National prime minister who succeeded the Fourth Labour Government argued in his memoirs, "[Douglas] knew Labour's supporters cared about the labour movement and to acknowledge that he protected the old order for unions. This in turn created serious distortions in the Labour

Government's reform programme. What Douglas was doing was deregulating every market in sight with the exception of the single most important one of all, the labour market."[110] As a former National Party minister explained,

> In 1990, we were able to move in the area of the economy where they were unable to move because they had union support. ... Now we were free to move further, particularly ... to free up the labour market, which a left wing, trade union-affiliated political party was unable to do. So that was one of the areas that we were free to move, whereas they were free to move in areas that we would have difficulty in, I think ... [for instance] in terms of removing subsidies and the like from the agricultural community, which caused a major problem for farming incomes for some time and as a conservative party we were more dependent on farmers for support. So they could move there; we could move in the labour market.[111]

Or, as Walsh describes the Labour approach,

> Labour's reluctance to [radically reform the labour market] was in part a legacy of traditional union-party links. These gave unions institutional opportunities to influence party and government policy. They combined with Department of Labour officials to turn back the radical agenda of deregulation. ... Labour's approach to industrial relations sought to balance efficiency and equity concerns. Efficiency concerns drove its restructuring of State sector industrial relations, including corporatization and privatization. ... However, Labour's equity concerns led it to retain union registration, and thus monopoly membership and bargaining rights, blanket award coverage, provision for compulsory union membership, and compulsory arbitration in the Labour Court for disputes of rights and personal grievances.[112]

In short, then, neoliberalism became the economic ideology of the day in Australia and New Zealand, as in Britain. But the way in which it was applied – to what sectors and with what speed – differed significantly along the left–right divide. A New Zealand National Party minister put it succinctly: "Some [people] did some things, some did others. The Labour Party tackled farmers; they didn't have a constituency there. The National Party tackled unions; it didn't have a constituency there. But there is a seamlessness of neoliberal diagnosis and prescription being offered."[113]

Conclusion

As the example of industrial relations and labour market policy in Britain, Australia, and New Zealand illustrates, traditional social structures and practices can have very significant effects on the success, nature, and extent of ideational change. In the cases considered here, one such key social element was the traditional structure of partisanship. As a key element of these countries' polities, traditional partisan differences had a profound effect on the course of neoliberal reform there.

As this chapter illustrates, the long-standing institutional linkages between the Antipodean Labor parties and trade unions critically affected the neoliberal programs these parties pursued once in government. In general, the programs of market liberalization in Labor-led Australia and New Zealand bore remarkable similarities to those pursued in Conservative-governed Britain and Canada. In fact, as detailed earlier in this book, the case of New Zealand stands out as one in which a Labour Party pushed the logic of market liberalization even further, in some respects, than even the better-known, archetypal case of Thatcherism in Britain. Nevertheless, partisanship made its very important influence felt – and quite dramatically so – with respect to that one area of public policy most central to the historic institutional linkages and traditional class interests of Labor parties: the rights and privileges of workers. While neoliberalism as applied to a wide range of other policy areas seemed largely unimpeded and unaffected by partisan considerations, here it took dramatically divergent paths. In Thatcher's Britain, neoliberalism was the motivation behind a coercive assault on the traditional privileges and immunities of trade unions. In Australia and New Zealand, by contrast, neoliberalism was adapted and modified – in Australia, as a result of direct negotiations between the government and the peak trade union organization – to reflect the interests of Labor's traditional union allies.

This, I argue, speaks to the significant effect that the "residue" of traditional social structures and institutions can have on the process of ideational change. As discussed in the introduction to this chapter, ideational change of any sort – and especially that as significant as the replacement of one political-economic imaginary by another – is unlikely to be uniform across various societies. Nor is it likely to have the same effect on various social institutions within societies. Rather, what is more probable – as confirmed by the case of labour market policy in the three countries discussed here – is that ideational change may succeed in some respects, but not in others. While such attempts may completely transform old practices and attitudes in the intended way, other social structures may be only partially affected – if at all. A key determinant in the degree to which these attempts succeed or fail is the extent to which they confront the basic foundational elements of a society's practices, norms, and institutions. Simply put, the more basic a social institution is to the structure of society generally, the more resistant it is likely to be to the efforts of norm entrepreneurs. Such was the case with partisanship – a key foundational element in modern democratic polities that, while itself changed in important ways by the experience of neoliberalism, also demonstrated a remarkable resilience in what was a period of rapid and unprecedented change.

6 "The Market Has Won": Norm Entrepreneurs and the Anglo-American Neoliberal Imaginary

A central emphasis of this book has been the ways in which norm entrepreneurs were central to the shift to a new neoliberal political-economic imaginary in the Anglo-American democracies. As discussed in theoretical terms in chapter one, and as illustrated in succeeding chapters by the examples of Britain, Canada, Australia, and New Zealand, norm entrepreneurs are able to play a strategically catalytic role in the process of large-scale ideational change. While much social change surely occurs gradually and seemingly organically, without the conspicuous advocacy of a few readily identifiable norm entrepreneurs, it nonetheless remains true that marked ideational shifts can be associated with, and in important ways the results of, such advocacy. Armed with a clear sense of how they would like to shift central elements of their societies' social imaginaries, and taking advantage of propitious contextual factors that serve to advance their goals, norm entrepreneurs are, under the right set of circumstances, able to effect significant change. The ways in which such change proved possible in the context of Anglo-American neoliberalism were the primary focus of this book. In this concluding chapter, I seek to restate a number of key points about successful norm entrepreneurialism as evidenced by the neoliberal reformers in these four countries. These concluding comments, it bears noting, are by no means comprehensive in the sense of exhausting all that could be said about the phenomenon of neoliberal change in the Anglo-American cases, to say nothing of other cases of ideational change. Nor are they intended as general statements or hypotheses about how and why ideational change takes place generally or universally – something that the highly diverse, contingent cases in this book would clearly not support. Rather, what follows are simply a number of important points highlighted in this study – ones that were important in the Anglo-American cases and that may prove useful in the interrogation of norm entrepreneurialism elsewhere.

1. Norm entrepreneurs can play important roles in strategically initiating, promoting, and guiding ideational change

The neoliberal reformers discussed in this book provide ample evidence of the ways in which determined, ideologically committed, strategically conscious advocacy can advance the cause of thoroughgoing ideational change.[1] In this respect, the example of Margaret Thatcher is often cited as the archetypal model of a (self-described) "conviction politician" committed to effecting a philosophical approach and policy program that quickly came to bear her name. As discussed in chapter four, however, each of the other three countries was also pushed toward neoliberalism by committed norm entrepreneurs: chiefly, Brian Mulroney in Canada, Bob Hawke and Paul Keating in Australia, and Roger Douglas in New Zealand. This analysis of their examples of norm entrepreneurialism reveals several important features.

First, each of these political elites was committed to ideational change and determined to see it effected across a range of government policies. While this might seem a trite and seemingly obvious conclusion, it nonetheless remains true that what distinguished these cases of change from less successful attempts – for instance, Thatcher's success at deregulating the British labour market compared to the failures of the Wilson and Heath governments to effect much more modest change – was in part the determination and, in some instances, heedlessness to resistance evinced by these governments. That is not to say, of course, that commitment and determination are sufficient conditions for change – even these largely successful leaders had their share of failures. But these traits may well prove critical for successful norm entrepreneurialism.

Closely related to the commitment of these reformers was the clarity with which they envisioned their goals of policy and ideational change. These goals were clearly and carefully delineated in such a way as to strategically focus their efforts and political capital. Indeed, it was this often single-minded focus that gave rise to the charge that these governments were acting in ways that were fundamentally dogmatic or doctrinaire. The Douglas blitzkrieg of reform in New Zealand is perhaps neoliberalism's most obvious case of a single clear economic doctrine driving the process of ideational and policy change. As discussed in chapter three, Douglas's goal was so clearly defined and his determination so great that what one respondent called the "coldturkeying" of New Zealand[2] with doctrinaire neoliberalism was seemingly inevitable. Much the same could be said for Thatcherism in Britain. While the Canadian Tories and Australian Labor pursued a much more gradual and moderate path, the goals of free trade (for Mulroney) and financial and trade deregulation (for Hawke and Keating) were clearly defined and directly pursued.

Third, and perhaps most importantly, these leaders were *strategic* norm entrepreneurs – that is, they consciously developed political, social, and economic strategies to accomplish their ideational goals. As discussed repeatedly throughout this study, neoliberalism in the Anglo-American countries did not just "happen." Rather, it was the result of deliberate strategies by committed norm entrepreneurs operating in propitious political, economic, and social contexts. In the process of change, then, these deliberate strategies played a key role. In Britain, for instance, *The Right Approach to the Economy*, released in 1977 while the Conservatives were still in opposition, laid the philosophical groundwork for the future Thatcher program. Moreover, the Conservatives' emasculation of the trade unions and deregulation of the labour market was the product of a well-planned, incremental strategy of ever more stringent legal strictures combined with an equally well-planned defeat of the miners in their 1984–5 strike. Similarly, in New Zealand, Roger Douglas's blitzkrieg had been presaged by his own book on economic reform and, bolstered by the encouragement of a strongly neoliberal Treasury, was planned in some detail by Douglas, Richard Prebble, and David Caygill in the days just prior to Labour's accession to power.

Much the same could be said for Mulroney's conscious courting of the Western provinces and their predilections for free trade and the deregulation of the energy sector, as well as the entire, well-planned Accord process in Australia. In each case, a deliberate, conscious strategy underlay each attempt at neoliberal change. While not guaranteeing success in any individual effort at policy change, such conscious strategizing about how best to achieve neoliberal change by these elites reveals an important facet of the ways in which norm entrepreneurs can pursue ideational change. Attempts to shift key elements of political-economic imaginaries, no less than other sizeable social changes, are, at their heart, fundamentally controversial and contestable – and thus inherently political and strategic.

2. Norm entrepreneurialism is likely to be most successful when pursued in a conducive political, social, economic, and institutional environment

Put somewhat differently, norm entrepreneurs do not operate within a vacuum, pursuing their goals in the absence of influence from the political, social, and institutional milieux within which they work. Rather, as this analysis of Anglo-American neoliberalism has shown, the environmental context in which norm entrepreneurialism occurs can be critically important. Addressing the classic constructivist "How possible?" question thus means examining the underlying contextual conditions faced by norm entrepreneurs. While these factors may not prove to be sufficient (or perhaps even necessary) conditions for significant ideational change, they certainly can and do play an important role in advancing or retarding, shaping, or transforming that change.

In chapters three and four, a number of such factors – and the role they played in shaping Anglo-American neoliberalism – were discussed. Perhaps the most important political and social contextual factor facilitating the advocates of neoliberalism was the sense of crisis, national economic decline, and prior policy failure that marked these countries in different ways in the late 1970s and early 1980s. The sense that "something has to be done" was a common thread running through political and social discourse in these countries – most obviously in Britain after the Winter of Discontent and in New Zealand as the country appeared threatened with insolvency in the wake of recession and the Think Big schemes. In Canada, rising protectionism from the United States was perceived as an emerging threat, and in Australia, drought and falling terms of trade evoked a similar sense of urgency. In all four cases, norm entrepreneurs were able to capitalize on the belief that government must "do something," exploiting this powerful, yet often vague and ill-formed public desire for change to push through their plans for both policy and ideational change.

However, the norm entrepreneurs discussed in this study did not merely utilize, or seek to exploit, a preexisting or exogenous sense of crisis in order to argue for change. Instead, as discussed in chapter four, they also actively sought to use the "exogenous shock" to create the "endogenous construction" of crisis and to portray their policies as the only available solution to it.[3] Paul Keating's "banana republic" speech is perhaps the best example of such active, strategic construction and utilization of the crisis frame. In this way, neoliberalism served as a set of "crisis-defining ideas," to use Mark Blyth's term – it offered a ready diagnosis of "what went wrong" and a self-confident answer to "what to do about it."[4] The relationship, then, between ideational change and economic crisis was dynamic and interactive: the neoliberal norm entrepreneurs did not unilaterally or single-handedly create a sense of crisis. They did, however, help construct and magnify that frame in order to serve their own political ends. Thus, the Anglo-American cases confirm the now near commonplace argument that a sense of failure and crisis can open windows of opportunity for agents of political change. Had such a sense not existed in these countries, the argument for the radically different policies that neoliberalism represented would have been, at a minimum, significantly more difficult to sustain.

However, political elites in these countries benefitted from more than simply a public sense of crisis and the need for change. They also found themselves operating in political-institutional contexts particularly conducive to their plans for radical change. Most obviously, all four governments wielded political power in majoritarian parliamentary systems that offered very little institutional resistance – much less formal "veto players" – to their plans for change. All four governments had workable, and in some cases, substantial parliamentary majorities in systems that, with strong party discipline, afford prime ministers nearly untrammeled potential influence and power. Moreover, three of the four governments faced virtually no potential opposition from upper houses of parliament. The British and Canadian upper houses – the House of the Lords and the Senate, respectively – have only limited powers of legislative delay and are severely restricted by their lack of democratic legitimacy as unelected and, in some ways, vestigial institutions. Furthermore, in New Zealand, the model of a majoritarian system was almost complete, with its first-past-the-post electoral system (before the 1996 election) coupled to a unicameral parliament. Only the Australian Senate stands out as a powerful upper house among the four cases. Elected on the basis of proportional representation – and thus without a Labour majority – the Senate had to be consciously attended to by the Hawke and Keating Labour governments. In the event, however, these governments were usually able to secure the support of the Australian Democrats or other parties in the Senate to ensure passage of their legislation, particularly as much of its neoliberal agenda came to be taken up with even greater fervor subsequently by the conservative Liberal and National parties. Finally, to the institutional conduciveness of parliamentary institutions could be added the encouragement of a variety of other key political and social actors, especially economic bureaucracies and trade unions (particularly the ACTU). Taken together, they provided a nexus of institutional factors that supported and made possible the radical policy shifts inherent in neoliberalism.

3. The "residue" of traditional ideas, practices, institutions, and policies can play an important role in advancing, retarding, transforming, and shaping attempts at ideational change

Attempts at ideational change – and particularly those as far-reaching as changes in a society's basic political-economic imaginary – will likely encounter the resistance and transformative potential of prior ideas, values, practices, and institutions. This point is related to the previous one in that it speaks to the influence of environmental factors that may condition norm entrepreneurs' chances of success. Here, however, the focus is less on such extant, contemporaneous factors as economic crisis or the role of civil servants, and more on the ideational and policy traditions that serve as the targets of norm entrepreneurs' efforts at change, but also have profound effects in and of themselves on these efforts. In fact, it is this simultaneous transformation of both the new ideational structures and of traditional practices and values that speaks to constructivism's notion of co-constitution. Put in the context of neoliberalism, co-constitution means that just as new economic ideas in the Anglo-American countries transformed the nature of economic policy and structure there, so these traditional values, structures, and practices also affected the nature of neoliberalism. Thus, new ideational constructs are not likely to be either successful or unsuccessful, accepted or rejected in toto. Instead, they are transformed even as they seek to transform. They are adapted and changed even as they seek to effect new political-economic imaginaries. Moreover, as exemplified by the politically strategic behaviour of the Anglo-American neoliberals, successful norm entrepreneurs intuitively sense these facts and are able to mould and adjust their tactics to best suit the actual political, social, and economic environments they face.

While the Anglo-American cases offer many such examples, this book focuses primarily on the residual power of a key structuring element in modern democratic polities: that of traditional partisanship. What we saw was that while neoliberalism successfully transformed many aspects of Anglo-American society and politics – everything from the pattern of state ownership and union rights all the way to public conceptions of the proper role of the state – much from the past remained in recognizable form. Such was the case with partisanship and traditional party differences. As discussed in detail in chapter five, partisanship proved to be both transformative and transformed by the experience of neoliberalism. On the one hand, the neoliberal period saw a decided shift of the partisan spectrum in these countries in a right-ward direction. Policies once thought as the exclusive preserve of free market liberals on the right became integral parts of the policy agenda of putatively centre-left parties. In the process, the traditional left–right divide narrowed and moved right.

On the other hand, while the traditional partisan divide changed, it also had a powerful transformative effect in its own right on neoliberalism, particularly as it came to be pursued and implemented by both conservative and Labor parties in the Anglo-American countries. In particular, labour market policy as pursued by the Australian and New Zealand Labor parties differed markedly from that pursued by British, Australian, and New Zealand conservatives. Much of neoliberalism was indistinguishable as pursued by either the centre-left or centre-right – with New Zealand Labour challenging the British Conservatives for the distinction of having been the most radically neoliberal government of the 1980s. However, on the single most salient point of difference between these parties historically – that concerning Labor's historic connection to trade unions – a clear distinction emerged.

The British Conservatives launched a coercive frontal attack on the traditional power and prerogatives of trade unions, succeeding in liberalizing the UK labour market where earlier, much more limited efforts had failed. Meanwhile, Australian and New Zealand Labor took a consciously gradual, moderate approach to labour market reform – in the case of the ALP, even going so far as to negotiate its liberalization of industrial relations with the country's peak trade union organization. The contrast with the British Tories was stark – as it was with the conservatives who succeeded Antipodean Labor. The Liberal/National Coalition in Australia and the National Party in New Zealand took Labor's moderate liberalizations and expanded them into some of the most comprehensive examples of labour market deregulation in the OECD. Where Labor had refused to tread, the conservatives stridently marched ahead. In this way, traditional partisan differences – a foundational building block of modern democratic politics – exerted their influence in remarkably traditional ways. An important "residue" remained.

4. Norm entrepreneurs strategically employ a wide range of tactics to achieve their goals, combining both rhetorical and material forms of persuasion and coercion

A key argument made in chapter one was that the challenge of shifting a society's key political-economic imaginary is often one requiring a war on many fronts. Thus, I contend that norm entrepreneurs are likely to employ a wide range of tactics in the pursuit of their goals of ideational change. To this end, I identified persuasion and coercion as two potential tactics, conceptually distinguishing between rhetorical and material forms of each (see Figure 2). Combining these alternatives, we have therefore the following conceptual possibilities: rhetorical persuasion ("appropriate"), rhetorical coercion ("no alternative"), material persuasion ("advantage"), and material coercion ("compulsion"). While these by no means exhaust the full range of possible tactics available to norm entrepreneurs, nor do these conceptual categories represent any sort of "law" or generalizable theory of norm entrepreneurialism, they do provide us with a number of heuristic categories that may help us identify and more fully understand the range of strategies available and potentially deployed by advocates of ideational change.

What we saw in the Anglo-American countries was that norm entrepreneurs used all four of these tactics in attempting to achieve political-economic imaginary change. Persuasion and coercion were used in both rhetorical and material forms as these norm entrepreneurs strategically adapted to the political vicissitudes of the day. A brief review summarizing the ways in which each of these approaches was employed will illustrate the point.

As discussed in chapter one, *rhetorical persuasion* has traditionally been the primary focus of those seeking to explain norm entrepreneurialism. In such cases, norm entrepreneurs seek to persuade others of the appropriateness of their points of view and of the necessity for normative change. This form of argumentation – closely linked to Habermas's analyses of rhetoric, persuasion, and "communicative action" – thus rests on the persuasiveness of one's argument and on the effectiveness of its advocates in convincing others to change. As a fundamental tool in the norm entrepreneur's toolkit, rhetorical persuasion is perhaps the most ubiquitous strategy in the effort to change social imaginaries.

This was no less true in the Anglo-American democracies. There, the fundamental neoliberal argument revolved around the assertion that a globalizing world was fundamentally different from that which had preceded it, that the old certainties and nostrums of the proper balance between state and society were anachronistic, and that only a radical reconfiguration of economic philosophy and ideology could save the country from inevitable decline. The case for neoliberalism thus diagnosed both the problem – the traditional post-war body of "consensus" policies – and provided the solution – a shift to freer, deregulated markets. These arguments were, of course, given added credibility by the conditions of economic downturn and crisis that these countries experienced in the late 1970s and early 1980s. In such conditions of anxiety and uncertainty, the door was opened for those with new and different plans to better and more convincingly make their cases. Thus, the Winter of Discontent lent implicit credence to the British Conservatives' claims that the "old way" of doing things had proven to be a failure. In the same way, the apparent threats to small countries in an increasingly globalizing world seemed to confirm the calls of the Canadian, Australian, and New Zealand governments for significant change.

This is not to say, of course, that the rhetorical efforts of the neoliberal norm entrepreneurs were always met with success. In fact, as the case of free trade in Canada shows, some aspects of the neoliberal program remained highly contested for years – and, of course, still are. However, the cumulative effect of calls for change, reinforced by the other tactics discussed in the following paragraphs, was to gradually shift the overall thrust of public attitudes to eventually accept many of the major elements – and in particular the underlying deregulationist philosophy – of the neoliberal program.

Coupled to rhetorical persuasion was *material persuasion*, or what I have labelled appeals to *advantage*. While rhetorical persuasion attempts to convince hearers that a new set of norms and ideas is appropriate to the task at hand, material persuasion essentially presents the new normative structure as advantageous and beneficial in quite tangible ways. Norm entrepreneurs are thus able to move beyond simply arguing – in what to many may be an esoteric way – the theoretical benefits of ideational and policy shifts, to instead focusing on "what's in it" for individual citizens. As discussed in chapter one, what the norm entrepreneur argues is objectively "good" in and of itself becomes dramatically more appealing if she can argue that it is also "good for you." While some may be convinced of the rightness of an argument simply on theoretical grounds, many more may be brought to accept it if it promises tangible rewards as well.

In this regard, one must never forget that the chief Anglo-American norm entrepreneurs were elected politicians who faced the constant pressures of public opinion and opposition criticism, as well as the ongoing challenge of winning future elections. Thus, it should come as no surprise that they were keen to emphasize the advantages neoliberalism allegedly promised for the nation, society, and individual. Neoliberalism was presented as perhaps, at times, a painful medicine, but one that would ultimately result in a more competitive, efficient, and prosperous economy and society – with all its attendant long-term benefits.

In this regard, perhaps the best example is the argument advanced by Hawke and Keating that economic rationalism in Australia was necessary, not only to create a more prosperous society, but also to achieve the traditional social goals advocated by Labor parties. Thus, what was (and is) generally portrayed by the left as a set of policies fundamentally at odds with the interests of working people was reworked by Australian Labor in order to appear advantageous – that is, as part of an overall plan to boost living standards, enhance social justice, and, in so doing, maintain the primary social goals of traditional Laborism. While often criticized for deviating from its historic tradition,[5] Labor leaders nonetheless maintained that they had kept the traditional faith, simply refitting the party's policies to suit the new and challenging world of globalization. An Australian Labor prime minister made this very argument in a personal interview:

> From my point of view, the fundamental Labor philosophy is the improvement of the standard of living of the community, the creation of equality of opportunity for everyone in the community. Economic growth is fundamental to doing those things. ... I say that everything we did was absolutely in the [Labor] tradition – what I see and have always seen as the Labor philosophy. We were making policy developments in light of what the changing economic realities were. Somebody [could take] the view that we should say, "Oh, we're not part of the world. We can pop off the world and have our own little artificial oasis." It's unadulterated bullshit. You can't do that.[6]

This view was echoed in nearly identical terms by a former minister in the Fourth Labour Government in New Zealand:

> What any minister in any government is aware of is [that] in order to get a larger share for your investment in health, education, welfare, etc., if you're trying to get a bigger share of a diminishing cake, you're on the road to disaster. What you have to have is a larger cake and out of that

larger cake, you can do the social things that you want to do. And while it's always more fashionable at Labour Party conferences to talk about how we spend money than how we generate it, the realities of life are that you have to generate it first in order to spend it, and there's not a person in any family in this country that's working for a living that doesn't understand that in terms of their own life. The same thing applies to the economy. It's not a complex problem.[7]

Thus, to the neoliberal norm entrepreneurs, neoliberalism was necessary for prosperity, for economic growth, for international competitiveness, and – especially for the Labor parties – in order to achieve traditional social democratic goals. In other words, neoliberalism was argued to be not only objectively good economic policy, but it was claimed to hold the promise of real material advantages for citizens.

The third potential strategy available to norm entrepreneurs is *material coercion,* or what might be labelled "compulsion." While scholars are generally quite skeptical of the role played by compulsion in ideational change, I argue that, particularly when coupled with rhetorical coercion (discussed next), it can be a useful strategy for norm entrepreneurs. Prior to a full acceptance of their ideas by citizens, norm entrepreneurs in positions of political power may be able to compel compliance with policies informed by these new ideas. What they aspire to, however, is not simply grudging compliance. They also hope that experience will work to produce the gradual acceptance of these new policies – and the ideas underlying them – as "normal," unquestioned, and "taken-for-granted." If and when such "taken-for-grantedness" emerges, ideational change can truly be said to have occurred.

One particular example of compulsion stands out clearly in three of the four Anglo-American cases: labour market deregulation and especially the prohibition of the closed shop. As discussed in chapter five, the closed shop was banned by the British Conservatives in 1990, by New Zealand National in 1991, and by the Coalition parties in Australia in 1996. Clearly, this was an act of legislative compulsion: rather than relying solely on appeals to norms of appropriateness ("the closed shop is wrong") or to potential advantage ("you'll do better without the closed shop"), these conservative governments passed legislation to outlaw such arrangements. In this way, unions and union members were compelled to behave in ways consistent with the neoliberal commitment to deregulated labour markets, their own personal views notwithstanding. In such a case, argumentation and appeals to advantage were ultimately transcended by legal coercion.

As it turns out, the banning of the closed shop also illustrates the observation made previously – that what begins as legal compulsion can, over time, come to be seen as appropriate, "taken-for-granted," and even advantageous. In all three of these cases where conservative parties acted to ban the closed shop – traditionally a jealously-guarded trade union prerogative and a hallmark of industrial relations during the "consensus" period – the Labor parties that followed them in power consciously declined to reverse this key neoliberal policy. The Blair Labour government in Britain, the Clark Labour government in New Zealand, and the Rudd Labor government in Australia did move, in various ways, to reverse certain aspects of the industrial relations laws of their predecessors. However, each did so in ways that proved quite moderate, and in each case, the ban on the closed shop was explicitly retained.

Consequently, one could argue that the prohibition of closed shops has largely taken on the status of "taken-for-granted."[8] While opposed by Labor when first introduced by conservatives, the ban has now become accepted Labor policy in Britain, Australia, and New Zealand. What had been taken for granted during the consensus period – that workers could be required to join a trade union as a condition of employment – has been replaced by the equally taken-for-granted notion that a worker's right to join, or not join, a union is paramount. This speaks to the ultimate success of compulsion as a tactic of norm entrepreneurs, at least in this particular instance. What began as legal compulsion has become part of a new ideational structure, with both sides of the political divide accepting as a given what was once strenuously contested.

Perhaps the most important tactic of norm entrepreneurialism in the Anglo-American democracies, however, was *rhetorical coercion*. In chapter one, such coercion was described as rhetoric that, rather than attempting to convince the hearer of the rightness of one's position (that is, rhetorical persuasion), is manipulated in such a way as to appear uncontestable, unanswerable, and therefore, by default, true. When rhetorically coerced, a hearer often finds herself unable to adequately contest or rebut the assertions made. Rhetorical coercion thus can successfully deprive would-be opponents of adequate means of argument, closing off debate and contestation, and forcing hearers – however reluctantly – to accept the argument itself.

In the case of Anglo-American neoliberalism, rhetorical coercion proved to be the ultimate weapon of norm entrepreneurialism. Specifically, in all four countries, the TINA argument was repeatedly deployed to assert that neoliberal policies were not derived from some esoteric philosophy, but rather represented a recognition that, as a law of economic science, deregulation and freer markets were unquestionably in the best of interests of society and the nation. Alternatives, to the extent they existed, had been tried and found wanting. Free markets were the only conclusion that rational, responsible policy-makers could draw.

TINA thus proved particularly useful – as rhetorical coercion is intended to do – in silencing opposition and arresting debate. Interview respondents in both Australia and New Zealand pointed out that Labor politicians there, particularly those outside the central economic ministries, were concerned about the spread of economic rationalism – and the deviation from traditional Labor policies that this shift seemed to represent. Yet, many reported that, despite these misgivings, they believed that there was, indeed, no alternative to these policies. Thus, in an atmosphere in which top decision-makers preached the inescapability of a competitive world environment that would brook no deviation from economic orthodoxy, even more circumspect Labor politicians and supporters acceded to what seemed the inevitable and necessary "facts of life." For instance, when asked whether he recalled any concerns about a possible "sellout" of Labor traditions to the new economic orthodoxy, a leading minister in the Hawke government responded as follows:

> There was a lot of concern about those issues. I think the truth is that in terms of some of the major economic decisions, there was nobody in the government with sufficient knowledge and conviction to state an alternative to what was done. That is to say, you could state alternatives, but they always seemed to be old hat alternatives. Saying, "Let's leave things as they are, let's leave things as we used to like to have them." And, in some ways, in a dynamic situation, that's not a very attractive or sustainable alternative.[9]

The coerciveness inherent in the TINA argument was evidenced by the underlying message that opposition to neoliberalism was a sign of economic stupidity. Opponents were cast as economic illiterates, antediluvians, and supporters of obviously failed command economies.

Their concerns about neoliberalism were born out of failed ideologies, and their unwillingness to accede to the demands of a globalizing world economy was, at best, naïve and, at worst, irresponsible. As a former Labor Treasurer in Australia recalled,

> Keating, being the bully that he is, ... if he wanted to get his way [in cabinet], he'd just really bully us with, "Unless you go along with this, the financial markets will monster us." So it was always the financial markets – we had to worry about the financial markets from then on. ... It assumed the air of inevitability. "You've got to be worried about the money markets, you know." ... [The Labor left] just got run over by the [Labor] right. Eventually they became – what's the word – the word is marginalized, I guess. ... If you attack economic rationalism, they say, "Well, you're in favor of economic irrationalism," which is a pretty lousy argument. And the latest one in that context is, "Well, do you want an economy like North Korea?" – that's the throwaway [line].[10]

Thus, in a remarkably effective way, this basic argument – that "there is no alternative" to neoliberalism – was used to deliver the coup de grâce to those arguing against it and in favour of maintaining elements of the old consensus status quo.

5. Norm entrepreneurialism can be said to succeed when the new political-economic imaginary comes to be accepted as relatively uncontested, obvious, and appropriate

That is, a key marker of the successful instantiation of a new political-economic imaginary is when the norms, values, and orientations comprising it take on the quality of "taken-for-grantedness." As discussed in chapter one, one of the hallmarks of social imaginaries is that they operate largely unseen and unfelt, shaping attitudes and behaviours in ways of which individuals are largely unaware. Because they are (usually unconsciously) accepted as organic parts of the ideational landscape, such imaginaries often work to constrain the range of ideas, attitudes, and values that seem "normal," "natural," or appropriate. Alternative values, norms, or behaviours that fall outside the boundaries set by the imaginary often do not "make sense" or seem grossly inappropriate – and are thus quickly rejected.

Because social imaginaries operate in this largely uncontested, even unconscious realm, the true test of whether norm entrepreneurs have been successful in their promotion of new political-economic imaginaries is whether the ideas contained in them have displaced the old values and themselves come to be seen as natural, appropriate, and taken-for-granted. To use Gramscian terminology, a new political-economic imaginary becomes truly hegemonic when it ceases to be seen as new, radical, and contested and instead becomes a largely unquestioned part of a society's "common sense" – or, in Colin Hay's vivid description, when the "spectacular" becomes the "vernacular."[11] When this occurs, those few recalcitrants who continue to oppose the new imaginary and its central ideas are increasingly marginalized in social discourse and come to be seen as retrogrades or extremists. The fact that some individuals may, for instance, support socialist central economic planning does not undermine the fundamental ideational hegemony of the new imaginaries that ultimately displaced this now largely anachronistic idea. In fact, the social and political marginalization of such individuals serves as evidence of the extent to which new normative structures have taken root.

The goal of the Anglo-American norm entrepreneurs was clearly to instantiate a new neoliberal political-economic imaginary as normative – or, in Bob Jessop's words, "as natural, spontaneous, inevitable, [and] technological."[12] In fact, a key strategy they employed was to argue that neoliberal ideas were beyond the realm of reasonable debate and thus should be understood as organic, natural "facts." In the approach adopted by many of these norm entrepreneurs, neoliberalism was not – as its detractors claimed – a particular political or economic ideology. Whereas ideologies are contestable, unverifiable, and thus ultimately "biased," free market ideas were presented as emanating from the laws of economics. As Jacqueline Best puts it, neoliberalism "denies its own normative and discursive practices, pretending instead that it is timeless, ahistorical and inevitable."[13] Thus, in the discourse of neoliberalism, its acceptance as the basis for a new political-economic imaginary was only natural – it was, in fact, the recognition of what had been objectively true all along.

When asked about neoliberalism as an ideology, a number of interview respondents specifically denied that it was ideological, instead arguing that it was simply a recognition of (now) obvious empirical facts. As argued by a finance minister in the decidedly un-neoliberal Trudeau government in Canada, " 'We are all neoliberals' – I suppose that is correct to say, but … I don't think there has been an ideological seachange. It has been a gradual realization that things had to be done ... There was a recognition by the public that something had to be done about the deficit and the debt – politicians, journalists, everybody was talking about it. ... I wouldn't call it ideological."[14] Such a view was echoed by a minister in Mulroney's Conservative government: "I think it's a combination of the global march to understanding the central predominance of the market in determining the course of actions of governments ... Look at the economic program of [Conservative leader Jean] Charest or [Reform Party leader Preston] Manning. Are they strikingly different from the Liberals? I don't think so. So that tells us something. It's certainly not the party that is ideological. The ideology is the market."[15]

This last sentence is revealing in that ideology is said to have given way to fact. No longer an ideology in the ideational sense, neoliberalism is said to be a recognition of what simply already exists. Thus, a critically important part of the neoliberal argument was its "facticity," as Pusey describes it[16] – the notion that markets are ontological realities to which governments must accede. In Best's formulation, "Neoliberalism tells us that the market is not only the best mode of organising economic life; it is the only mode."[17] This uncritically universalist[18] view was one that in particular permeated the advice coming from neoliberals in the key financial ministries. To them, the adoption of neoliberal economics was simply a matter of convincing government ministers that their old policy preconceptions were quaint relics of a simpler past, ones that must be supplanted by the reality of the "real world" around them. In the words of one top Treasury official in Australia,

> It's what I've always termed – I used to say this to my staff in the Treasury – what I call reality breaking in. From time to time, when governments used to do things – and I'm talking about both sides of politics here – the Treasury would go back to its offices and sit around the table and have a post mortem on the subject and shake its collective head and say, "You know, this is ridiculous." And then I would say, "Well, yes, but don't despair. Reality will keep on breaking in." Sometimes it took years for it to do so, but it always did so to some degree. ... What these politicians have gradually found, often in the face of their own quite strongly-held ideological convictions, is that their own ideologies don't work. ... The truth is that the reason why you had people who have begun to adopt these [economic rationalist] policies is that they found the previous ones didn't work.[19]

This supposed facticity was echoed by Roger Douglas. Early in the Fourth Labour Government's tenure, announcing the decision to float the New Zealand dollar, he declared in Parliament, "For the past 9 years the former Government lived a big lie. It closed the door on reality – the problem for all of us was that reality continued to come in through the window."[20] Or, as a former Australian Liberal minister quipped, Labor's adoption of neoliberalism was the result of "getting mugged by reality."[21] When asked to explain how the ALP could pursue policies so seemingly at odds with its own traditional policies, he said, "Well, there were just powerful movements that occur and they can be global in nature and, you know, you just get infections of common sense. Raging infections after a while – it's pretty hard to escape the virus."[22] A former Australian Labor prime minister largely concurred:

> The failure of the [command economies] is not an esoteric truth known only to [me]. It's obvious. The world knows it, the social democratic parties know it, and the conservative parties know it. So, basically, within democracies, they're going to be operating within a market system and trying to make your markets more efficient. Your arguments are just as likely to be within parties, in some ways, as between parties as to the extent to which you will recognize *the truth about the market*.[23]

What we see, then, in the Anglo-American cases is the acceptance across the traditional political divide that neoliberalism represented economic facts – ones that were largely beyond partisan contestation and that governments ignored at their peril. Whether or not individuals wish to label these ideas neoliberal or economically rationalist (something Labor is often reluctant to do), and despite the fact that differences still exist about the extent to which market logic should predominate, it is nonetheless the case that the central neoliberal ideas of competition, deregulation, privatization, entrepreneurialism, and "free markets" have become deeply entrenched in these societies' public policies and ideational constructs, spanning the traditional divide between centre-left and centre-right parties. As Colin Hay terms it, neoliberal economics is no longer simply "normative," in the sense of being a politically contestable ideology; it is now "normalized" and "necessaritarian" – that is, seen as a settled and non-negotiable mandate of economic science.[24] With that shift, one can say that a new political-economic imaginary has taken hold.

The extent to which this new political-economic imaginary is taken for granted and now underlies the policy positions of both left and right in these countries is evidenced, as discussed elsewhere in this book, by the lack of partisan debate and difference on the key tenets of neoliberal economics. Policies that, at the time of their introduction by the early neoliberals, were the cause of heated political debate are now generally accepted without question. In Britain, for example, there is no mainstream argument to renationalize large parts of the country's industrial sector. Nor in Canada is there any chance that NAFTA will be repealed – what had been *the* issue of the 1988 general election is now taken for granted by both major parties. In Australia, both conservatives and Labor accept the principle of a largely deregulated labour market. And, in New Zealand, no effort has ever been made to return the country to the highly regulated society and economy it was prior to 1984 – or even to move in any meaningful way in that direction.

Moreover, as a potent symbol of their longer-term entrenchment in these countries' political-economic imaginaries, neoliberal policies have also remained intact despite a number of alternations of government between left and right. In Britain, the Labour governments of Tony Blair and Gordon Brown (1997–2010) that succeeded the Conservatives left the Thatcherite legacy virtually untouched, and even extended its logic in some respects (granting operational independence to the Bank of England, for instance). In Canada, the Liberal Party under Jean Chrétien and Paul Martin (1993–2006) reconciled itself to NAFTA, reformed the country's system of unemployment insurance, introduced fiscal austerity measures, and reversed no major policy of the Mulroney Conservatives. The examples of Australia and New Zealand are even more informative. In each case, the Labor parties that initiated neoliberal change in the 1980s were succeeded by conservative parties that, in the 1990s, enacted radically deregulationalist policies (particularly, as discussed in chapter five, concerning the labour market) far beyond where Labor had been willing to go. Yet, when Labor returned to power – first in New Zealand under Helen Clark in 1999, then later in Australia under Kevin Rudd in 2007 – it made only marginal changes to the conservatives' labour laws, accepting the fundamentally deregulationist logic underlying them and leaving intact the accumulated body of neoliberal policy reform that had been enacted in the rest of the economy since the mid-1980s.

Thus, what we have seen is that the language of the "free" market, the priority placed on economic growth and efficiency, and the acceptance of market logic as factual and uncontested have become firmly entrenched in the political-economic imaginaries of the Anglo-American democracies. Whatever differences remain between the parties of these countries, whatever policy and partisan competition take place, they do so on a playing field that has been significantly narrowed by the instantiation of this new ideational construct. As a former Australian prime minister, a leader of the Labor Party, and one of neo-liberalism's chief norm entrepreneurs expressed the essence of the new political-economic imaginary: "Markets are a fact of life. You've not going to uncreate or disinvent the market. ... In other words, the market has won."[25]

Appendix 1: Unemployment, 1968–94 (percent unemployed)

	68	69	70	71	72	73	74	75	76	77	78	79	80	81	82	83	84	85	86	87	88	89	90	91	92	93	94
Britain	2.1	2.0	2.2	2.8	3.1	2.2	2.1	3.2	4.8	5.2	5.1	4.7	5.6	9.0	10.4	11.2	11.2	11.5	11.6	10.4	8.3	6.1	5.5	7.9	9.7	10.3	9.6
Canada	4.4	4.4	5.6	6.1	6.2	5.5	5.3	6.9	7.1	8.0	8.3	7.4	7.4	7.5	10.9	11.8	11.2	10.5	9.5	8.8	7.7	7.5	8.1	10.3	11.3	11.2	10.3
Australia	1.8	1.8	1.6	1.9	2.6	2.3	2.6	4.8	4.7	5.6	6.4	6.1	6.0	5.7	7.0	9.8	8.9	7.8	7.9	7.8	6.8	5.9	7.2	9.7	10.8	11.0	9.7
New Zealand	0.8	0.3	0.2	0.2	0.4	0.2	0.1	0.2	0.4	0.3	1.7	1.9	2.2	3.7	3.5	5.6	5.7	4.1	4.0	4.0	5.5	7.1	7.7	10.2	10.3	9.4	8.1
OECD Average	3.1	3.8	3.3	3.5	3.9	3.5	3.9	5.4	5.5	5.5	5.4	5.4	6.1	7.0	8.3	8.8	8.4	7.8	7.8	7.4	6.9	6.4	6.2	6.6	7.3	7.6	7.6

Source: OECD Historical Statistics, various years.

Appendix 2: Inflation, 1970–1994, Change on previous year (percent)

	70	71	72	73	74	75	76	77	78	79	80	81	82	83	84	85	86	87	88	89	90	91	92	93	94
Britain	6.4	9.4	7.1	9.2	16.0	24.2	16.5	15.8	8.3	13.4	18.0	11.9	8.6	4.6	5.0	6.1	3.4	4.1	4.9	7.8	9.5	5.9	3.7	1.6	2.5
Canada	3.4	2.8	4.8	7.6	10.9	10.8	7.5	8.0	8.9	9.2	10.2	12.5	10.8	5.8	4.3	7.0	4.2	4.4	4.0	5.0	4.8	5.6	1.5	1.8	0.2
Australia	3.9	6.1	5.8	9.5	15.1	15.1	13.5	12.3	7.9	4.1	10.2	9.7	11.2	10.1	3.9	6.7	9.1	8.5	7.3	7.5	7.3	3.2	1.0	1.8	1.9
New Zealand	6.5	10.4	6.9	8.2	11.1	14.7	16.9	14.3	12.0	13.8	17.1	15.4	16.1	7.4	6.1	15.4	13.2	15.7	6.4	5.7	6.1	2.6	1.0	1.3	1.8
OECD Average	5.6	5.3	4.7	7.8	13.4	11.3	8.6	8.9	7.9	9.8	12.8	10.5	10.1	9.4	8.2	7.0	6.0	7.9	8.7	6.3	6.8	6.1	4.9	4.3	4.4

Source: OECD Historical Statistics, various years.

Appendix 3: Real Per Capita GDP Growth, 1968–94, Change on previous year (percent)

	68	69	70	71	72	73	74	75	76	77	78	79	80	81	82	83	84	85	86	87	88	89	90	91	92	93	94
Britain	3.7	1.1	1.9	2.1	2.3	7.6	-1.1	-0.7	3.9	1.0	3.7	2.0	-2.3	-1.3	1.6	3.4	2.3	3.2	4.1	4.5	4.7	1.8	0.0	-2.4	-0.9	1.8	3.5
Canada	4.0	3.7	1.2	5.6	4.7	6.3	2.0	-0.4	4.8	1.1	2.8	2.4	-0.2	2.7	-5.5	2.2	5.4	3.8	2.2	2.8	3.6	0.6	-1.8	-3.0	-0.7	0.8	3.0
Australia	4.1	4.3	4.0	3.8	1.9	3.9	0.2	1.2	2.1	-0.1	1.6	3.4	0.5	2.4	-2.3	-0.4	6.1	3.3	0.6	3.2	2.4	2.4	-0.3	-2.7	1.4	2.9	4.3
New Zealand	0.2	6.6	0.1	2.4	2.2	5.7	4.9	-3.0	2.1	-5.3	-0.6	1.1	1.8	3.2	1.0	1.4	3.9	0.3	1.9	-0.2	-1.0	0.4	-1.5	-2.5	0.1	5.1	4.1
OECD Average	4.4	4.3	2.4	2.5	4.2	5.2	-0.2	-1.1	4.0	3.0	3.1	2.5	0.4	1.2	-0.9	1.5	3.5	2.5	2.0	2.4	3.3	2.6	1.5	-0.2	0.9	0.2	2.0

Source: OECD Historical Statistics, various years.

Notes

1. The Construction of Political-Economic Imaginaries

1 Macmillan 1969, 314.
2 Thatcher 1997, 516.
3 Chifley 1953, 102.
4 Personal interview, 14 November 1996, Menlo Park, CA.
5 Hay 2007, 97.
6 The point of reference here is, of course, Polanyi's landmark argument that modern, capitalist societies experienced a "double movement" in economic principles and policy: a drive toward free, supposedly self-regulating markets on the one hand, and on the other, a "countermovement" that opposed this shift and promoted institutions to shield and protect society from the deleterious effects of free markets (Polanyi [1944] 1957).
7 Blyth 2002, 5; see also the definition in Best 2008, 365–6.
8 The United States – and, in particular, the shift toward more liberal economic policies in the Reagan era – is not considered here. Despite a general similarity with the four countries discussed in this book, neoliberalism in the United States did not represent the much more radical shift that it did in Britain, Canada, Australia, and New Zealand. The US economy in the postwar period was generally much more liberal than the other four and, most significantly, evinced nothing comparable to the protectionist, interventionist "consensus" to which neoliberalism elsewhere was largely a response. For that reason, in addition to a desire to keep the analysis as compact as possible, the United States has not been included.
9 On economic constructivism, see Abdelal, Blyth, and Parsons 2010a; Best 2005, 2007, 2010; Woods 1995; McNamara 1998; Spillman 1999; Finnemore 1996b, 2003; Abdelal 2001; Blyth 2001, 2002; Culpepper 2003; Kirshner

2003; Parsons 2003; Best and Paterson 2010; Dickins 2006; Hobson and Seabrooke 2007; Seabrooke 2006, 2007a, 2007b, 2007c. Other standard constructivist works include Wendt 1987, 1992, 1999; Onuf 1989, 1997; Adler 1997; Kratochwil 1989; Katzenstein 1996b; Checkel 1998; Hopf 1998; Ruggie 1998a, 1998b; Guzzini 2000.

10 The phrase is Wendt's (1999).

11 Wendt 1992, 1999, 24; Burch 2002, 62. On ideas generally, see Goldstein 1989; Goldstein and Keohane 1993; Hall 1986, 1989; Lieberman 2002; Campbell 1998, 2002. See also Jacobsen 1995, 2003; Checkel 1999; Hay 2004b.

12 Sunstein 1996b, 907; see also, 910–14 passim. I follow Sunstein in defining norms as "social attitudes of approval or disapproval, specifying what ought to be done and what ought not to be done" (1996b, 914). Finnemore and Sikkink contend that a norm is "a standard of appropriate behavior for actors with a given identity" (1998, 891). See similar definitions in Katzenstein 1996b, 5; Checkel 1999, 83; Payne 2001, 37; Florini 1996, 364–5.

13 Finnemore and Sikkink 1998, 894; see also Jepperson, Wendt, and Katzenstein 1996, 60–2; Finnemore 2003, 67.

14 Biernacki 1995, 35.

15 Ibid.

16 Meyer, Frank, et al. 1997, 148.

17 Meyer, Boli, et al. 1997; Drori, Meyer, and Hwang 2006; Meyer 2000; Strang and Meyer 1993; Bergersen 1980; Thomas et al. 1987. On diffusion in various contexts, see, among others, Meyer et al. 1977; Benavot et al. 1991; Meyer, Frank, et al. 1997; Meyer, Ramirez, and Soysal 1992; Schofer and Meyer 2005; Dobbin 1993, 2005; Dobbin, Simmons, and Garrett 2007; Simmons, Dobbin, and Garrett 2006; Strang 1991; Strang and Macy 2001; Strang and Soule 1998; Forsythe 1991; Ramirez and McEneaney 1997.

18 Meyer, Frank, et al. 1997, 628.

19 Finnemore 1996b, 136–7; 1996c, 341–4. For elaborations of this argument, see Hay 2000, 2004a.

20 Finnemore 1996b, 138–9.

21 Hay 2004a, 246.

22 Hay 2000, 512.

23 Weldes 1999, 10.

24 Castoriadis 1987, 145. A somewhat more specific meaning is given by Muppidi: "[T]he structuring principle underlying a set of meanings and social relations and constituting them into an organized set of under-standings and social identities that are productive of worlds" (1999, 124). For more discussion, see Thompson 1984, ch. 1; Tomlinson 1991, 154–63;

Muppidi 1999. A related discussion – though one that does not reference Castoriadis – is Charles Taylor's analysis of what he considers to be the dominant social imaginaries of modern life (2004).

25 As Castoriadis puts it, "We know of no society in which food, dress, and dwellings obey strictly 'utilitarian' or 'rational' considerations. We know of no culture in which there are not 'inferior' foods, and we would be surprised if any had ever existed. ... It is neither the availability of snails and frogs nor their scarcity that makes them for contemporary, nearby and related cultures, in one instance a gourmet's delight and in the other a sure cause of vomiting. One has only to draw up the catalogue of everything that humans can eat, and actually have eaten (not feeling any the worse for it) in different periods and in different societies, to see that what is edible for humans far exceeds what each culture has taken as its food, and that what has determined this choice has not been simply natural availability and technical possibilities" (1987, 150).

26 Castoriadis 1987, 135–6, 146–7; also partially quoted in Weldes 1999, 10; emphasis added.

27 My analysis shares a number of important features with Bob Jessop's discussion of imaginaries within his Cultural Political Economy (CPE) framework, particularly his interest in the ways in which "imaginaries identify, privilege, and seek to stabilize some economic activities from the totality of economic relations and transform them into objects of observation, calculation, and governance" (2008a, 18). On CPE and the role of imaginaries, see also Jessop 2004, 2005, 2008b, 2011; Jessop and Oosterlynck 2008; Jessop and Sum 2010; Sum and Jessop 2003.

28 Parsons 2003, 7.

29 Castoriadis claims that "These are not questions that are posed explicitly ... The questions are not even raised prior to the answers" (1987, 147).

30 One might object that imaginaries are more about the norms and values that construct our social desires and goals, rather than the technical means of achieving them. However, means and ends are not so easily divorced. The same normative structures that constrain our choice of ends are likely to inform our choice of means, no matter how technical and "un-ideational" the latter may seem. For instance, one's views on the appropriateness of state-sponsored redistribution of wealth are likely to color one's choice of taxation type and instrument.

31 Blyth 2002, 275.

32 Castoriadis 1987, 156.

33 Quoted in Emerson 2010.

34 Best 2006, 325.

35 And, of course, also ideas about whether and to what extent these worlds are (or should be) distinct.

36 As Craig Simon nicely puts it, "We can think of a phenomenon and its practitioners separately, but they are not separable. One cannot exist without the other. A path cannot be called a path without the people who walk it. This is no subtle point; the notion of co-constitution is at the heart of constructivism's critique of both positivism and the post-modern movement" (1998, 158).

37 Craig Parsons comments that "the existing literature ... tends to privilege structure over agency, consensus over conflict, and persuasion over political maneuvering" (2003, 22). See also Checkel 1998, 340–2; 1999; Shannon 2000, 311.

38 On slavery, see Finnemore 1996a, 170–2; on apartheid, see Klotz 1995a, 1995b.

39 Wendt 1999, 165–89; Adler 2002, 101; Khan 2004, 7, 50–2; Solomon 2006, 44.

40 Barnett 1998, 27. For the effects of ideas on economic structures, see Biernacki 1995, 2001, 2002; Dobbin 2001.

41 Finnemore and Sikkink 1998, 896. Sunstein in first popularizing the term describes norm entrepreneurs quite simply as "people interested in changing social norms" (1996b, 909). See also Checkel 1997, 8–11.

42 Among other studies of norm entrepreneurialism, see Klotz 1995a, 1995b; Finnemore 1996a; Bernstein 2000; Ingebritsen 2002; Brysk 2005; Nielson, Tierney, and Weaver 2006. For studies of policy entrepreneurialism, see Mintrom 1997, 2000; Kingdon 1984; Baumgartner and Jones 1993. See also - Frohlich, Oppenheimer, and Young 1971; Young 1991; Schneider and Teske 1992; Moon 1993.

43 In this schema, I expand on and rework a number of ideas found in Peter Hall's very useful work on first-, second-, and third-order change (1993).

44 These are identities, it might be pointed out, that are in large part socially constructed in and of themselves. The very term *consumer*, for instance, identifies not only a particular role or identity, but also a range of expected, and appropriate, action for that agent.

45 In Ann Florini's incisive comment, "The realm of *conceivable* behavior in a given social structure is normatively determined and it is not as wide as the realm of behavior that is physically possible. At the same time, which behaviors are conceivable, that is, which norms are accepted, varies over time" (1996, 366; emphasis in original). On Gramsci, see Halliday 2000, 59–64; Bieler 2001; Bieler and Morton 2001; Cox 1981, 1983.

46 Peet 2002, 57.

47 Taylor 2004, 17.

48 Wyatt 2005, 467.
49 Blyth 2002, 37; emphasis in original.
50 Jessop 2008a, 28.
51 Lord, Ross, and Lepper 1979; Anderson 1995; Devine 1989; Hamilton and Trolier 1986; Greenwald and Banaji 1995.
52 Jessop 2008a, 16; Jessop 2011.
53 Zald 1996, 262; quoted in Barnett 1998, 40. See also Barnett 1999; Goffman 1974; Snow and Benford 1992; Snow et al. 1986; Payne 2001; Keck and Sikkink 1998, 17–19.
54 Snow et al. 1986, 464; quoted in Finnemore and Sikkink 1998, 897.
55 I borrow the term from Payne (2001, 39), who uses it in a slightly different way.
56 Jacobsen 1995, 291–2.
57 Blyth 2001, 2002. See also Hamilton and Rolander 1993.
58 Kowert and Legro 1996, 463.
59 On the multilevel impact of imaginaries, see Jessop 2008b.
60 Sum and Jessop 2003, 1013.
61 Ibid., 8. For discussions of negotiations and contestation, see also Elgström 2000 and van Kersbergen and Verbeek 2007.
62 Muppidi 1999, 140.
63 The affinity to Thomas Kuhn's analysis of "normal science" and paradigm shifts is obvious (1970).
64 Of course, as discussed previously, even "ordinary" contestation of policy settings can unwittingly feedback into the imaginary itself. In this case, "policy entrepreneurs" may become the unwitting agents of normative change as their contestation effects change in the imaginary itself. For instance, the elimination of a particular social welfare benefit may originate as a narrowly conceived policy option. However, over the longer term, this policy choice can cause a shift in the imaginary if this kind of benefit comes to be perceived as a no longer desirable or appropriate government action.
65 The term is Katzenstein's (1996a).
66 Parsons 2003, 238; see also Florini 1996, 375; Weldes et al. 1999, 17–19.
67 Goldstein 1989, 71.
68 See Hopf for a critique of this tendency (2002, ch. 6).
69 See, for instance, Finnemore 2003, 152–4; Nadelmann 1990, 479–86; Price 1998. See also Majone 1989, ch. 2.
70 Finnemore 2003, 153; Habermas 1979, 1984. Risse refers to this as a "logic of truth seeking or arguing" (2000, 6–11).
71 Finnemore and Sikkink 1998, 914.

72 Ibid., 897.
73 See Finnemore and Sikkink 1998, 910; Khan 2004; Payne 2001, 47; Barnett 1999.
74 Finnemore 2003, 143; emphases added.
75 Parsons 2003, 238, 239.
76 Jacobsen 1995, 298–300; Seabrooke 2006, 37.
77 Krebs and Jackson 2007.
78 Ibid., 36; emphasis in original.
79 Ibid., 39, 40.
80 Ibid., 40; emphasis in original.
81 Ibid., 45.
82 Ibid., 45, 47; emphasis in original.
83 Ibid., 52.
84 Ibid., 48–55.
85 On this point, see Kübler 2001, 452–3.
86 For instance, Risse et al. 1999; Larsen 1999; Christiansen, Jørgensen, and Wiener 2001. For a review of competing theoretical approaches on this topic, including constructivism, see Pollack 2005.
87 For instance, Price 1997, 1998.
88 That is, totally self-interested acts without regard to appropriateness or morality certainly occur, as do (although perhaps less often?) acts motivated only by normative demands irrespective of advantage or rational self-interest.
89 Furthermore, there can be an additional, "bandwagon" effect where, in Kübler's words, "once a critical proportion of the population follows the norm, it becomes very costly in terms of reputation not to follow it" (2001, 469).
90 Finnemore and Sikkink discuss internalization as the final stage in the three-step process of normative change (1998, 904–5). However, their analysis concentrates on successful rhetorical, not material, persuasion.
91 Karakatsanis 2001, 2008. On such "political learning," see also Levy 1994; Stein 1994; Mo 1996; Bermeo 1992.
92 See, for instance, Knight 1992; Bates 2001; Pennock and Chapman 2006.
93 Ellickson 1998; Mahoney and Sanchirico 2001, 2003; McAdams 2000; Sugden 1998; Sunstein 1996a.
94 Although, see the argument for the effectiveness and ubiquity of coercion in Giustozzi 2011.
95 Finnemore 2003, 16–18, 146–7.
96 In a similar vein, Kübler argues that "the regulation of motives [which would include coercion and the manipulation of (dis)incentives] and of

meaning reinforce each other in many cases and should be used simultaneously" (2001, 472).

97 A related idea is Risse's "self-entrapment" (2000, 32).
98 Risse 2000, 6; Hall 1988, 44; Weldes 1996, 303–4.
99 Jessop 2011, 5.
100 Weldes 1996, 303; Weldes et al. 1999, 17; Jacobsen 2003, 47.
101 Sum and Jessop 2003, 1008; emphasis added.
102 Berk 1994, 16; quoted in Parsons 2003, 239.
103 Hall 1985, 105; quoted in Weldes et al. 1999, 17.
104 Parsons 2003, 240.
105 Ibid., 239.

2. Prelude to Neoliberalism

1 Kavanagh and Morris 1989; Hay 1994b; Beer 1969, 1982.
2 Cairncross 1992, ch. 1, 2.
3 This discussion is based in part on Kavanagh and Morris (1989), who set
out a similar enumeration of consensus characteristics.
4 A clause that would remain in this form until the reforms of the Labour
Party led by Tony Blair in 1995.
5 Morgan 1984, ch. 3.
6 Kavanagh and Morris 1989, 26.
7 Forman-Peck and Millward 1994; Gamble 1988.
8 Esping-Andersen 1985; Marshall 1950; Castles 1978.
9 Laybourn 1995.
10 Beveridge 1942; Hills, Ditch, and Glennerster 1994.
11 Klein 1983, 146.
12 Personal interview, 24 June 1997, London.
13 Thatcher 1993, 603; Pierson 1994.
14 Hall 1986, 71; see also Weir 1989, 79–84.
15 Mowat 1955, 465.
16 Ibid.; Stevenson and Cook 1994.
17 Keynes 1935; Schott 1982.
18 Kavanagh and Morris 1989, 36.
19 Personal interview, 10 April 1997, London.
20 Personal interview, 21 May 1997, London.
21 Personal interview, 3 June 1997, London.
22 Hall 1986; Brittan 1970, 448–56.
23 Widmaier 2008, 2010, 155–7.
24 Britton 1991, 94–8.

25 Ibid., ch. 16; Kavanagh and Morris 1989, ch. 3.
26 The 1920s was a period of open conflict between government and unions, characterized by tight statutory controls on union activities and culminating in the General Strike of 1926 (McDonald 1975; Mowat 1955, ch. 6, 7).
27 Kavanagh and Morris 1989, 51–2; Morgan 1984.
28 Hall 1986, 80–5; Clegg 1971, 1979.
29 Widmaier 2003, 2005, 2007b, 2008, 2010; Best and Widmaier 2006.
30 Castle 1984; Jenkins 1970.
31 Moran 1977; Crouch 1977, ch. 13.
32 Schmitter and Lehmbruch 1979, 1982.
33 Personal interview, 21 May 1997, London.
34 Conservative Central Office 1973.
35 Kavanagh and Morris 1989, 68.
36 Quoted in Wearing 1988, 73.
37 Stairs and Winham 1985; Laxer 1991; Riekhokk and Neuhold 1993.
38 Brown 1964; Waite 1971; Lamb 1977.
39 Lusztig 1996, 72.
40 Doern and Tomlin 1991, 58–60.
41 A former Trudeau cabinet minister emphasized the fundamentally pragmatic nature of Canadian parties this way: "You seem to have a very different concept of a party than I have. You think a party is the European type where it has a slogan, a platform, nails its colors up and stands with tests of faith every now and again, expelling the dissidents or the people who don't meet the theology of the time. [Canadian] parties aren't like that. Parties have to govern. Parties have to make compromises. … The objective of a politician is to make things work. The objective of a political party is to provide good government. And it can only provide good government in a sense of compromise and being very practical in terms of what you can do" (personal interview, 9 December 1997, Ottawa).
42 Horowitz 1966; Forbes 1987.
43 Major issues in both world wars were the role Canada would play in helping defend Britain and the Empire. French Canada, in particular, was overwhelmingly hostile to Canadian involvement. Conscription operated in the First World War but was only implemented over French Canadian opposition very late in the Second World War (Granatstein and Hitsman 1977).
44 Holmes 1993; Johnson 1993; U.S.-Canada Automotive Agreement Policy Research Project 1985.
45 Martin 1993, 26.
46 Sharp 1994, 184–6; Finlayson and Bertasi 1992, 27–9.
47 Deigan 1991; Hayden and Burns 1976; Beckman 1984.

48 Doern and Toner 1985; James 1990; Plourde 2005; Lusztig 1996, 78–81.
49 Banting 1982, 48–9.
50 Personal interview, 9 December 1997, Ottawa.
51 Pope 1987; Pincus 1987.
52 Castles 1988. See also Goldfinch 2000, 13–17.
53 Hawke 1985; Dyster and Meredith 1990, ch. 2, 3.
54 Castles 1988, 44–5; Freebairn 1987.
55 Anderson 1987; Reitsma 1960; Anderson and Garnaut 1987; Hawke 1985; Chatterjee 1988.
56 Castles 1988, 95–7.
57 Personal interview, 18 May 1998, Canberra.
58 Garnaut 1994, 51, 55–6.
59 Leigh 2002, 491–4.
60 It must be said, however, that Muldoon did agree, reluctantly, to sign the Closer Economic Relations (CER) treaty with Australia in 1983 (Massey 1995, 107; Templeton 1995).
61 Castles 1985, 82–8; Castles 1988, 97–100; Holt 1986.
62 Castles 1988, 98.
63 Macarthy 1967.
64 Quoted in Castles 1988, 99.
65 Castles 1988, 99, 100.
66 Bray and Neilson 1996, 72; Hancock and Rawson 1993; Matthews 1994.
67 Walsh 1997, 190–2; Walsh 1993.
68 Walsh 1997, 192–3.
69 Walsh 1993, 1994; Boston 1984.
70 Several efforts to model agreements on the Australian Accord – particularly the government's Compact and Growth Agreement with the Council of Trade Unions (CTU) – were unsuccessful (Kelsey 1993, 100–1; Walsh 1997, 194; Eichbaum 1992, 224).
71 Walsh 1989; Boxall 1991.
72 Hancock 1930, 72–3; quoted in Goldfinch 2003, 552.
73 Catley 1996, 55–9; Butlin 1987.
74 Catley 1996, 59; Edwards and Watson 1978.
75 Catley, 1996, 59.
76 Ibid.
77 Quoted in Puplick 1994, 54.
78 Horne 1976, 62.
79 Nagel 1998, 236–8; Massey 1995, ch. 2; Gustafson 1986; Gould 1982; Muldoon 1977, 1981; Templeton 1995.
80 Douglas 1993, 257; emphasis in original.

81 13 January 1996, 21.
82 Dorey 1995a, ch. 4; Dutton 1997, ch.4; Prasad 2006, 152–4; Ball and Seldon 1996.
83 Which, in percentage terms, is the now relatively low figure of around 4.5 percent (OECD [United Kingdom] 1976, 16, 17).
84 Personal interview, 10 June 1997, London.
85 Hall 1986, 89–90; Cairncross 1996.
86 Taylor 1996a, 1996b.
87 Morgan 1990, 328; Hall 1981; Taylor 1984.
88 Personal interview, 3 June 1997, London.
89 Butler and Kavanagh 1974, 1975.
90 Tebbit 1988, 95.
91 Whitehead 1985; Holmes 1985; Coates 1980; Callaghan 1987.
92 Morgan 1990, 376.
93 Quoted in Day 1993.
94 Barnett 1982.
95 Morgan 1990, 397.
96 This account is drawn from Morgan 1990, 397–433. See also Barnes and Reid 1980; Dorfman 1979.
97 Morgan 1990, 420.
98 Personal interview, 11 March 1997, London.
99 Personal interview, 6 May 1997, Broadstairs, Kent.
100 Mann 2002.
101 Sharp 1994, 167–8.
102 Personal interview, 12 February 1998, Columbus, Ohio.
103 Personal interview, 10 December 1997, Toronto.
104 See Doern and Toner 1985; James and Michelin 1989; James 1990, 1993; Uslaner 1989; Laxer 1989.
105 Simpson 1980.
106 Personal interview, 17 February 1998, Columbus, Ohio.
107 Perry 1989.
108 OECD (Canada) 1985, 20.
109 Whitlam 1985; Emy, Hughes, and Mathews 1993.
110 Personal interview, 13 August 1998, Sydney. The following anecdote is also instructive: "At a function to mark Bill Hayden's twenty-five years in Parliament, Whitlam recalled Hayden coming to him anxiously to report that an American agency was considering downgrading Australia's credit rating. Whitlam said: 'Sounds serious, comrade. What does it mean?'" (Stubbs 1989, 119).
111 Personal interview, 21 October 1998, Sydney.

112 Personal interview, 21 May 1998, Canberra.
113 Kelly 1995.
114 Ayres 1989; Weller 1989.
115 Personal interview, 29 May 1998, Canberra.
116 Personal interview, 26 November 1998, Wellington.
117 Muldoon 1977, 40, 43; emphasis in original.
118 Bollard 1994, 74–5; Roper 1997, 2003, 579.
119 Muldoon 1977, 1981.
120 Bassett 1998, 338; Bollard 1994, 88.
121 Massey 1995, 33.
122 Personal interview, 5 November 1998, Wellington.
123 Massey 1995, 48–50.
124 Quoted in Massey 1995, 50. At the time Douglas made this comment, the price of oil was about NZ$23 a barrel (United Nations 1986, 59).
125 Bollard 1994, 98–9; Goldfinch 2000, 20–4.
126 Upton 1985, 35; quoted in Massey 1995, 52.

3. The Neoliberal Revolution of the 1980s and Beyond

1 Finnemore 1996b, 138.
2 Mulgan 1990, 15.
3 Bollard 1994; Nagel 1998, 244–5.
4 Personal interview, 12 November 1998, Wellington.
5 Brian Easton, however, points out that Douglas in 1980 was not as purely neoliberal as he was to become only three or four years later. The book is a "confused document," with calls for not only deregulation, but also development proposals that were suspiciously akin to "Think Big" projects (Easton 1997, 76). See also Bollard 1994, 88–90.
6 Personal interview, 12 November 1998, Wellington.
7 Quoted in Davies 1995, 49; H. Young 1989, 406; Riddell 1989, 1.
8 Personal interview, 24 June 1997, London.
9 Easton 1997, 81.
10 On this period, see Riddell 1985, ch. 2; Gamble 1994, ch. 2; Evans 2004, ch. 1; H. Young 1989, ch. 8; Denham and Garnett 2001b, ch. 11.
11 Conservative Central Office 1976, 71.
12 Quoted in Young 1988, n.p.
13 Personal interview, 8 April 1997, London.
14 Hay 2004c, 513–16; De Long 2000; Prasad 2006, 105–21; Riddell 1985, ch. 4, 5; Smith 1988; Hall 1992; Pepper and Oliver 2001.
15 Britton 1991, ch. 7–9; Pepper and Oliver 2001, 34–6; Pepper 1998, ch. 1–3.

16 Conservative Central Office 1975, 22.

17 On Joseph, see Denham and Garnett 2001a, 2001b.

18 Britton 1991, ch. 7; Friedman 1968, 1970; Barro 1976.

19 Hall 1986, 101; emphasis added.

20 The phrase was Nigel Lawson's (quoted in Jenkins 1988, 54).

21 Hall 1986, 101.

22 Quoted in Hall 1986, 101.

23 Personal interview, 3 June 1997, London.

24 Thain 1985; Tomlinson 2007, 8–10; Minford 1990, 96–8.

25 De Long 2000, 92; Riddell 1985, ch. 5.

26 For descriptions of these, see Pliatzky 1989, 121.

27 Goodhart 1989.

28 Healey 1993, 140.

29 See Davies 1989 for a discussion.

30 Jenkins 1988, 263.

31 Personal interview with a Labour minister, 14 March 1997, London. Keith Joseph had already signalled his opposition to full employment policies, beginning in 1974. See Joseph 1975; Wood 1975; Skidelsky 1990, 14.

32 Personal interview, 3 June 1997, London.

33 Lawson 1982, 10; emphasis added.

34 Jenkins 1988, 98.

35 Farnham 1990; Roberts 1989; Riddell 1985, 186–91; Marsh 1992.

36 International Labour Office, *Year Book of Labour Statistics*, various years.

37 31 January 1970, 14.

38 Conservative Central Office 1980, 4.

39 Conservative Central Office 1979, 5.

40 Kavanagh 1987, 237.

41 Creighton 1987, 76.

42 Morgan 1990, 472–5; Adeney and Lloyd 1986; Beynon 1985; Winterton 1989; Walker 1991; Parker 2000.

43 Glyn and Machin 1996.

44 Clarke 1994; Abromeit 1988; Letwin 1988; Marsh 1991b; Swann 1988, part III; Feigenbaum, Henig, and Hamnett 1999, ch. 3; Zahariadis 1995; Riddell 1985, 170–83; Stevens 2004; Prasad 2006, 121–35; Veljanovski 1987.

45 Howe 1981, 4–5.

46 Sanders and Harris 1994; Heath and Garrett 1991.

47 Conservative Central Office 1977, 34.

48 OECD (United Kingdom) 1995, 91.

49 Parker 1993, 174.

50 The phrase was allegedly that of Harold Macmillan. In actual fact, he warned of the dangers of selling off the Georgian silver before going on to the furniture and the Canaletto paintings (Evans 2004, 37).

51 The success of Thatcher's program to create a property-owning society is not uncontested. Some point out that many of the first-time shareowners sold their stock very quickly, pocketing a quick, easy profit without becoming some sort of long-term "little capitalist." For instance, within a year of the sale of Cable and Wireless in 1981–2, the number of shareholders in the company dropped from 150,000 to less than 26,000. By 1990, the number of shareholders in British Airways had dropped from one million to less than 350,000, those owning shares in British Gas fell from four-and-a-half million to less than three million, and the number of owners of Rolls-Royce shares declined from two million to 925,000 (Dorey 1995a, 203). For a similar analysis, see also Clarke 1994, 218–20.

52 Thatcher 1995, 574; Coxall and Robins 1998, 62.

53 Atkinson and Durden 1990; Murie 1989; Prasad 2006, 136–42.

54 Horton 1990; K. Young 1989; Evans 2004, 58–64.

55 On health, see Kendall and Moon 1990; Webster 1989; Giaimo 2002; Ruggie 1996. On education, see McVicar 1990; Tomlinson 1989; Scott 1989.

56 Douglas turned out to be perhaps the truest of true believers – eventually leaving the Labour Party to, in 1994, form ACT New Zealand, an essentially libertarian party committed to the driest of economic principles.

57 James 1992, 149.

58 Bollard 1994, 86–88.

59 Easton 1994, 215.

60 Kelsey 1995, 33.

61 Personal interview, 19 November 1998, Wellington.

62 Kelsey 1995, 38. On the framing and policy effects of the "Polish shipyard" metaphor, see Goldfinch and Malpass 2007.

63 Massey 1995, 133.

64 Goldfinch 2000, 86–91; Massey 1995, 112–15; Harper and Karacaoglu 1987; Buckle 1987.

65 Massey 1995, 108–10, 115–16; Bremer and Brooking 1993; Evans 1987.

66 Massey 1995, 110–12, 117–18; Bollard 1987; Wooding 1987.

67 Castles 1978, 25, 125–8.

68 Quoted in Massey 1995, 62; emphasis added.

69 Goldfinch 2000, 108–12.

70 Quoted in Dalziel 1993, 84.

71 Dalziel 1993, 84.

72 OECD (New Zealand) 1989, 49.

73 Kelsey 1995, 118–19.

74 Duncan and Bollard 1992; Kelsey 1993; Kelsey 1995, 127–36; Kelsey 2000, 178–83; Boston 1992a; Bollard and Mayes 1994; Goldfinch 2000, 102–8.

75 Kelsey 1995, 128; Goldfinch 2003, 552.

76 OECD (New Zealand) 1996, 97.

77 Personal interview, 21 October 1998, Sydney.

78 Personal interview, 19 November 1998, Wellington.

79 Goldfinch 2000, 13. On Hawke's gradualist, consultative style, see Garnaut 1994, 66–70.

80 On fiscal policy under Mulroney, see Lewis 2004, 113–42; Savoie 1990; Baar 2002.

81 On privatization in Canada, see Jörgensen, Hafsi, and Demers 1994; Doern and Atherton 1987; Tupper and Doern 1988; Richardson 1990; Stanbury 1989.

82 See Plourde 2005; Safarian 1991; Clarkson 1991; Doern and Toner 1985; James 1990; James and Michelin 1989; Toner 1986.

83 Mulroney 1983, 98.

84 Doern and Toner 1985, 106–7.

85 OECD (Canada) 1986, 25.

86 Doern and Tomlin 1991, 17.

87 Ibid., 17–18.

88 *House of Commons Debates*, v. 28, p. 1089.

89 LeDuc and Murray 1989, 131.

90 Ibid., 132.

91 On Canada and free trade, see McDougall 2006; Kreinin 2000; Ritchie 1997; Hart, Dymond, and Richardson 1994; Lusztig 1996; Doran and Marchildon 1994.

92 Quoted in Martin 1993, 43–4.

93 *House of Commons Debates*, v. 128, p. 7055.

94 Ibid., p. 13559.

95 Personal interview, 8 December 1997, Ottawa.

96 For a comprehensive review of the Macdonald Commission, see Inwood 2005.

97 Royal Commission 1985, 1:60, 63.

98 Personal interview, 28 May 1998, Canberra.

99 Garnaut 1994, 59–62; Hall 1987; Perkins 1989; Pauly 1987; Argy 1995.

100 OECD (Australia) 1985, 10–11.

101 Garnaut 1994, 62–7.

102 OECD (Australia) 1998, 81.

103 Keating and Dixon 1989, ch. 7; Bell 1993.
104 Department of the Prime Minister and Cabinet 1991, 1.5, 1.22.
105 Frankel 1997; Matthews 1994; Stilwell 1986, 1990; Singleton 1990a, 1990b.
106 Mills 1993, 40–1.
107 Quoted in Mills 1993, 46.
108 Goldfinch 2000, 188–95; Fairbrother 1997; Teicher 1998.
109 Quoted in Henderson 1995, 102.
110 Personal interview, 14 November 1996, Menlo Park, CA.
111 The bulk of these were held by the states (OECD [Australia] 1992, 78).
112 Among many others, see Heffernan 2001; Ludlam and Smith 2001; Hay
      1999b; Driver and Martell 1998; Shaw 1994; Russell 2005; Coates and
      Lawler 2001.
113 The phrase was that of Labour MP Gerald Kaufman.
114 Hay 1999b. See also Hay 1994a, 2004c; Watson and Hay 2003.
115 See Hay 1999b, 137–8; 2007, 113–18.
116 This program was a modified form of the Conservatives' Private Finance
      Initiative of the early 1990s, which had largely the same goal.
117 Jessop 2003.
118 OECD (Canada) 1996, ch. 3.
119 It must be pointed out that this opposition was not universal within the
      Liberal Party. While the party officially opposed the FTA, many MPs sup-
      ported it. As one top Liberal declared, "I supported what the [Mulroney]
      government did on free trade, … [but the Liberal Party] was clearly
      divided. … A number of us who were free traders within the Liberal
      Party just bit our tongues. What else could we do?" (Personal interview,
      9 December 1997, Ottawa).
120 Among a large literature on this topic, see Schmidt 1996, 1997; Hibbs
      1977, 1986, 1992; Alesina and Sachs 1988; Alvarez, Garrett, and Lange
      1991; Castles and McKinlay 1979a, 1979b, 1997; Garrett and Lange 1989.
121 On the Coalition in Australia, see Garnaut 1994, 69; on the National Party
      in New Zealand, see Bollard 1994, 93–4.
122 Castles, Gerritsen, and Vowles 1996, 15.
123 OECD (Australia) 2003, 99; OECD (Australia) 2005, 186–8.
124 OECD (Australia) 2006, 124–5.
125 Kelsey 2000, 13; Easton 1999, 34–6; Goldfinch 2000, 208; Mulgan 1997.
126 Bray and Neilson 1996, 82–3; Goldfinch 2000, 117–20.
127 Clark 2000. See also Miller 2003, 246–8.
128 Walsh and Harbridge 2001; OECD (New Zealand) 2000, 75–80; Anderson
      2006.
129 OECD (New Zealand) 2000, 76–77.

4. The Strategic Construction of the Neoliberal Political-Economic Imaginary

1 Abdelal, Blyth, and Parsons 2010b, 234.
2 On Thatcher's style, see King 1985, 1990; Moon 1993; Dyson 2009. See also Jim Bulpitt's discussion of Thatcher's particular form of "statecraft" (1986).
3 Dyson 2009, 38.
4 Personal interview, 16 June 1997, London.
5 Lawson 1993, 26; emphasis in original.
6 Doern and Tomlin 1991, 272–3.
7 Ludwig 2002, 339; Weber 1968, 18–27.
8 As Goldfinch and 't Hart put it, "The tandem worked despite the two members being very different individuals with very different political styles: Hawke, the academically trained yet folksy, popular, crowd-loving, politically pragmatic consensus-builder; Keating, the working-class autodidact with an acquired elitist taste, strong policy views, and a phenomenal yet highly divisive rhetorical ability" (2003, 259).
9 Quoted in Carew 1988, 146–7.
10 Goldfinch and 't Hart 2003, 259. On affect and the need for respect, see Best 2009.
11 Quoted in Ryan 1995, 7.
12 Douglas 1993, 220, 222, 225, 233.
13 Quoted in Deane 1995, 5.
14 Bolger 1998, 48.
15 Personal interview, 5 November 1998, Wellington.
16 On Douglas and his colleagues, see Bollard 1994, 88–90. See also Nagel 2004; Rudd and Taichi 1994.
17 Seabrooke 2007b, 796. On legitimacy generally, see also Seabrooke 2006; Best 2007.
18 Jessop 2004, 161.
19 Among a very substantial literature, see Kingdon 1984; Hay 1999a; Keeler 1993; Browne 1987, 1998; Birkland 1997; Lipsky and Smith, 1989; Polsby 1984; Nelson 1990; Aberbach and Christensen 2001.
20 As Bob Jessop puts it, "not only do economic imaginaries provide a semiotic frame for construing economic 'events' but they also help to construct such events and their economic contexts" (2004, 164).
21 Blyth 2001, 3.
22 Jessop and Oosterlynck 2008, 1159.

23 On the significance of crisis to ideational change, see Blyth 2001, 2002, 2007; Jessop 2004, 2011; Jessop and Oosterlynck 2008; Widmaier, Blyth, and Seabrooke 2007; Hay 1994a, 2001.

24 New Zealand was a partial exception to this pattern. There, full employment had essentially been achieved in the post-war period, and it persisted until the late 1970s. Widespread unemployment only emerged in full force in the 1980s.

25 On how the Winter of Discontent was discursively constructed, see Hay 1996.

26 Easton 1989; Boston 1992b; Goldfinch and Roper 1993; Walsh 1995; Goldfinch 2000, 41–4, 125–9.

27 Muetzelfeldt 1992, 188.

28 Pusey 1992b, 64.

29 Pusey 1991, 6; Pusey 1992a, 1992b; Whitwell 1986.

30 Personal interview, 20 May 1998, Canberra.

31 Personal interview, 24 June 1998, Canberra.

32 Kelsey 1995, 49.

33 Deane 1995, 8; See also Miskin 1997.

34 Goldfinch and Roper 1993, 64, 68. See also Bollard 1994, 90–2, 94–8; Easton 1997, ch. 6; Kelsey 2000, 8–10.

35 Miskin 1997, 28.

36 Harris 1988, 96; Savoie 1994, 90–1.

37 Doern and Tomlin 1991, 275; Savoie 1994, 91, 94.

38 Lawson 1993, 26.

39 Hall 1986, 248–9; Lawson 1993, 26.

40 Quoted in Hall 1986, 97.

41 Thatcher, for her part, rejected a 1988 proposal for Bank independence (Kynaston 1995, 53–4). See also Burnham 2007; Prasad 2006, 114.

42 Doern and Tomlin 1991, 97–8.

43 Ibid., 274–6, 179; emphasis in original.

44 An objection could be raised that such a focus on institutional factors detracts from, or even is at odds with, a constructionist, ideational account of economic policy change. However, this would be true only if my approach was a rather crude institutionalist one, considering institutions and their effects in a way largely divorced from the ideas producing and governing them. Rather, I view institutions as *themselves* primarily ideational in that they both are rooted in and comprised by sets of ideas. Thus, for example, the institutions, rules, and practices of parliamentary government should themselves be seen as complexes of ideas instantiated in more or less concrete ways. While a discussion of the ideational origins

and structure of these institutions is beyond the scope of this study, such an analysis is possible – and would be entirely compatible with, and complementary to, the present constructivist account, which takes them largely as a given. (I wish to thank an anonymous reader of this manuscript for explicating these points to me.)

45 Tsebelis 1995, 1999, 2002. See also Crepaz and Moser 2004.
46 On these differences, see Lijphart 1984, 1999; see also Powell 1982, 2000; Huber and Powell 1994; Schmidt 2002; Reynolds 2002; Steiner 1971.
47 Blyth 2001, 24.
48 On oppositions, see Nelson 1990, 335.
49 Bollard 1994, 88; Bollard and Mayes 1994, 310.
50 The British Conservatives had majorities of 43 (in 1979), 144 (1983), 102 (1987), and 21 (1992). Mulroney had majorities of 140 (1984) and 43 (1988). The ALP's majorities were 25 (1983), 16 (1984), 24 (1987), 8 (1990), and 13 (1993). New Zealand Labour had majorities of 17 (1984) and 17 (1987).
51 On the honeymoon period in Australia, see McAllister 2003.
52 On bicameralism, see Tsebelis and Money 1997.
53 As Jack Nagel puts it, "Scholars of comparative politics have given significant theoretical significance to New Zealand's pre-1993 system because it was the purest example of ... [pluralitarian] democracy. Its chief features ... included parliamentary sovereignty, fusion of legislative and executive power through cabinet government, a unicameral legislature, a unitary system with weak local authorities and no provinces or states, frequent (usually triennial) elections and single-member-district plurality elections that promoted the dominance of two political parties, one or the other of which normally had a disciplined parliamentary majority" (1998, 225).
54 Kelly 2000, 224.
55 Personal interview, 12 June 1997, London.
56 Douglas 1980, 9.
57 OECD (Australia) 1987, 7–8.
58 Quoted in Carew 1988, 157.
59 Personal interview, 20 May 1998, Canberra.
60 Personal interview, 5 November 1998, Wellington.
61 Personal interview, 19 January 1998, Ottawa.
62 An entire literature in Britain grew up around the issue of decline, its causes and potential remedies. See Gamble 1990; Budge 1993; Clarke and Trebilcock 1997; Allen 1976; Wiener 1981; Pollard 1982.
63 Personal interview, 3 June 1997, London.
64 Mulroney 1983, 22–3, 38.
65 *Parliamentary Debates (Hansard)* [United Kingdom], v. 967, col. 893–4.

66 Douglas and Callan 1987, 13–14.
67 *Parliamentary Debates (Hansard)* [New Zealand], v. 450, p. 15.
68 Quoted in Whitwell 1986, 253–4; emphasis added.
69 For this argument regarding New Zealand, see Goldfinch and Malpass 2007.
70 McAllister and Vowles 1994, 388.
71 For a review of this argument, see Drezner 2001. See also Giddens 1999; Krugman 1997; Strange 1996; Stiglitz 2002; Schwartz 2000b.
72 For various contributions to the debate on the relative autonomy of the state, see Mosley 2005; Gritsch 2005; Drache 1996; Falk 1997; Habermas 1999; Rodrik 1997; Evans 1997; Sassen 1996, 1998, 1999; Strange 1996, 1997.
73 Douglas 1993, 11–12; emphasis added.
74 Destler 1992; Nollen and Quinn 1994; Nollen and Iglarsh 1990; Czinkota 1985.
75 Royal Commission 1985, 1:300.
76 Department of the Prime Minister and Cabinet 1991, 1.1; emphasis added.
77 Personal interview, 5 November 1998, Wellington.
78 Personal interview, 3 June 1997, London.
79 Personal interview, 14 May 1998, Canberra.
80 Personal interview, 14 May 1998, Canberra.
81 On this framing strategy, see Hay 2004b; Hay and Rosamond 2002.
82 Blyth 2001, 2002.
83 Thatcher 1993, 7–8.
84 Conservative Central Office 1976, 19; emphasis in original.
85 Young 1989, 204–5.
86 Carrington 1988, 309.
87 Personal interview, 3 June 1997, London.
88 Personal interview, 19 January 1998, Ottawa.
89 Quoted in Martin 1993, 101; emphasis added.
90 Australian Centre for Industrial Relations Research and Training 1999, 157.
91 Personal interview, 23 November 1998, Wellington.
92 Personal interview, 14 November 1996, Menlo Park, Ca.
93 Personal interview, 19 November 1998, Wellington.

5. Labour Markets and the Power of Partisanship

1 Klingemann et al. 1994, 5, 48.
2 Hofferbert and Cingranelli 1996, 594.
3 Ibid., 607.
4 Schmidt 1996, 156.

5 See Klingemann et al. 1994.
6 Godard 2003; Singh and Jain 2001; Abraham 1997.
7 For a wide range of measures indicating the essentially deregulated nature of Canada's labour market – and its similarities to that of the United States – see OECD 1999, ch. 2.
8 Godard 2003, 460.
9 For reviews, see OECD (Canada) 1995, 1996. See also OECD 1994, 1995.
10 Lipset 1960, 229; Lipset and Rokkan 1967.
11 Catley 1996, 65.
12 Taylor 1993, 369.
13 Ibid., 2.
14 The phrase is Taylor's (1993).
15 Personal interview, 21 May 1997, London.
16 See, for instance, Browne 1979; Pelling 1992; Taylor 1993; McIlroy 1995; Fraser 1999, ch. 8–10; Aldcroft and Oliver 2000, ch. 3–4.
17 On the Act, see Mack 1959; Thompson 1998.
18 Quoted in Hanson 1991, 21.
19 Ibid., 22–3.
20 Taylor 1993, 4–14. See also Flanders 1974; Rogin 1962.
21 Garbarino 1973, 797.
22 Personal interview, 21 May 1997, London.
23 For general treatments of *In Place of Strife*, see Dorfman 1979, ch. 2; Crouch 1979, ch. 2; Tyler 2006; Whiting 2007; Dorey 2006.
24 Personal interview, 6 May 1997, Broadstairs, Kent.
25 Taylor 1993, 164–8.
26 Ibid., 186.
27 See Moran 1977; Dorfman 1979, ch. 3; Marsh 1992, ch. 1; Dorey 1995b, ch. 5; Whiting 2007.
28 Personal interview, 21 May 1997, London.
29 Taylor 1993, 190–1.
30 Personal interview, 6 May 1997, Broadstairs, Kent.
31 Taylor 1993, ch. 6.
32 Jones 1986, 259; quoted in Taylor 1993, 203.
33 On the industrial relations policies of the 1974–9 Labour governments, see Marsh 1992, ch. 2; Crouch 1979, ch. 4; Brown 1991. See also Holmes 1985; Coates 1980.
34 Taylor 1993, 228.
35 Personal interview, 11 March 1997, London.
36 Personal interview, 28 May 1997, London.
37 Personal interview, 3 June 1997, London.

38 Among a very large literature on Thatcher and the unions, see Crouch 1986; Hyman 1987; Towers 1989; Marsh 1991a, 1992; Dorey 1993, 1995b, ch. 7; Fredman 1992; Howell 2005, ch. 5.

39 Personal interview, 20 March 1997, London.

40 Thatcher 1995, 109–10.

41 Lawson 1993, 437.

42 Quoted in Hall 1986, 101.

43 See chapter 3, note 31.

44 Black 2004, 130.

45 A comprehensive review of the relationship between the Conservative Party and the unions can be found in Dorey 1995b.

46 Personal interview, 21 May 1997, London.

47 For discussion of these legislative efforts, see Fredman 1992; Hendy 1991; Miller and Steele 1993.

48 Hanson 1991, 7–8.

49 For a discussion of the Conservative Party and its approach to closed shops, see Dorey 2009.

50 Hanson 1991, 17–19; OECD (United Kingdom) 1985, 26; OECD (United Kingdom) 1986, 30; OECD (United Kingdom) 1993, 53.

51 On the link between trade union legislation and union membership, see Freeman and Pelletier 1991; Disney, Gosling, and Machin 1995.

52 OECD (United Kingdom) 1991, 83.

53 Personal interview, 6 May 1997, Broadstairs, Kent.

54 Personal interview, 17 March 1997, London.

55 Quiggin 2001, 80.

56 On this connection in Britain, see Reid 2000; Taylor 1987; Minkin 1992; in Australia, Jupp 1982, 103–5; James and Markey 2006; Marsh 2006; Bramble and Kuhn 2009; in New Zealand, Milne 1966, 101–14; Vowles 2002.

57 However, the nature of that linkage should not be taken as a kind of fixed, institutional given, but rather as itself an ideational phenomenon, subject to change, reformulation, and reinterpretation.

58 Harbridge and Honeybone 1996, 427.

59 Personal interview, 28 May 1998, Canberra.

60 Castles 1988, 98–9. See also Callaghan 1983; McQueen 1983; Goldfinch and Smith 2006.

61 Bray and Walsh 1998, 365.

62 Lansbury 1978, 619.

63 Ibid., 620–1.

64 Bray and Walsh 1998, 366; Bray and Neilson 1996, 73–4.

65 Personal interview, 14 May 1998, Canberra.

66 Easton and Gerritsen 1996, 45; Castles 1996, 106–7, 110.
67 The Australian case, of course, stands in sharp contrast to the unwilling-ness of workers in other countries, as discussed by Widmaier (2003, 2005, 2007b, 2008, 2010), to voluntarily limit wage demands.
68 Quoted in Anson 1991, 85.
69 Personal interview, 14 November 1996, Menlo Park, CA.
70 Bray and Walsh 1998, 380.
71 Personal interview, 14 November 1996, Menlo Park, CA.
72 For a discussion of ALP factions, see Leigh 2000; McAllister 1991; Lloyd and Swan 1987; Bean and McAllister 1989; Parkin and Warhurst 1983.
73 Personal interview, 14 May 1998, Canberra.
74 Wooden 2000, 31–2; Ogden 1993. See also Huzzard, Gregory, and Scott 2004.
75 Personal interview, 2 July 1998, Canberra.
76 Bramble and Heal 1997, 134–5.
77 Personal interview, 21 May 1998, Canberra.
78 OECD (Australia) 1995, 54–5; OECD (Australia) 1990, 73.
79 Quoted in Hancock 1999, 42–3.
80 OECD (Australia) 1995, 56.
81 OECD (Australia) 1994, 89; OECD (Australia) 1995, 55–8; Campbell and Brosnan 1999.
82 Australian Centre for Industrial Relations Research and Training 1999, 58.
83 Bray and Neilson 1996, 80.
84 Bell 1997, 193–4; Australian Centre for Industrial Relations Research and Training 1999, 58.
85 Pusey 2003, 11; Mendes 2003.
86 Bray and Walsh 1998, 375–6; McCallum 1997; Creighton 1997; Naughton 1997; OECD (Australia) 1998, 55–65.
87 Cooper and Ellem 2008; Ellem et al. 2005; Hall 2006; Stewart 2006; OECD (Australia) 2006, 117–32.
88 Dabscheck 2008; Cooper 2009; Hall 2008.
89 Personal interview, 14 May 1998, Canberra.
90 Personal interview, 9 June 1998, Canberra.
91 Personal interview, 28 May 1998, Canberra.
92 Kaufman 2004, 293. See also Goldfinch and Smith 2006.
93 Schwartz 2000a, 105.
94 Burton 2001; Walsh 1994.
95 Boston 1984; Roper 1993, 160–1.
96 Bray and Walsh 1998, 365–6; Bray and Neilson 1996.
97 Kelsey 1993, 100–1; Walsh 1997, 194.

98 Bray and Neilson 1996, 77.
99 Personal interview, 28 May 1998, Canberra.
100 Maloney and Savage 1996, 184; Harbridge and Walsh 1985.
101 Boxall 1990; Dannin 1997, 33–5; Walsh 1989; Wood 1988.
102 OECD (New Zealand) 1989, 44.
103 Rudd 1990, 91.
104 OECD (New Zealand) 1991, 70.
105 OECD (New Zealand) 1996, 54. Among many treatments of the ECA, see Dannin 1997; Hince and Vranken 1991; Walsh and Ryan 1993; Anderson 1991; Boxall 1991.
106 Dalziel and Lattimore 2001, 95.
107 Chaison 1996, 140.
108 Leybourne and Mizen 1999, 803.
109 Personal interview, 5 November 1998, Wellington.
110 Bolger 1998, 49.
111 Personal interview, 10 November 1998, Wellington.
112 Walsh 1993, 184–5.
113 Personal interview, 5 November 1998, Wellington.

6. "The Market Has Won"

1 However, for the argument that attention should be shifted away from elites toward the "everyday politics" and "everyday discourses" occurring at the mass level, see Seabrooke 2006, 2007a, 2007b, 2007c, 2010; Hobson and Seabrooke 2007; Seabrooke and Tsingou 2009.
2 Personal interview, 21 October 1998, Sydney.
3 The terms are Widmaier's (2003, 2007a, 2007b).
4 Blyth 2007, 762.
5 See, for instance, Beilharz 1994; Maddox 1989; Jaensch 1989.
6 Personal interview, 13 August 1998, Sydney.
7 Personal interview 6 November 1998, Wellington.
8 On Labour and industrial relations in Britain, see Jessop 2003.
9 Personal interview, 25 May 1998, Canberra.
10 Personal interview, 19 May 1998, Canberra.
11 Hay 2004b, 514.
12 Jessop 2002, 468.
13 Best 2003, 371.
14 Personal interview, 17 February 1998, Columbus, Ohio.
15 Personal interview, 24 February 1998, Columbus, Ohio.
16 Pusey 1991, 10, 175; Kirkby 1993, 107.

17 Best 2003, 371.
18 Ibid., 372.
19 Personal interview, 20 May 1998, Canberra.
20 *Parliamentary Debates (Hansard)* [New Zealand], 1985, v. 461, p. 3418.
21 Personal interview, 28 May 1998, Canberra.
22 Personal interview, 28 May 1998, Canberra.
23 Personal interview, 14 November 1996, Menlo Park, CA; emphasis added.
24 Hay 2004c, 503–4.
25 Personal interview, 14 November 1996, Menlo Park, CA.

References

Abdelal, Rawi. 2001. *National Purpose in the World Economy: Post-Soviet States in Comparative Perspective*. Ithaca, NY: Cornell University Press.

Abdelal, Rawi, Mark Blyth, and Craig Parsons, eds. 2010a. *Constructing the International Economy*. Ithaca, NY: Cornell University Press.

Abdelal, Rawi, Mark Blyth, and Craig Parsons. 2010b. "Reconstructing IPE: Some Conclusions Drawn from a Crisis." In *Constructing the International Economy*, ed. Rawi Abdelal, Mark Blyth, and Craig Parsons, 227–40. Ithaca, NY: Cornell University Press.

Aberbach, Joel D., and Tom Christensen. 2001. "Radical Reform in New Zealand: Crisis, Windows of Opportunity, and Rational Actors." *Public Administration* 79 (2): 403–22. http://dx.doi.org/10.1111/1467-9299.00262.

Abraham, Steven E. 1997. "Relevance of Canadian Labour Law to US Firms Operating in Canada." *International Journal of Manpower* 18 (8): 662–74. http://dx.doi.org/10.1108/01437729710192791.

Abromeit, Heidrun. 1988. "British Privatisation Policy." *Parliamentary Affairs* 41 (1): 68–85.

Adeney, Martin, and John Lloyd. 1986. *The Miners' Strike, 1984–5: Loss without Limit*. London: Routledge and Kegan Paul.

Adler, Emanuel. 1997. "Seizing the Middle Ground: Constructivism in World Politics." *European Journal of International Relations* 3 (3): 319–63. http://dx.doi.org/10.1177/1354066197003003003.

Adler, Emanuel. 2002. "Constructivism and International Relations." In *Handbook of International Relations*, ed. Walter Carlnaes, Thomas Risse-Kappen, and Beth A. Simmons, 95–118. London: Sage. http://dx.doi.org/10.4135/9781848608290.n5.

Aldcroft, Derek H., and Michael J. Oliver. 2000. *Trade Unions and the Economy: 1870–2000*. Aldershot: Ashgate.

Alesina, Alberto, and Jeffrey D. Sachs. 1988. "Political Parties and the Business Cycle in the United States, 1948–1984." *Journal of Money, Credit and Banking* 20 (1): 63–87. http://dx.doi.org/10.2307/1992667.

Allen, G.C. 1976. *The British Disease: A Short Essay on the Nature and Cause of the Nation's Lagging Wealth*. London: Institute of Economic Affairs.

Alvarez, R. Michael, Geoffrey Garrett, and Peter Lange. 1991. "Government Partisanship, Labor Organization, and Macroeconomic Performance." *American Political Science Review* 85 (2): 539–56. http://dx.doi.org/10.2307/1963174.

Anderson, Craig A. 1995. "Implicit Personality Theories and Empirical Data: Biased Assimilation, Belief Perseverance and Change, and Covariation Detection Sensitivity." *Social Cognition* 13 (1): 25–48. http://dx.doi.org/10.1521/soco. 1995.13.1.25.

Anderson, Gordon J. 1991. "The Employment Contracts Act 1991: An Employers' Charter?" *New Zealand Journal of Industrial Relations* 16: 127–42.

Anderson, Gordon J. 2006. "Transplanting and Growing Good Faith in New Zealand Labour Law." *Australian Journal of Labour Law* 19 (1): 1–29.

Anderson, Kym. 1987. "Tariffs and the Manufacturing Sector." In *The Australian Economy in the Long Run*, ed. Rodney Maddock and Ian W. McLean, 165–94. Cambridge: Cambridge University Press.

Anderson, Kym, and Ross Garnaut. 1987. *Australian Protectionism: Extent, Causes and Effect*. Sydney: Allen and Unwin.

Anson, Stan. 1991. *Hawke: An Emotional Life*. Ringwood, Vic.: McPhee Gribble.

Argy, Fred. 1995. *Financial Deregulation: Past Promise, Future Realities*. Melbourne: Committee for Economic Development of Australia.

Atkinson, Rob, and Paul Durden. 1990. "Housing Policy in the Thatcher Years." In *Public Policy under Thatcher*, ed. Stephen P. Savage and Lynton Robins, 117-30. New York: St. Martin's Press.

Australian Centre for Industrial Relations Research and Training. 1999. *Australia at Work: Just Managing?* Sydney: Prentice Hall.

Ayres, Philip. 1989. *Malcolm Fraser: A Biography*. Port Melbourne, Vic.: Mandarin Australia.

Baar, David W. 2002. "The Sequencing of Deficit Reduction and Disinflation in Canada." *Canadian Public Policy—Analyse de Politiques* 28 (4): 547–61.

Ball, Stuart, and Anthony Seldon, eds. 1996. *The Heath Government 1970–74: A Reappraisal*. London: Longman.

Banting, Keith G. 1982. *The Welfare State and Canadian Federalism*. Montreal: McGill-Queen's University Press.

Barnes, Denis, and Eileen Reid. 1980. *Governments and Trade Unions: The British Experience, 1964–79*. London: Heinemann.

Barnett, Joel. 1982. *Inside the Treasury*. London: Deutsch.

Barnett, Michael. 1999. "Culture, Strategy and Foreign Policy Change: Israel's Road to Oslo." *European Journal of International Relations* 5 (1): 5–36. http://dx.doi.org/10.1177/1354066199005001001.

Barnett, Michael N. 1998. *Dialogues in Arab Politics: Negotiations in Regional Order*. New York: Columbia University Press.

Barro, Robert J. 1976. *Money, Employment and Inflation*. Cambridge: Cambridge University Press. http://dx.doi.org/10.1017/CBO9780511895654.

Bassett, Michael. 1998. *The State in New Zealand 1840–1984: Socialism without Doctrines?* Auckland: Auckland University Press.

Bates, Robert H. 2001. *Prosperity and Violence: The Political Economy of Violence*. New York: W. W. Norton.

Baumgartner, Frank R., and Bryan D. Jones. 1993. *Agendas and Instability in American Politics*. Chicago: University of Chicago Press.

Bean, Clive, and Ian McAllister. 1989. "Factions and Tendencies in the Australian Party System." *Politics* 24 (2): 79–99.

Beckman, Christopher C. 1984. *The Foreign Investment Review Agency: Images and Realities*. Ottawa: Conference Board of Canada.

Beer, Samuel H. 1969. *British Politics in the Collectivist Age* . New York: Vintage.

Beer, Samuel H. 1982. *Modern British Politics: Parties and Pressure Groups in the Collectivist Age*. London: Faber.

Beilharz, Peter. 1994. *Transforming Labor: Labour Tradition in the Labor Decade*. Cambridge: Cambridge University Press.

Bell, Stephen. 1993. *Australian Manufacturing and the State: The Politics of Industry Policy in the Post-War Era*. Cambridge: Cambridge University Press.

Bell, Stephen. 1997. *Ungoverning the Economy: The Political Economy of Australian Economic Policy*. Melbourne: Oxford University Press.

Benavot, Aaron, Yun-Kyung Cha, David Kamens, John W. Meyer, and Suk-Ying Wong. 1991. "Knowledge for the Masses: World Models and National Curricula, 1920–1986." *American Sociological Review* 56 (1): 85–100. http://dx.doi.org/10.2307/2095675.

Bergersen, Albert, ed. 1980. *Studies of the Modern World-System*. New York: Academic Press.

Berk, Gerald. 1994. *Alternative Tracks: The Constitution of the American Industrial Order, 1865–1917*. Baltimore: Johns Hopkins University Press.

Bermeo, Nancy. 1992. "Democracy and the Lessons of Dictatorship." *Comparative Politics* 24 (3): 273–92. http://dx.doi.org/10.2307/422133.

Bernstein, Steven. 2000. "Ideas, Social Structure and the Compromise of Liberal Environmentalism." *European Journal of International Relations* 6 (4): 464–512. http://dx.doi.org/10.1177/1354066100006004002.

Best, Jacqueline. 2003. "From the Top-Down: The New Financial Architecture and the Re-embedding of Global Finance." *New Political Economy* 8 (3): 363–84. http://dx.doi.org/10.1080/1356346032000138069.

Best, Jacqueline. 2005. *The Limits of Transparency: Ambiguity and the History of International Finance*. Ithaca, NY: Cornell University Press.

Best, Jacqueline. 2006. "Co-opting Cosmopolitanism? The International Monetary Fund's New Global Ethics." *Global Society* 20 (3): 307–27. http://dx.doi.org/10.1080/13600820600816316.

Best, Jacqueline. 2007. "Legitimacy Dilemmas: The IMF's Pursuit of Country Ownership." *Third World Quarterly* 28 (3): 469–88. http://dx.doi.org/10.1080/01436590701192231.

Best, Jacqueline. 2008. "Ambiguity, Uncertainty, and Risk: Rethinking Indeterminacy." *International Political Sociology* 2 (4): 355–74. http://dx.doi.org/10.1111/j.1749-5687. 2008.00056.x.

Best, Jacqueline. 2009. "How to Make a Bubble: Toward a Cultural Political Economy of the Financial Crisis." *International Political Sociology* 3 (4): 461–5. http://dx.doi.org/10.1111/j.1749-5687. 2009.00086_5.x.

Best, Jacqueline. 2010. "Bringing Power Back In: The IMF's Constructivist Strategy in Critical Perspective." In *Constructing the International Economy*, ed. Rawi Abdelal, Mark Blyth, and Craig Parsons, eds., 194–210. Ithaca, NY: Cornell University Press.

Best, Jacqueline, and Matthew Paterson, eds. 2010. *Cultural Political Economy*. London: Routledge.

Best, Jacqueline, and Wesley Widmaier. 2006. "Micro- or Macro-Moralities? Economic Discourses and Policy Possibilities." *Review of International Political Economy* 13 (4): 609–31. http://dx.doi.org/10.1080/09692290600839881.

Beveridge, Sir William. 1942. *Social Insurance and Allied Services*. New York: Macmillan.

Beynon, Huw, ed. 1985. *Digging Deeper: Issues in the Miners Strike*. London: Verso.

Bieler, Andreas. 2001. "Questioning Cognitivism and Constructivism in IR Theory: Reflections on the Material Structure of Ideas." *Politics* 21 (2): 93–100. http://dx.doi.org/10.1111/1467-9256.00140.

Bieler, Andreas, and Adam David Morton. 2001. "The Gordian Knot of Agency-Structure in International Relations: A Neo-Gramscian Perspective." *European Journal of International Relations* 7 (1): 5–35. http://dx.doi.org/10.1177/1354066101007001001.

Biernacki, Richard. 1995. *The Fabrication of Labor: Germany and Britain, 1640–1914*. Berkeley: University of California Press.

Biernacki, Richard. 2001. "Labor as an Imagined Commodity." *Politics &*
   Society 29 (2): 173–206. http://dx.doi.org/10.1177/0032329201029002002.
Biernacki, Richard. 2002. "Culture and Know-How in the 'Satanic Mills': An
   Anglo-German Comparison." *Textile History* 33 (2): 219–37. http://dx.doi.
   org/10.1179/004049602793710035.
Birkland, Thomas A. 1997. *After Disaster: Agenda Setting, Public Policy, and*
   Focusing Events. Washington: Georgetown University Press.
Black, Jeremy. 2004. *Britain Since the Seventies: Politics and Society in the*
   Consumer Age. London: Reaktion Books.
Blyth, Mark. 2001. "The Transformation of the Swedish Model: Economic
   Ideas, Distributional Conflict, and Institutional Change." *World Politics* 54
   (1): 1–26. http://dx.doi.org/10.1353/wp. 2001.0020.
Blyth, Mark. 2002. *Great Transformations: Economic Ideas and Institutional Change*
   in the Twentieth Century. Cambridge: Cambridge University Press. http://
   dx.doi.org/10.1017/CBO9781139087230.
Blyth, Mark. 2007. "Powering, Puzzling, or Persuading? The Mechanisms of
   Building Institutional Orders." *International Studies Quarterly* 51 (4): 761–77.
   http://dx.doi.org/10.1111/j.1468-2478. 2007.00475.x.
Boix, Carles. 1997. "Privatizing the Public Business Sector in the Eighties:
   Economic Performance, Partisan Responses and Divided Governments."
   British Journal of Political Science 27 (4): 473–96. http://dx.doi.org/10.1017/
   S0007123497000239.
Bolger, Jim. 1998. *Bolger: A View from the Top*. Auckland: Viking.
Bollard, Alan. 1987. "More Market: The Deregulation of Industry." In
   Economic Liberalisation in New Zealand, ed. Alan Bollard and Robert Buckle,
   25–45. Wellington: Allen and Unwin.
Bollard, Alan. 1994. "New Zealand." In *The Political Economy of Policy Reform*,
   ed. John Williamson, 73–110. Washington: Institute for International
   Economics.
Bollard, Alan, and David Mayes. 1994. "Corporatization and Privatization in
   New Zealand." In *The Political Economy of Privatization*, ed. Thomas Clarke
   and Christos Pitelis, 308–336. London: Routledge.
Boston, Jonathan. 1984. *Incomes Policy in New Zealand, 1968–1984*. Wellington:
   Victoria University Press.
Boston, Jonathan. 1992a. "New Zealand's Privatization Programme:
   Objectives, Principles, Problems, and Outcomes." *Annals of Public and*
   Cooperative Economics 63 (4): 573–600. http://dx.doi.org/10.1111/j.1467-8292.
   1992.tb02108.x.
Boston, Jonathan. 1992b. "The Treasury: Its Role, Philosophy and Influence."
   In *New Zealand Politics in Perspective*, ed. Hyam Gold, 194–215. Auckland:
   Longman Paul.

Boxall, Peter. 1990. "Towards the Wagner Framework: Change in New Zealand Industrial Relations." *Journal of Industrial Relations* 32 (4): 523–43. http://dx.doi.org/10.1177/002218569003200404.

Boxall, Peter. 1991. "New Zealand's Employment Contracts Act 1991: An Analysis of Background, Provisions and Implications." *Australian Bulletin of Labour* 17 (4): 284–309.

Bramble, Tom, with Sarah Heal. 1997. "Trade Unions." In *The Political Economy of New Zealand*, ed. Chris Rudd and Brian Roper, 119–40. Auckland: Oxford University Press.

Bramble, Tom, and Rick Kuhn. 2009. "Continuity or Discontinuity in the Recent History of the Australian Labor Party." *Australian Journal of Political Science* 44 (2): 281–94. http://dx.doi.org/10.1080/10361140902862792.

Bray, Mark, and David Neilson. 1996. "Industrial Relations Reform and the Relative Autonomy of the State." In *The Great Experiment: Labour Parties and Public Policy Transformation in Australia and New Zealand*, ed. Francis G. Castles, Rolf Gerritsen, and Jack Vowles, 68–87. St. Leonards, NSW: Allen and Unwin.

Bray, Mark, and Pat Walsh. 1998. "Different Paths to Neo-Liberalism? Comparing Australia and New Zealand." *Industrial Relations* 37 (3): 358–87. http://dx.doi.org/10.1111/0019-8676.00092.

Bremer, Robert, and Tom Brooking. 1993. "Federated Farmers and the State." In *State and Economy in New Zealand*, ed. Brian Roper and Chris Rudd, 108–27. Auckland: Oxford University Press.

Brittan, Samuel. 1970. *Steering the Economy.* Harmondsworth: Penguin.

Britton, Andrew. 1991. *Macroeconomic Policy in Britain 1974–87.* Cambridge: Cambridge University Press.

Brown, Robert Craig. 1964. *Canada's National Policy, 1883–1900: A Study in Canadian-American Relations.* Princeton: Princeton University Press.

Brown, William. 1991. "Industrial Relations." In *Labour's Economic Policies 1974–1979*, ed. Michael Artis and David Cobham, 213–28. Manchester: Manchester University Press.

Browne, Harry. 1979. *The Rise of British Trade Unions, 1825–1914.* London: Longman.

Browne, William P. 1987. "Some Social and Political Conditions of Issue Credibility: Legislative Agendas in American States." *Polity* 20 (2): 296–315. http://dx.doi.org/10.2307/3234784.

Browne, William P. 1998. *Groups, Interests, and U.S. Public Policy.* Washington: Georgetown University Press.

Brysk, Alison. 2005. "Global Good Samaritans? Human Rights Foreign Policy in Costa Rica." *Global Governance* 11 (3): 445–66.

Buckle, Robert. 1987. "Sequencing and the Role of the Foreign Exchange Market." In *Economic Liberalisation in New Zealand*, ed. Alan Bollard and Robert Buckle, 236–30. Wellington: Allen and Unwin.

Budge, Ian. 1993. "Relative Decline as a Political Issue: Ideological Motivations of the Politico-Economic Debate in Post-War Britain." *Contemporary Review (London, England)* 7 (1): 1–23. http://dx.doi.org/10.1080/13619469308581234.

Bulpitt, Jim. 1986. "The Discipline of the New Democracy: Mrs Thatcher's Domestic Statecraft." *Political Studies* 34 (1): 19–39. http://dx.doi.org/10.1111/j.1467-9248. 1986.tb01870.x.

Burch, Kurt. 2002. "Toward a Constructivist Comparative Politics." In *Constructivism and Comparative Politics*, ed. Daniel M. Green, 60–87. Armonk, NY: M.E. Sharpe.

Burnham, Peter. 2007. "The Politicisation of Monetary Policy-Making in Postwar Britain." *British Politics* 2 (3): 395–419. http://dx.doi.org/10.1057/palgrave.bp.4200074.

Burton, Jocelyn. 2001. "Changing the Rules: The Nil Wage Order and New Zealand Industrial Relations in the 1960s." M.A. Thesis, Wellington, Victoria University of Wellington.

Butler, David, and Dennis Kavanagh. 1974. *The British General Election of February 1974*. London: Macmillan.

Butler, David, and Dennis Kavanagh. 1975. *The British General Election of October 1974*. London: Macmillan.

Butlin, Matthew W. 1987. "Capital Markets." In *The Australian Economy in the Long Run*, ed. Rodney Maddock and Ian W. McLean, 229–247. Cambridge: Cambridge University Press.

Cairncross, Alec. 1992. *The British Economy since 1945*. Oxford: Blackwell.

Cairncross, Alec. 1996. "The Heath Government and the British Economy." In *The Heath Government 1970–1974: A Reappraisal*, ed. Stuart Ball and Anthony Seldon, 107–38. London: Longman.

Callaghan, James. 1987. *Time and Chance*. London: Collins.

Callaghan, P.S. 1983."Idealism and Arbitration in H.B. Higgins' New Province for Law and Order." *Journal of Australian Studies* 7 (13): 56–66. http://dx.doi.org/10.1080/14443058309386874.

Campbell, Iain, and Peter Brosnan. 1999. "Labour Market Deregulation in Australia: The Slow Combustion Approach to Workplace Change." *International Review of Applied Economics* 13 (3): 353–94. http://dx.doi.org/10.1080/026921799101599.

Campbell, John L. 1998. "Institutional Analysis and the Role of Ideas in Political Economy." *Theory and Society* 27 (3): 377–409. http://dx.doi. org/10.1023/A:1006871114987.

Campbell, John L. 2002."Ideas, Politics and Public Policy." *Annual Review of Sociology* 28 (1): 21–38. http://dx.doi.org/10.1146/annurev.soc.28.110601.141111.

Carew, Edna. 1988. *Keating: A Biography.* Sydney: Allen and Unwin.

Carrington, Peter. 1988. *Reflect on Things Past: The Memoirs of Lord Carrington.* London: Collins.

Castle, Barbara. 1984. *The Castle Diaries 1968–70.* London: Weidenfeld and Nicolson.

Castles, Francis G. 1978. *The Social Democratic Image of Society.* London: Routledge and Kegan Paul.

Castles, Francis G. 1985. *The Working Class and Welfare: Reflections on the Political Development of the Welfare States in Australia and New Zealand, 1890–1980.* Sydney: Allen and Unwin.

Castles, Francis G. 1988. *Australian Public Policy and Economic Vulnerability: A Comparative and Historical Perspective.* Sydney: Allen and Unwin.

Castles, Francis G. 1996. "Needs-Based Strategies of Social Protection in Australia and New Zealand." In *Welfare States in Transition: National Adaptations in Global Economies,* ed. Gøsta Esping-Andersen, 88–115. London: Sage. http://dx.doi.org/10.4135/9781446216941.n4.

Castles, Francis G., Rolf Gerritsen, and Jack Vowles. 1996. "Introduction: Setting the Scene for Economic and Political Change." In *The Great Experiment: Labour Parties and Public Policy Transformation in Australia and New Zealand,* ed. Francis G. Castles, Rolf Gerritsen, and Jack Vowles, 1–12. St. Leonards, NSW: Allen and Unwin.

Castles, Francis G., and Robert D. McKinlay. 1979a. "Public Welfare Provision, Scandinavia, and the Sheer Futility of the Sociological Approach to Politics." *British Journal of Political Science* 9 (2): 157–71. http://dx.doi. org/10.1017/S0007123400001708.

Castles, Francis G., and Robert D. McKinlay. 1979b. "Does Politics Matter? An Analysis of Public Welfare Commitment in Advanced Democratic States." *European Journal of Political Research* 7 (2): 169–86. http://dx.doi. org/10.1111/j.1475-6765. 1979.tb01274.x.

Castles, Francis G., and Robert D. McKinlay. 1997. "Does Politics Matter? Increasing Complexity and Renewed Challenges." *European Journal of Political Research* 31 (1): 102–7.

Castoriadis, Cornelius. 1987. *The Imaginary Institution of Society.* Cambridge, MA: The MIT Press.

Catley, Robert. 1996. *Globalising Australian Capitalism*. Cambridge: Cambridge University Press. http://dx.doi.org/10.1017/CBO9780511597145.

Chaison, Gary N. 1996. *Union Mergers in Hard Times: The View from Five Countries*. Ithaca, NY: Cornell University Press.

Chatterjee, Srikanta. 1988. "International Trade: Structure and Policy." In *The New Zealand Economy: Issues and Policy*, ed. Stuart Birks and Srikanta Chatterjee, 274–97. Auckland: Dunmore Press.

Checkel, Jeffrey T. 1997. *Ideas and International Political Change: Soviet/Russian Behavior and the End of the Cold War*. New Haven: Yale University Press.

Checkel, Jeffrey T. 1998. "The Constructivist Turn in International Relations Theory." *World Politics* 50 (2): 324–48. http://dx.doi.org/10.1017/S0043887100008133.

Checkel, Jeffrey T. 1999. "Norms, Institutions, and National Identity in Contemporary Europe." *International Studies Quarterly* 43 (1): 83–114. http://dx.doi.org/10.1111/0020-8833.00112.

Chifley, J.B. 1953. *Things Worth Fighting For: Speeches by Joseph Benedict Chifley*. Melbourne: Australian Labor Party.

Christiansen, Thomas, Knud Erik Jørgensen, and Antje Wiener, eds. 2001. *The Social Construction of Europe*. London: Sage.

Clark, Helen. 2000. "Speech to Auckland Chamber of Commerce, 16 June 2000." Accessed 12 October 2004. http://www.executive.govt.nz/speech.cfm?speechralph=31400&SR=1.

Clarke, Peter, and Clive Trebilcock, eds. 1997. *Understanding Decline: Perceptions and Realities of British Economic Performance*. Cambridge: Cambridge University Press.

Clarke, Thomas. 1994. "The Political Economy of the UK Privatization Programme: A Blueprint for Other Countries?" In *The Political Economy of Privatization*, ed. Thomas Clarke and Christos Pitelis, 205–33. London: Routledge.

Clarkson, Stephen. 1991. "Disjunctions: Free Trade and the Paradox of Canadian Development." In *The New Era of Global Competition: State Policy and Market Power*, ed. Daniel Drache and Meric S. Gertler, 103–26. Montreal: McGill-Queen's University Press.

Clegg, Hugh A. 1971. *How to Run an Incomes Policy*. London: Heinemann.

Clegg, Hugh A. 1979. *The Changing System of Industrial Relations in Great Britain*. Oxford: Blackwell.

Coates, David. 1980. *Labour in Power? A Study of the Labour Government 1974–1979*. London: Longman.

Coates, David, and Peter Lawler, eds. 2001. *New Labour in Power*. Manchester: Manchester University Press.

Conservative Central Office. 1973. *We're Going Through with It*. London: Conservative Central Office.

Conservative Central Office. 1975. *Margaret Thatcher in North America*. London: Conservative Central Office.

Conservative Central Office. 1976. *The Right Approach: A Statement of Conservative Aims*. London: Conservative Central Office.

Conservative Central Office. 1977. *The Right Approach to the Economy: Outline of an Economic Strategy for the Next Conservative Government*. London: Conservative Central Office.

Conservative Central Office. 1979. *The Prime Minister's Address at the Conservative Conference 1979*. London: Conservative Central Office.

Conservative Central Office. 1980. *Extract from a Speech by the Rt. Hon. The Lord Hailsham of St. Marylebone, CH, Lord Chancellor, on the Subject of 'The Individual and the State'*. London: Conservative Central Office.

Cooper, Rae. 2009. "Forward with Fairness? Industrial Relations Under Labor in 2008." *Journal of Industrial Relations* 51 (3): 285–96. http://dx.doi.org/10.1177/0022185609104298.

Cooper, Rae, and Bradon Ellem. 2008. "The Neoliberal State, Trade Unions and Collective Bargaining in Australia." *British Journal of Industrial Relations* 46 (3): 532–54. http://dx.doi.org/10.1111/j.1467-8543.2008.00694.x.

Cox, Robert W. 1981. "Social Forces, States and World Orders: Beyond International Relations Theory." *Millennium: Journal of International Studies* 10 (2): 126–55. http://dx.doi.org/10.1177/03058298810100020501.

Cox, Robert W. 1983. "Gramsci, Hegemony and International Relations: An Essay on Method." *Millennium: Journal of International Studies* 12 (2): 162–75. http://dx.doi.org/10.1177/03058298830120020701.

Coxall, Bill, and Lynton Robins. 1998. *British Politics since the War*. Basingstoke: Macmillan.

Creighton, Breen. 1987. "Trade Unions, the Law and the New Right." In *The New Right's Australian Fantasy*, ed. Ken Coghill, 74–92. Fitzroy, Vic.: McPhee Gribble.

Creighton, Breen. 1997. "The Workplace Relations Act in International Perspective." *Australian Journal of Labour Law* 10 (1): 31–49.

Crepaz, Markus M.L., and Ann W. Moser. 2004. "The Impact of Collective and Competitive Veto Points on Public Expenditures in the Global Age." *Comparative Political Studies* 37 (3): 259–85. http://dx.doi.org/10.1177/0010414003262067.

Crouch, Colin. 1977. *Class Conflict and the Industrial Relations Crisis*. London: Heinemann.

Crouch, Colin. 1979. *The Politics of Industrial Relations*. Manchester: Manchester University Press.

Crouch, Colin. 1986. "Conservative Industrial Relations Policy: Towards Labour Exclusion?" In *Economic Crisis, Trade Unions, and the State*, ed. Otto Jacobi, Bob Jessop, Hans Kastendiek, and Marino Regini, 131–53. London: Croom Helm.

Culpepper, Pepper D. 2003. *Creating Cooperation: How States Develop Human Capital in Europe*. Ithaca, NY: Cornell University Press.

Czinkota, Michael R. 1985. "U. S. Trade Policy and Congress." *Columbia Journal of World Business* 20 (4): 71–7.

Dabscheck, Braham. 2008. "Industrial Relations Under the Rudd Labor Government: Establishing a New Safety Net." *The Otemon Journal of Australian Studies* 34: 67–73.

Dalziel, Paul. 1993. "The Reserve Bank Act: Reflecting Changing Relationships between State and Economy in the Twentieth Century." In *State and Economy in New Zealand*, ed. Brian Roper and Chris Rudd, 74–90. Auckland: Oxford University Press.

Dalziel, Paul, and Ralph Lattimore. 2001. *The New Zealand Macroeconomy: A Briefing on the Reforms and their Legacy*. South Melbourne: Oxford University Press.

Dannin, Ellen J. 1997. *Working Free: The Origins and Impact of New Zealand's Employment Contracts Act*. Auckland: Auckland University Press.

Davies, Andrew. 1995. *We, the Nation: The Conservative Party and the Pursuit of Power*. London: Little, Brown.

Davies, Gavyn. 1989. "A Critique of Monetarism, Old and New." In *Conquering Unemployment: The Case for Economic Growth*, ed. Jon Shields, 49–144. Basingstoke: Macmillan.

Day, Sir Robin. 1993. *But with Respect*. London: Weidenfeld and Nicolson.

De Long, J. Bradford. 2000. "The Triumph of Monetarism?" *Journal of Economic Perspectives* 14 (1): 83–94. http://dx.doi.org/10.1257/jep.14.1.83.

Deane, Roderick S. 1995. *People, Power and Politics: The Dynamics of Economic Change*. Wellington: New Zealand Institute of Economic Research.

Deigan, Russell. 1991. *Investing in Canada: The Pursuit and Regulation of Foreign Investment*. Scarborough, Ont: De Boc.

Denham, Andrew, and Mark Garnett. 2001a. "From 'Guru' to 'Godfather': Keith Joseph, 'New' Labour and the British Conservative Tradition." *Political Quarterly* 72 (1): 97–106. http://dx.doi.org/10.1111/1467-923X.00347.

Denham, Andrew, and Mark Garnett. 2001b. *Keith Joseph*. London: Acumen.

Department of the Prime Minister and Cabinet. 1991. *Building a Competitive Australia*. Canberra: Australian Government Printing Service.

Destler, I.M. 1992. *American Trade Politics: System under Stress*. Washington: Institute for International Economics.

Devine, Patricia G. 1989. "Stereotypes and Prejudice: Their Automatic and Controlled Components." *Journal of Personality and Social Psychology* 56 (1): 5–18. http://dx.doi.org/10.1037/0022-3514.56.1.5.

Dickins, Amanda. 2006. "The Evolution of International Political Economy." *International Affairs* 82 (3): 479–92. http://dx.doi.org/10.1111/j.1468-2346. 2006.00546.x.

Disney, Richard, Amanda Gosling, and Stephen Machin. 1995. "British Unions in Decline: Determinants of the 1980s Fall in Union Recognition." *Industrial & Labor Relations Review* 48 (3): 403–19. http://dx.doi. org/10.2307/2524771.

Dobbin, Frank. 2001. "Why the Economy Reflects the Polity: Early Rail Policy in Britain, France, and the United States." In *The Sociology of Economic Life*, ed. Mark Granovetter and Richard Swedberg, 401–24. Boulder, CO: Westview Press.

Dobbin, Frank. 2005. "Is Globalization Making Us All the Same?" *British Journal of Industrial Relations* 43 (4): 569–76. http://dx.doi. org/10.1111/j.1467-8543.2005.00471.x.

Dobbin, Frank, Beth Simmons, and Geoffrey Garrett. 2007. "The Global Diffusion of Public Policies: Social Construction, Coercion, Competition, or Learning?" *Annual Review of Sociology* 33 (1): 449–72. http://dx.doi. org/10.1146/annurev.soc.33.090106.142507.

Dobbin, Frank R. 1993. "The Social Construction of the Great Depression: Industrial Policy during the 1930s in the United States, Britain, and France." *Theory and Society* 22 (1): 1–56. http://dx.doi.org/10.1007/BF00993447.

Doern, G. Bruce and John Atherton. 1987. "The Tories and the Crowns: Restraining and Privatizing in a Political Minefield." In *How Ottawa Spends, 1987–88: Restraining the State*, ed. Michael J. Prince, 129–75. Toronto: Methuen.

Doern, G. Bruce and Brian W. Tomlin. 1991. *Faith and Fear: The Free Trade Story*. Toronto: Stoddart.

Doern, G. Bruce and Glen Toner. 1985. *The Politics of Energy: The Development and Implementation of the NEP*. Toronto: Methuen.

Doran, Charles F., and Gregory P. Marchildon, eds. 1994. *The NAFTA Puzzle: Political Parties and Trade in North America*. Boulder: Westview.

Dorey, Peter. 1993. "One Step at a Time: The Conservative Government's Approach to the Reform of Industrial Relations Since 1979." *Political Quarterly* 64 (1): 24–36. http://dx.doi.org/10.1111/j.1467-923X. 1993.tb00311.x.

Dorey, Peter. 1995a. *British Politics since 1945*. Oxford: Blackwell.

Dorey, Peter. 1995b. *The Conservative Party and the Trade Unions*. London: Routledge. http://dx.doi.org/10.4324/9780203202807.

Dorey, Peter. 2006. "Industrial Relations Imbroglio." In *The Labour Governments 1964–1970*, ed. Peter Dorey, 92–107. London: Routledge. http://dx.doi.org/10.4324/9780203327227_chapter_6.

Dorey, Peter. 2009. "Individual Liberty Versus Industrial Order: Conservatives and the Trade Union Closed Shop 1946–90." *Contemporary British History* 23 (2): 221–44. http://dx.doi.org/10.1080/13619460802636458.

Dorfman, Gerald. 1979. *Government versus Trade Unionism in British Politics*. London: Macmillan.

Douglas, Roger. 1980. *There's Got to be a Better Way! A Practical ABC to Solving New Zealand's Major Problems*. Wellington: Fourth Estate Books.

Douglas, Roger. 1993. *Unfinished Business*. Auckland: Random House New Zealand.

Douglas, Roger, and Louise Callan. 1987. *Toward Prosperity*. Auckland: D. Bateman.

Drache, Daniel. 1996. "From Keynes to K-Mart: Competitiveness in a Corporate Age." In *States Against Markets: The Limits of Globalization*, ed. Robert Boyer and Daniel Drache, 31–61. London: Routledge.

Drezner, Daniel W. 2001. "Globalization and Policy Convergence." *International Studies Review* 3 (1): 53–78.

Driver, Stephen, and Luke Martell. 1998. *New Labour: Politics after Thatcherism*. Cambridge: Polity Press.

Drori, Gili S., John W. Meyer, and Hokyu Hwang, eds. 2006. *Globalization and Organization: World Society and Organizational Change*. Oxford: Oxford University Press.

Duncan, Ian, and Alan Bollard. 1992. *Corporatization and Privatization: Lessons from New Zealand*. Auckland: Oxford University Press.

Dutton, David. 1997. *British Politics since 1945: The Rise, Fall and Rebirth of Consensus*. Oxford: Blackwell.

Dyson, Stephen Benedict. 2009. "Cognitive Style and Foreign Policy: Margaret Thatcher's Black-and-White Thinking." *International Political Science Review* 30 (1): 33–48. http://dx.doi.org/10.1177/0192512108097055.

Dyster, Barrie, and David Meredith. 1990. *Australia in the International Economy in the Twentieth Century*. Cambridge: Cambridge University Press.

Easton, Brian, ed. 1989. *The Making of Rogernomics*. Auckland: Auckland University Press.

Easton, Brian. 1994. "How Did the Health Reforms Blitzkrieg Fail?" *Political Science (Wellington, N.Z.)* 46 (2): 215–33. http://dx.doi.org/10.1177/003231879404600205.

Easton, Brian. 1997. *The Commercialisation of New Zealand*. Auckland: Auckland University Press.

Easton, Brian. 1999. *The Whimpering of the State: Policy after MMP*. Auckland: Auckland University Press.

Easton, Brian H., and Rolf Gerritsen. 1996. "Economic Reform: Parallels and Divergences." In *The Great Experiment: Labour Parties and Public Policy Transformation in Australia and New Zealand*, ed. Francis G. Castles, Rolf Gerritsen, and Jack Vowles, 22–47. St. Leonards, NSW: Allen and Unwin.

Edwards, Geoff W., and Alistair S. Watson. 1978. "Agricultural Policy." In *Surveys of Australian Economics*, ed. Fred H. Gruen, 189–239. Sydney: Allen and Unwin.

Eichbaum, Chris. 1992. "Market Liberalisation in New Zealand: Fightback! in Practice?" In *Markets, Morals and Manifestos: Fightback! and the Politics of Economic Rationalism in the 1990s*, ed. Peter Vintila and John Phillimore, 221–36. Murdoch, WA: Institute for Science and Technology, Murdoch University.

Elgström, Ole. 2000. "Norm Negotiations: The Construction of New Norms Regarding Gender and Development in EU Foreign Aid Policy." *Journal of European Public Policy* 7 (3): 457–76. http://dx.doi.org/10.1080/13501760050086125.

Ellem, Bradon, Marian Baird, Rae Cooper, and Russell Lansbury. 2005. "'WorkChoices': Myth-Making at Work." *Journal of Australian Political Economy* 56: 13–31.

Ellickson, Robert C. 1998. "Law and Economics Discovers Social Norms." *Journal of Legal Studies* 27 (S2): 537–52. http://dx.doi.org/10.1086/468033.

Emerson, Craig. 2010. "The Future of Trade Policy in an Uncertain World." Australian Government, Department of Foreign Affairs and Trade. Accessed 31 August 2011. http://www.trademinister.gov.au/speeches/2010/ce_sp_101210.html.

Emy, Hugh V., Owen E. Hughes, and Race Mathews, eds. 1993. *Whitlam Re-visited: Policy Development, Policies, and Outcomes*. Leichhardt, NSW: Pluto Press.

Esping-Andersen, Gøsta. 1985. *Politics against Markets: The Social Democratic Road to Power*. Princeton: Princeton University Press.

Evans, Eric J. 2004. *Thatcher and Thatcherism*. London: Routledge.

Evans, Lewis. 1987. "Farming in a Changing Economic Environment." In *Economic Liberalisation in New Zealand*, ed. Alan Bollard and Robert Buckle, 102–20. Wellington: Allen and Unwin.

Evans, Peter. 1997. "The Eclipse of the State? Reflections on Stateness in an Era of Globalization."*World Politics* 50 (1): 62–87. http://dx.doi.org/10.1017/S0043887100014726.

Fairbrother, Peter. 1997. *The Withering Away of the Australian State: Privatisation and its Implications for Labour*. Melbourne: National Key Centre in Industrial Relations, Monash University.

Falk, Richard. 1997. "State of Siege: Will Globalization Win Out?" *International Affairs* 73 (1): 123–36. http://dx.doi.org/10.2307/2623553.

Farnham, David. 1990. "Trade Union Policy 1979–89: Restriction or Reform?" In *Public Policy under Thatcher*, ed. Stephen P. Savage and Lynton Robins, 60–74. New York: St. Martin's Press.

Feigenbaum, Harvey, Jeffrey Henig, and Chris Hamnett. 1999. *Shrinking the State: The Political Underpinnings of Privatization*. Cambridge: Cambridge University Press.

Finlayson, Jock A., with Stefano Bertasi. 1992. "Evolution of Canadian Postwar International Trade Policy." In *Canadian Foreign Policy and International Economic Regimes*, ed. A. Claire Cutler and Mark W. Zacher, 19–46. Vancouver: UBC Press.

Finnemore, Martha. 1996a. "Constructing Norms of Humanitarian Intervention." In *The Culture of National Security: Norms and Identity in World Politics*, ed. Peter J. Katzenstein, 153–85. New York: Columbia University Press.

Finnemore, Martha. 1996b. *National Interests in International Society*. Ithaca, NY: Cornell University Press.

Finnemore, Martha. 1996c. "Norms, Culture, and World Politics: Insights from Sociology's Institutionalism." *International Organization* 50 (2): 325–47. http://dx.doi.org/10.1017/S0020818300028587.

Finnemore, Martha. 2003. *The Purpose of Intervention: Changing Beliefs about the Use of Force*. Ithaca, NY: Cornell University Press.

Finnemore, Martha, and Kathryn Sikkink. 1998. "International Norm Dynamics and Political Change." *International Organization* 52 (4): 887–917. http://dx.doi.org/10.1162/002081898550789.

Flanders, Allan D. 1974. "The Tradition of Voluntarism." *British Journal of Industrial Relations* 12 (3): 352–70. http://dx.doi.org/10.1111/j.1467-8543. 1974. tb00012.x.

Florini, Ann. 1996. "The Evolution of International Norms." *International Studies Quarterly* 40 (3): 363–89. http://dx.doi.org/10.2307/2600716.

Forbes, H.D. 1987. "Hartz-Horowitz at Twenty: Nationalism, Toryism and Socialism in Canada and the United States." *Canadian Journal of Political Science* 20 (2): 287–315. http://dx.doi.org/10.1017/S0008423900049453.

Forman-Peck, James, and Robert Millward. 1994. *Public and Private Ownership of British Industry, 1820–1990*. Oxford: Clarendon Press. http://dx.doi.org/10.1093/acprof:oso/9780198203599.001.0001.

Forsythe, David P. 1991. *The Internationalization of Human Rights*. Lexington, MA: Lexington Books.

Frankel, Boris. 1997. "Beyond Labourism and Socialism: How the Australian Labor Party Developed the Model of 'New Labor'." *New Left Review* 221: 3–33.

Fraser, W. Hamish. 1999. *A History of British Trade Unionism 1700–1988*. Basingstoke: Macmillan.

Fredman, Sandra. 1992. "The New Rights: Labour Law and Ideology in the Thatcher Years." *Oxford Journal of Legal Studies* 12 (1): 24–44. http://dx.doi.org/10.1093/ojls/12.1.24.

Freebairn, John W. 1987. "Natural Resource Industries." In *The Australian Economy in the Long Run*, ed. Rodney Maddock and Ian W. McLean, 133–164. Cambridge: Cambridge University Press.

Freeman, Richard, and Jeffrey Pelletier. 1991. "The Impact of Industrial Relations Legislation on British Union Density." NBER Working Paper No. 3167. Cambridge, MA: National Bureau of Economic Research.

Friedman, Milton. 1968. *Dollars and Deficits: Inflation, Monetary Policy and the Balance of Payments*. Englewood Cliffs, NJ: Prentice-Hall.

Friedman, Milton. 1970. *The Optimum Quantity of Money, and Other Essays*. Chicago: Aldine.

Frohlich, Norman, Joe A. Oppenheimer, and Oran R. Young. 1971. *Political Leadership and Collective Goods*. Princeton: Princeton University Press.

Gamble, Andrew. 1988. "Privatisation, Thatcherism and the British State." *Journal of Law and Society* 16 (1): 1–20. http://dx.doi.org/10.2307/1409974.

Gamble, Andrew. 1990. *Britain in Decline: Economic Policy, Political Strategy and the British State*. New York: St. Martin's Press.

Gamble, Andrew. 1994. *The Free Economy and the Strong State*. Basingstoke: Macmillan.

Garbarino, Joseph W. 1973. "The British Experiment with Industrial Relations Reform." *Industrial & Labor Relations Review* 26 (2): 793–804. http://dx.doi.org/10.2307/2521682.

Garnaut, Ross. 1994. "Australia." In *The Political Economy of Policy Reform*, ed. John Williamson, 51–72. Washington: Institute for International Economics.

Garrett, Geoffrey, and Peter Lange. 1989. "Government Partisanship and Economic Performance: When and How Does 'Who Governs' Matter?" *Journal of Politics* 51 (3): 676–93. http://dx.doi.org/10.2307/2131501.

Giaimo, Susan. 2002. *Markets and Medicine: The Politics of Health Care Reform in Britain, Germany, and the United States.* Ann Arbor: University of Michigan Press.

Giddens, Anthony. 1999. *Runaway World: How Globalisation is Reshaping our Lives.* London: Profile Press.

Giustozzi, Antonio. 2011. *The Art of Coercion: The Primitive Accumulation and Management of Coercive Power.* New York: Columbia University Press.

Glyn, Andrew, and Stephen Machin. 1996. *Colliery Closures and the Decline of the UK Coal Industry.* Oxford: Institute of Economics and Statistics, University of Oxford. http://dx.doi.org/10.1111/1467-8543.00048.

Godard, John. 2003. "Do Labor Laws Matter? The Density Decline and Convergence Thesis Revisited." *Industrial Relations* 42 (3): 458–92. http://dx.doi.org/10.1111/1468-232X.00300.

Goffman, Erving. 1974. *Frame Analysis.* Cambridge, MA: Harvard University Press.

Goldfinch, Shaun. 2000. *Remaking New Zealand and Australian Economic Policy: Ideas, Institutions and Policy Communities.* Washington: Georgetown University Press.

Goldfinch, Shaun. 2003. "The State." In *New Zealand Government and Politics,* ed. Raymond Miller, 547–56. Oxford: Oxford University Press.

Goldfinch, Shaun, and Daniel Malpass. 2007. "The Polish Shipyard: Myth, Economic History and Economic Policy Reform in New Zealand." *Australian Journal of Politics and History* 53 (1): 118–37. http://dx.doi.org/10.1111/j.1467-8497. 2007.00446.x.

Goldfinch, Shaun, and Brian Roper. 1993. "Treasury's Role in State Policy Formation during the Post-War Era." In *State and Economy in New Zealand,* ed. Brian Roper and Chris Rudd, 50–73. Auckland: Oxford University Press.

Goldfinch, Shaun, and Philippa Mein Smith. 2006. "Compulsory Arbitration and the Australasian Model of State Development: Policy Transfer, Learning, and Innovation." *Journal of Policy History* 18 (4): 419–45. http://dx.doi.org/10.1353/jph. 2006.0012.

Goldfinch, Shaun, and Paul 't Hart. 2003. "Leadership and Institutional Reform: Engineering Macroeconomic Policy Change in Australia." *Governance: An International Journal of Policy, Administration and Institutions* 16 (2): 235–70. http://dx.doi.org/10.1111/1468-0491.00215.

Goldstein, Judith. 1989. "The Impact of Ideas on Trade Policy: The Origins of U.S. Agricultural and Manufacturing Policies." *International Organization* 43 (1): 31–71. http://dx.doi.org/10.1017/S0020818300004550.

Goldstein, Judith, and Robert O. Keohane. 1993. "Ideas and Foreign Policy: An Analytical Framework." In *Ideas and Foreign Policy: Beliefs, Institutions, and Political Change*, ed. Judith Goldstein and Robert O. Keohane, 3–30. Ithaca, NY: Cornell University Press.

Goodhart, Charles. 1989. "The Conduct of Monetary Policy." *Economic Journal* 99 (396): 293–346. http://dx.doi.org/10.2307/2234028.

Gould, J.D. 1982. *The Rake's Progress? The New Zealand Economy Since 1945*. Auckland: Hodder and Stoughton.

Granatstein, Jack L. and J. Mackay Hitsman. 1977. *Broken Promises: A History of Conscription in Canada*. Toronto: Oxford University Press.

Greenwald, Anthony J., and Mahzarin R. Banaji. 1995. "Implicit Social Cognition: Attitudes, Self-Esteem, and Stereotypes." *Psychological Review* 102 (1): 4–27. http://dx.doi.org/10.1037/0033-295X.102.1.4.

Gritsch, Maria. 2005. "The Nation-State and Economic Globalization: Soft Geo-politics and Increased State Autonomy?" *Review of International Political Economy* 12 (1): 1–25. http://dx.doi.org/10.1080/09692290500049854.

Gustafson, Barry. 1986. *The First 50 Years: A History of the New Zealand National Party*. Auckland: Reed Methuen.

Guzzini, Stefano. 2000. "A Reconstruction of Constructivism in International Relations." *European Journal of International Relations* 6 (2): 147–82. http://dx.doi.org/10.1177/1354066100006002001.

Habermas, Jürgen. 1979. *Communication and the Evolution of Society*. Boston: Beacon Press.

Habermas, Jürgen. 1984. *The Theory of Communicative Action, Volume One*. Boston: Beacon Press.

Habermas, Jürgen. 1999. "The European Nation-State and the Pressures of Globalization." *New Left Review* 235: 46–59.

Hall, Maximilian. 1987. *Financial Deregulation: A Comparative Study of Australia and the United Kingdom*. Basingstoke: Macmillan.

Hall, Peter A. 1986. *Governing the Economy: The Politics of State Intervention in Britain and France*. Oxford: Blackwell.

Hall, Peter A. 1989. "Conclusion: The Politics of Keynesian Ideas." In *The Political Power of Economic Ideas: Keynesianism across Nations*, ed. Peter A. Hall, 361–91. Princeton: Princeton University Press.

Hall, Peter A. 1992. "The Movement from Keynesianism to Monetarism: Institutional Analysis and British Economic Policy in the 1970s." In *Structuring Politics: Historical Institutionalism in Comparative Analysis*, ed. Sven Steinmo, Kathleen Thelen, and Frank Longstreth, 90-113. Cambridge: Cambridge University Press. http://dx.doi.org/10.1017/CBO9780511528125.005.

Hall, Peter A. 1993. "Policy Paradigms, Social Learning, and the State: The Case of Economic Policymaking in Britain." *Comparative Politics* 25 (3): 275–96. http://dx.doi.org/10.2307/422246.

Hall, Richard. 2006. "Australian Industrial Relations in 2005—The WorkChoices Revolution." *Journal of Industrial Relations* 48 (3): 291–303. http://dx.doi.org/10.1177/0022185606064786.

Hall, Richard. 2008. "The Politics of Industrial Relations in Australia in 2007." *Journal of Industrial Relations* 50 (3): 371–82. http://dx.doi.org/10.1177/0022185608089994.

Hall, Stuart. 1985. "Signification, Representation, Ideology: Althusser and the Post-Structuralist Debates." *Critical Studies in Mass Communication* 2 (2): 91–114. http://dx.doi.org/10.1080/15295038509360070.

Hall, Stuart. 1988. "The Toad in the Garden: Thatcherism Among the Theorists." In *Marxism and the Interpretation of Culture*, ed. Cary Nelson and Lawrence Grossberg, 35–57. Urbana, IL: University of Illinois Press.

Hall, Tony. 1981. *King Coal: Miners, Coal and Britain's Industrial Future*. Harmondsworth: Penguin.

Halliday, Fred. 2000. "Culture and International Relations: A New Reductionism?" In *Confronting the Political in International Relations*, ed. Michi Ebata and Beverly Neufeld, 47–71. New York: St. Martin's Press.

Hamilton, Carl, and Dag Rolander. 1993. *Att leda Sverige in i Krisen: moral och politik i nedgångstid*. Stockholm: Norstedts.

Hamilton, David L., and Tina K. Trolier. 1986. "Stereotypes and Stereotyping: An Overview of the Cognitive Approach." In *Prejudice, Discrimination, and Racism*, ed. Samuel L. Gaertner and John F. Dovidio, 127–63. New York: Academic Press.

Hancock, Keith. 1999. "Labour Market Deregulation in Australia." In *Reshaping the Labour Market: Regulation, Efficiency and Equality in Australia*, ed. Sue Richardson, 38–85. Cambridge: Cambridge University Press.

Hancock, Keith, and Don Rawson. 1993. "The Metamorphosis of Australian Industrial Relations." *British Journal of Industrial Relations* 31 (4): 489–513. http://dx.doi.org/10.1111/j.1467-8543. 1993.tb00410.x.

Hancock, W.K. 1930. *Australia*. London: Ernest Benn.

Hanson, Charles. 1991. *Taming the Trade Unions: A Guide to the Thatcher Government's Employment Reforms, 1980–1990*. London: Macmillan.

Harbridge, Raymond, and Anthony Honeybone. 1996. "External Legitimacy of Unions: Trends in New Zealand." *Journal of Labor Research* 17 (3): 425–44. http://dx.doi.org/10.1007/BF02685858.

Harbridge, Raymond, and Pat Walsh. 1985. "Legislation Prohibiting the Closed Shop in New Zealand: Its Introduction and Consequences." *Journal*

of Industrial Relations 27 (2): 191–206. http://dx.doi.org/10.1177/0022185685
02700204.

Harper, David, and Girol Karacaoglu. 1987. "Financial Policy Reform in New
Zealand." In *Economic Liberalisation in New Zealand,* ed. Alan Bollard and
Robert Buckle, 206–35. Wellington: Allen and Unwin.

Harris, Kenneth. 1988. *Thatcher.* London: Weidenfeld and Nicolson.

Hart, Michael, with Bill Dymond and Colin Richardson. 1994. *Decision at
Midnight: Inside the Canada-US Free-Trade Negotiations.* Vancouver: UBC
Press.

Hawke, G.R. 1985. *The Making of New Zealand: An Economic History.*
Cambridge: Cambridge University Press.

Hay, Colin. 1994a. "Labour's Thatcherite Revisionism: Playing the 'Politics of
Catch-Up'." *Political Studies* 42 (4): 700–7. http://dx.doi.org/10.1111/j.1467-9248.
1994.tb00307.x.

Hay, Colin. 1994b. "The Structural and Ideological Contradictions of Britain's
Post-War Reconstruction." *Capital and Class* 18 (3): 25–59. http://dx.doi.
org/10.1177/030981689405400103.

Hay, Colin. 1996. "Narrating Crisis: The Discursive Construction of the
'Winter of Discontent'." *Sociology* 30 (2): 253–77. http://dx.doi.org/10.1177/003
8038596030002004.

Hay, Colin. 1999a. "Crisis and the Structural Transformation of the State:
Interrogating the Process of Change." *British Journal of Politics and
International Relations* 1 (3): 317–44. http://dx.doi.org/10.1111/1467-856X.00018.

Hay, Colin. 1999b. *The Political Economy of New Labour: Labouring under False
Pretences?* Manchester: Manchester University Press.

Hay, Colin. 2000. "Contemporary Capitalism, Globalization, Regionalization
and the Persistence of National Variation." *Review of International Studies* 26
(4): 509–31. http://dx.doi.org/10.1017/S026021050000509X.

Hay, Colin. 2001. "The 'Crisis' of Keynesianism and the Rise of Neoliberalism
in Britain: An Ideational Institutional Approach." In *The Rise of
Neoliberalism and Institutional Analysis,* ed. John L. Campbell and Ove K.
Pedersen, 192–218. Princeton: Princeton University Press.

Hay, Colin. 2004a. "Common Trajectories, Variable Paces, Divergent
Outcomes? Models of European Capitalism under Conditions of Complex
Economic Interdependence." *Review of International Political Economy* 11 (2):
231–62. http://dx.doi.org/10.1080/09692290420001672796.

Hay, Colin. 2004b. "Ideas, Interests and Institutions in the Comparative
Political Economy of Great Transformations." *Review of International Political
Economy* 11 (1): 204–26. http://dx.doi.org/10.1080/0969229042000179811.

Hay, Colin. 2004c. "The Normalizing Role of Rationalist Assumptions in the Institutional Embedding of Neoliberalism." *Economy and Society* 33 (4): 500–27. http://dx.doi.org/10.1080/0308514042000285260.

Hay, Colin. 2007. *Why We Hate Politics*. Cambridge: Polity Press.

Hay, Colin, and Ben Rosamond. 2002. "Globalization, European Integration and the Discursive Construction of Economic Imperatives." *Journal of European Public Policy* 9 (2): 147–67. http://dx.doi.org/10.1080/13501760110120192.

Hayden, Peter R., and Jeffrey H. Burns. 1976. *The Regulation of Foreign Investment in Canada*. Scarborough, Ont.: Prentice-Hall.

Healey, Nigel M. 1993. "The Conservative Government's 'Fight against Inflation': Ten Years without Cheers." In *Britain's Economic Miracle: Myth or Reality?* ed. Nigel M. Healey, 127–48. London: Routledge. http://dx.doi.org/10.4324/9780203418482.

Heath, Anthony, and Geoffrey Garrett. 1991. "The Extension of Popular Capitalism." In *Understanding Political Change: The British Voter, 1964–1987*, ed. Anthony Heath , Roger Jowell, John Curtice, Geoff Evans, Julia Field, and Sharon Witherspoon, 120–35. Oxford: Pergamon Press.

Heffernan, Richard. 2001. *New Labour and Thatcherism*. Basingstoke: Palgrave. http://dx.doi.org/10.1057/9780230598430.

Henderson, Gerard. 1995. *A Howard Government? Inside the Coalition*. Pymble, NSW: HarperCollins.

Hendy, John. 1991. *The Conservative Employment Laws: A National and International Perspective*. London: Institute of Employment Rights.

Hibbs, Douglas A., Jr. 1977. "Political Parties and Macroeconomic Policy." *American Political Science Review* 71 (4): 1467–87. http://dx.doi.org/10.2307/1961490.

Hibbs, Douglas A., Jr. 1986. "Political Parties and Macroeconomic Policies and Outcomes in the United States." *American Economic Review* 76 (2): 66–70.

Hibbs, Douglas A., Jr. 1992. "Partisan Theory after Fifteen Years." *European Journal of Political Economy* 8 (3): 361–73. http://dx.doi.org/10.1016/0176-2680(92)90001-W.

Hills, John, John Ditch, and Howard Glennerster. 1994. *Beveridge and Social Security: An International Retrospective*. Oxford: Clarendon Press.

Hince, Kevin, and Martin Vranken. 1991. "A Controversial Reform of New Zealand Labour Law: The Employment Contracts Act 1991." *International Labour Review* 130 (4): 475–93.

Hobson, John M., and Leonard Seabrooke, eds. 2007. *Everyday Politics of the World Economy*. Cambridge: Cambridge University Press.

Hofferbert, Richard I., and David Louis Cingranelli. 1996. "Public Policy and Administration: Comparative Policy Analysis." In *A New Handbook of Political Science*, ed. Robert E. Goodin and Hans-Dieter Klingemann, 593–609. Oxford: Oxford University Press. http://dx.doi.org/10.1093/0198294 719.003.0025.

Holmes, John. 1993. "From Three Industries to One: Towards an Integrated North American Automobile Industry." In *Driving Continentally: National Policies and the North American Auto Industry*, ed. Maureen Appel Molot, 23–61. Ottawa: Carleton University Press.

Holmes, Martin. 1985. *The Labour Government, 1974–79: Political Aims and Economic Reality*. New York: St. Martin's Press.

Holt, James. 1986. *Compulsory Arbitration in New Zealand: The First Forty Years*. Auckland: Auckland University Press.

Hopf, Ted. 1998. "The Promise of Constructivism in International Relations Theory." *International Security* 23 (1): 171–200. http://dx.doi.org/10.2307/2539267.

Hopf, Ted. 2002. *Social Construction of International Politics: Identities and Foreign Policies, Moscow, 1955 and 1999*. Ithaca, NY: Cornell University Press.

Horne, Donald. 1976. *Death of the Lucky Country*. Ringwood, Vic.: Penguin.

Horowitz, Gad. 1966. "Conservatism, Liberalism and Socialism in Canada: An Interpretation." *Canadian Journal of Political Science* 32 (2): 143–71. http://dx.doi.org/10.2307/139794.

Horton, Sylvia. 1990. "Local Government 1979–89: A Decade of Change." In *Public Policy under Thatcher*, ed. Stephen P. Savage and Lynton Robins, 172–86. New York: St. Martin's Press.

House of Commons Debates, Official Report (Hansard). Various years. Ottawa: Supply and Services Canada.

Howe, Geoffrey. 1981. *Privatisation: The Way Ahead*. London: Conservative Political Centre.

Howell, Chris. 2005. *Trade Unions and the State: The Construction of Industrial Relations Institutions in Britain, 1890–2000*. Princeton: Princeton University Press.

Huber, John D., and G. Bingham Powell. 1994. "Congruence between Citizens and Policymakers in Two Visions of Liberal Democracy." *World Politics* 46 (3): 291–326. http://dx.doi.org/10.2307/2950684.

Huzzard, Tony, Denis Gregory, and Regan Scott, eds. 2004. *Strategic Unionism and Partnership: Boxing or Dancing?* Basingstoke: Palgrave Macmillan.

Hyman, Richard. 1987. "Trade Unions and the Law: Papering over the Cracks." *Capital and Class* 11 (1): 93–113. http://dx.doi.org/10.1177/030981688703100107.

Ingebritsen, Christine. 2002. "Norm Entrepreneurs: Scandinavia's Role in World Politics." *Cooperation and Conflict* 37 (1): 11–23. http://dx.doi.org/10.117 7/0010836702037001689.

International Labour Office. Various years. *Year Book of Labour Statistics.* Geneva: International Labour Office.

Inwood, Gregory J. 2005. *Continentalizing Canada: The Politics and Legacy of the Macdonald Royal Commission.* Toronto: University of Toronto Press.

Jacobsen, John Kurt. 1995. "Much Ado about Ideas: The Cognitive Factor in Economic Policy." *World Politics* 47 (2): 283–310. http://dx.doi.org/10.1017/ S0043887100016117.

Jacobsen, John Kurt. 2003. "Duelling Constructivisms: A Post-Mortem on the Ideas Debate in Mainstream IR/IPE." *Review of International Studies* 29 (1): 39–60. http://dx.doi.org/10.1017/S0260210503000032.

Jaensch, Dean. 1989. *The Hawke-Keating Hijack: The ALP in Transition.* Sydney: Allen and Unwin.

James, Colin. 1992. *New Territory: The Transformation of New Zealand, 1984–92.* Wellington: Bridget Williams Books.

James, Leighton, and Raymond Markey. 2006. "Class and Labour: The British Labour Party and the Australian Labor Party Compared." *Labour History* 90: 23–42. http://dx.doi.org/10.2307/27516112.

James, Patrick. 1990. "The Canadian National Energy Program and Its Aftermath: A Game-theoretic Analysis." *Canadian Public Policy* 16 (2): 174– 90. http://dx.doi.org/10.2307/3550964.

James, Patrick. 1993. "Energy Policy in Canada, 1980–1981: Threat Power in a Sequential Game." *Canadian Journal of Political Science* 26 (1): 31–59. http:// dx.doi.org/10.1017/S0008423900002432.

James, Patrick, and Robert Michelin. 1989. "The Canadian National Energy Program and its Aftermath: Perspectives on an Era of Confrontation." *American Review of Canadian Studies* 19 (1): 59–81. http://dx.doi. org/10.1080/02722018909481732.

Jenkins, Peter. 1970. *The Battle of Downing Street.* London: Charles Knight.

Jenkins, Peter. 1988. *Mrs. Thatcher's Revolution: The Ending of the Socialist Era.* London: Pan Books.

Jepperson, Ronald L., Alexander Wendt, and Peter J. Katzenstein. 1996. "Norms, Identity, and Culture in National Security." In *The Culture of National Security: Norms and Identity in World Politics*, ed. Peter J. Katzenstein, 33–75. New York: Columbia University Press.

Jessop, Bob. 2002. "Liberalism, Neoliberalism, and Urban Governance: A State-Theoretical Perspective." *Antipode* 34 (3): 452–72. http://dx.doi. org/10.1111/1467-8330.00250.

Jessop, Bob. 2003. "From Thatcherism to New Labour: Neo-Liberalism, Workfarism, and Labour Market Regulation." Department of Sociology, Lancaster University. Accessed 30 September 2011. http://www.lancs.ac.uk/fass/sociology/papers/jessop-from-thatcherism-to-new-labour.pdf.

Jessop, Bob. 2004. "Critical Semiotic Analysis and Cultural Political Economy." *Critical Discourse Studies* 1 (2): 159–74. http://dx.doi.org/10.1080/17405900410001674506.

Jessop, Bob. 2005. "Cultural Political Economy, the Knowledge-Based Economy and the State." In *The Technological Economy*, ed. Andrew Barry and Don Slater, 142–64. New York: Routledge.

Jessop, Bob. 2008a. "A Cultural Political Economy of Competitiveness and its Implications for Higher Education." In *Education and the Knowledge-Based Economy in Europe*, ed. Bob Jessop, Norman Fairclough, and Ruth Wodak, 11–39. Rotterdam: Sense Publishers.

Jessop, Bob. 2008b. "The Knowledge-Based Economy." Institute for Advanced Studies, Lancaster University, unpublished paper.

Jessop, Bob. 2011. "Imagined Recoveries, Recovered Imaginaries: A Cultural Political Economy Perspective." Cultural Political Economy Research Centre, Lancaster University. Accessed 30 September 2011. http://www.lancs.ac.uk/cperc/docs/E-2012%20Jessop-CPE-Swansea-Recovery.pdf.

Jessop, Bob, and Stijn Oosterlynck. 2008. "Cultural Political Economy: On Making the Cultural Turn without Falling into Soft Economic Sociology." *Geoforum* 39 (3): 1155–69. http://dx.doi.org/10.1016/j.geoforum.2006.12.008.

Jessop, Bob, and Ngai-Ling Sum. 2010. "Cultural Political Economy: Logics of Discovery, Epistemic Fallacies, the Complexity of Emergence, and the Potential of the Cultural Turn." *New Political Economy* 15 (3): 445–51. http://dx.doi.org/10.1080/13563461003802051.

Johnson, Jon R. 1993. "The Effect of the Canada-US Free Trade Agreement on the Auto Pact." In *Driving Continentally: National Policies and the North American Auto Industry*, ed. Maureen Appel Molot, 255–84. Ottawa: Carleton University Press.

Jones, Jack. 1986. *Union Man: The Autobiography of Jack Jones*. London: Collins.

Jörgensen, Jan J., Taïeb Hafsi, and Christiane Demers. 1994. "Context and Process in Privatization: Canada/Quebec." In *The Political Economy of Privatization*, ed. Thomas Clarke and Christos Pitelis, 234–72. London: Routledge.

Joseph, Keith. 1975. *Reversing the Trend*. London: Centre for Policy Studies.

Jupp, James. 1982. *Party Politics: Australia 1966–1981*. Sydney: George Allen and Unwin.

Karakatsanis, Neovi M. 2001. *The Politics of Elite Transformation: The Consolidation of Greek Democracy in Comparative Perspective*. Westport, CT: Praeger.

Karakatsanis, Neovi M. 2008. "Political Learning as a Catalyst of Moderation: Lessons from Democratic Consolidation in Greece." *Democratization* 15 (2): 386–409. http://dx.doi.org/10.1080/13510340701846459.

Katzenstein, Peter J. 1996a. *Cultural Norms and National Security: Police and Military in Postwar Japan*. Ithaca, NY: Cornell University Press.

Katzenstein, Peter J., ed. 1996b. *The Culture of National Security: Norms and Identity in World Politics*. New York: Columbia University Press.

Kaufman, Bruce E. 2004. *The Global Evolution of Industrial Relations: Events, Ideas and the IIRA*. Geneva: International Labour Organization.

Kavanagh, Dennis. 1987. *Thatcherism and British Politics: The End of Consensus?* Oxford: Clarendon.

Kavanagh, Dennis, and Peter Morris. 1989. *Consensus Politics from Attlee to Thatcher*. Oxford: Basil Blackwell.

Keating, Michael, and Geoff Dixon. 1989. *Making Economic Policy in Australia 1983–1988*. Melbourne: Longman Cheshire.

Keck, Margaret E., and Kathryn Sikkink. 1998. *Activists beyond Borders: Advocacy Networks in International Politics*. Ithaca, NY: Cornell University Press.

Keeler, John T.S. 1993. "Opening the Window for Reform: Mandates, Crises and Extraordinary Policymaking." *Comparative Political Studies* 25 (4): 433–86. http://dx.doi.org/10.1177/0010414093025004002.

Kelly, Paul. 1995. *November 1975: The Inside Story of Australia's Greatest Political Crisis*. St. Leonard's, NSW: Allen and Unwin.

Kelly, Paul. 2000. "The Politics of Economic Change in Australia in the 1980s and 1990s." In *The Australian Economy in the 1990s: Proceedings of a Conference*, ed. David W.R. Gruen and Sona Shrestha, 222–34. Sydney: Reserve Bank of Australia.

Kelsey, Jane. 1993. *Rolling Back the State: The Privatisation of Power in Aotearoa/ New Zealand*. Wellington: Bridget Williams Books.

Kelsey, Jane. 1995. *Economic Fundamentalism*. London: Pluto Press.

Kelsey, Jane. 2000. *Reclaiming the Future: New Zealand and the Global Economy*. Toronto: University of Toronto Press.

Kendall, Ian, and Graham Moon. 1990. "Health Policy." In *Public Policy under Thatcher*, ed. Stephen P. Savage and Lynton Robins, 103–16. New York: St. Martin's Press.

Keynes, John Maynard. 1935. *The General Theory of Employment, Interest and Money*. London: Macmillan.

Khan, M.A. Muqtedar. 2004. *Jihad for Jerusalem: Identity and Strategy in International Relations*. Westport, CT: Praeger.

King, Anthony. 1985. "Margaret Thatcher: The Style of a Prime Minister." In *The British Prime Minister*, ed. Anthony King, 96–140. Durham, NC: Duke University Press.

King, Anthony. 1990. "Margaret Thatcher as a Political Leader." In *Thatcherism*, ed. Robert Skidelsky, 51–64. Oxford: Basil Blackwell.

Kingdon, John W. 1984. *Agenda, Alternatives, and Public Policies*. Boston: Little, Brown.

Kirkby, Elisabeth. 1993. "Broadening the Scope of Public Policy." In *Beyond the Market: Alternatives to Economic Rationalism*, ed. Stuart Rees, Gordon Ridley, and Frank Stilwell, 105–9. Leichhardt, NSW: Pluto Press.

Kirshner, Jonathan. 2003. "Money Is Politics." *Review of International Political Economy* 10 (4): 645–60. http://dx.doi.org/10.1080/09692290310001601911.

Klein, Rudolf. 1983. *The Politics of the National Health Service*. London: Longman. http://dx.doi.org/10.2307/3349893.

Klingemann, Hans-Dieter, Richard I. Hofferbert, Ian Budge, Hans Keman, François Petry, and Kaare Strøm. 1994. *Parties, Policies, and Democracy*. Boulder, CO: Westview.

Klotz, Audie. 1995a. "Norms Reconstituting Interests: Global Racial Equality and US Sanctions Against South Africa." *International Organization* 49 (3): 451–78. http://dx.doi.org/10.1017/S0020818300033348.

Klotz, Audie. 1995b. *Norms in International Relations: The Struggle Against Apartheid*. Ithaca, NY: Cornell University Press.

Knight, Jack. 1992. *Institutions and Social Conflict*. New York: Cambridge University Press. http://dx.doi.org/10.1017/CBO9780511528170.

Kowert, Paul, and Jeffrey Legro. 1996. "Norms, Identity, and Their Limits: A Theoretical Reprise." In *The Culture of National Security: Norms and Identity in World Politics*, ed. Peter J. Katzenstein, 451–97. New York: Columbia University Press.

Kratochwil, Friedrich. 1989. *Rules, Norms and Decisions: On the Conditions of Practical and Legal Reasoning in International Relations and Domestic Affairs*. Cambridge: Cambridge University Press. http://dx.doi.org/10.1017/CBO9780511559044.

Krebs, Ronald R., and Patrick Thaddeus Jackson. 2007. "Twisting Tongues and Twisting Arms: The Power of Political Rhetoric." *European Journal of International Relations* 13 (1): 35–66. http://dx.doi.org/10.1177/1354066107074284.

Kreinin, Mordechai, ed. 2000. *Building a Partnership: The Canada-United States Free Trade Agreement*. East Lansing: Michigan State University Press.

Krugman, Paul. 1997. *Pop Internationalism*. Cambridge: The MIT Press.

Kübler, Dorothea. 2001. "On the Regulation of Social Norms." *Journal of Law, Economics, and Organization* 17 (2): 449–76. http://dx.doi.org/10.1093/jleo/17.2.449.

Kuhn, Thomas S. 1970. *The Structure of Scientific Revolutions*. Chicago: University of Chicago Press.

Kynaston, David. 1995. "The Bank of England and the Government." In *The Bank of England: Money, Power and Influence 1694–1994*, ed. Richard Roberts and David Kynaston, 19–55. Oxford: Clarendon Press.

Lamb, W. Kaye. 1977. *History of the Canadian Pacific Railway*. New York: Macmillan.

Lansbury, Russell D. 1978. "The Return to Arbitration: Recent Trends in Dispute Settlement and Wages Policy in Australia." *International Labour Review* 117 (5): 611–24.

Larsen, Henrik. 1999. "British and Danish European Policies in the 1990s: A Discourse Approach." *European Journal of International Relations* 5 (4): 451–83. http://dx.doi.org/10.1177/1354066199005004003.

Lawson, Nigel. 1982. *What's Right with Britain*. London: Conservative Political Centre.

Lawson, Nigel. 1993. *The View from No. 11: Memoirs of a Tory Radical*. London: Corgi.

Laxer, Gordon. 1989. *Open for Business: The Roots of Foreign Ownership in Canada*. Toronto: Oxford University Press.

Laxer, Gordon. 1991. *Perspectives on Canadian Economic Development*. Oxford: Oxford University Press.

Laybourn, Keith. 1995. *The Evolution of British Social Policy and the Welfare State, c. 1800–1993*. Keele: Ryburn.

LeDuc, Lawrence, and J. Alex Murray. 1989. "Open for Business? Foreign Investment and Trade Issues in Canada." In *Economic Decline and Political Change: Canada, Great Britain, the United States*, ed. Harold D. Clarke, Marianne C. Stewart, and Gary Zuk, 127–39. Pittsburgh: University of Pittsburgh Press.

Leigh, Andrew. 2000. "Factions and Fractions: A Case Study of Power Politics in the Australian Labor Party." *Australian Journal of Political Science* 35 (3): 427–48. http://dx.doi.org/10.1080/713649348.

Leigh, Andrew. 2002. "Trade Liberalisation and the Australian Labor Party." *Australian Journal of Politics and History* 48 (4): 487–508. http://dx.doi.org/10.1111/1467-8497.00272.

Letwin, Oliver. 1988. *Privatising the World*. London: Cassell.

Levy, Jack S. 1994. "Learning and Foreign Policy: Sweeping a Conceptual Minefield." *International Organization* 48 (2): 279–312. http://dx.doi. org/10.1017/S0020818300028198.

Lewis, Timothy. 2004. *In the Long Run We're All Dead: The Canadian Turn to Fiscal Restraint.* Vancouver: UBC Press.

Leybourne, Stephen J., and Paul Mizen. 1999. "Understanding the Disinflations in Australia, Canada and New Zealand Using Evidence from Smooth Transition Analysis." *Journal of International Money and Finance* 18 (5): 799–816. http://dx.doi.org/10.1016/S0261-5606(99)00032-7.

Lieberman, Robert C. 2002. "Ideas, Institutions, and Political Order: Explaining Political Change." *American Political Science Review* 96 (4): 697–712. http://dx.doi.org/10.1017/S0003055402000394.

Lijphart, Arend. 1984. *Democracies: Patterns of Majoritarian and Consensus Government.* New Haven: Yale University Press.

Lijphart, Arend. 1999. *Government Forms and Performance in Thirty-Six Countries.* New Haven: Yale University Press.

Lipset, Seymour Martin. 1960. *Political Man: The Social Bases of Politics.* Garden City, NY: Doubleday.

Lipset, Seymour Martin, and Stein Rokkan, eds. 1967. *Party Systems and Voter Alignments: Cross-National Perspectives.* New York: The Free Press.

Lipsky, Michael, and Steven Rathgeb Smith. 1989. "When Social Problems Are Treated as Emergencies." *Social Service Review* 63 (1): 5–25. http://dx.doi. org/10.1086/603675.

Lloyd, Clem, and Wayne Swan. 1987. "National Factions and the ALP." *Politics* 22 (1): 100–10.

Lord, Charles G., Lee Ross, and Mark R. Lepper. 1979. "Biased Assimilation and Attitude Polarization: The Effects of Prior Theories on Subsequently Considered Evidence." *Journal of Personality and Social Psychology* 37 (11): 2098–109. http://dx.doi.org/10.1037/0022-3514.37.11.2098.

Ludlam, Steve, and Martin J. Smith, eds. 2001. *New Labour in Government.* Basingstoke: Macmillan.

Ludwig, Arnold M. 2002. *King of the Mountain: The Nature of Political Leadership.* Lexington, KY: University Press of Kentucky.

Lusztig, Michael. 1996. *Risking Free Trade: The Politics of Trade in Britain, Canada, Mexico, and the United States.* Pittsburgh: University of Pittsburgh Press.

Macarthy, Peter. 1967. "The Harvester Judgment: An Historical Assessment." Ph.D. Thesis, Canberra, Australian National University.

Mack, J.A. 1959."Trade Unions and the State." *Scottish Journal of Political Economy* 6 (2): 47–64. http://dx.doi.org/10.1111/j.1467-9485. 1959.tb00108.x.

Macmillan, Harold. 1969. *Tides of Fortune: 1945–1955*. London: Macmillan.

Maddox, Graham. 1989. *The Hawke Government and Labor Tradition*. Ringwood, Vic.: Penguin.

Mahoney, Paul G., and Christopher Sanchirico. 2001. "Competing Norms and Social Evolution: Is the Fittest Norm Efficient?" *University of Pennsylvania Law Review* 149 (6): 2027–62. http://dx.doi.org/10.2307/3312904.

Mahoney, Paul G., and Christopher Sanchirico. 2003. "Norms, Repeated Games, and the Role of Law." *California Law Review* 91 (5): 1281–329. http://dx.doi.org/10.2307/3481344.

Majone, Giandomenico. 1989. *Evidence, Argument and Persuasion in the Policy Process*. New Haven: Yale University Press.

Maloney, Tim, and John Savage. 1996. "Labour Markets and Policy." In *A Study of Economic Reform: The Case of New Zealand*, ed. Brian Silverstone, Alan Bollard, and Ralph Lattimore, 173–213. Amsterdam: Elsevier.

Mann, Susan. 2002. *The Dream of Nation: A Social and Intellectual History of Quebec*. Montreal: McGill-Queen's University Press.

Marsh, David. 1991a. "British Industrial Relations Policy Transformed: The Thatcher Legacy." *Journal of Public Policy* 11 (3): 291–313. http://dx.doi.org/10.1017/S0143814X00005341.

Marsh, David. 1991b. "Privatisation under Mrs Thatcher: A Review of the Literature." *Public Administration* 69 (4): 459–80. http://dx.doi.org/10.1111/j.1467-9299. 1991.tb00915.x.

Marsh, David. 1992. *The New Politics of British Trade Unionism: Union Power and the Thatcher Legacy*. Ithaca, NY: ILR Press.

Marsh, Ian, ed. 2006. *Political Parties in Transition?* Leichhardt, NSW: Federation Press.

Marshall, T.H. 1950. *Citizenship and Social Class and Other Essays*. Cambridge: Cambridge University Press.

Martin, Lawrence. 1993. *Pledge of Allegiance: The Americanization of Canada in the Mulroney Years*. Toronto: McClelland and Stewart.

Massey, Patrick. 1995. *New Zealand: Market Liberalization in a Developed Economy*. New York: St. Martin's Press.

Matthews, Trevor. 1994. "Employers' Associations, Corporatism and the Accord: The Politics of Industrial Relations." In *State, Economy and Public Policy in Australia*, ed. Stephen Bell and Brian Head, 194–224. Melbourne: Oxford University Press.

McAdams, Richard H. 2000. "An Attitudinal Theory of Expressive Law." *Oregon Law Review* 79 (2): 339–90.

McAllister, Ian. 1991. "Party Adaptation and Factionalism within the Australian Party System." *American Journal of Political Science* 35 (1): 206–27. http://dx.doi.org/10.2307/2111444.

McAllister, Ian. 2003. "Prime Ministers, Opposition Leaders and Government Popularity in Australia." *Australian Journal of Political Science* 38 (2): 259–77. http://dx.doi.org/10.1080/1036114032000092710.

McAllister, Ian, and Jack Vowles. 1994. "The Rise of New Politics and Market Liberalism in Australia and New Zealand." *British Journal of Political Science* 24 (3): 381–402. http://dx.doi.org/10.1017/S0007123400006906.

McCallum, Ronald C. 1997. "Australian Workplace Agreements—An Analysis." *Australian Journal of Labour Law* 10 (1): 50–61.

McDonald, Geoffrey. 1975. "The Defeat of the General Strike." In *The Politics of Reappraisal, 1918–1939*, ed. Gillian Peele and Chris Cook, 64–87. New York: St. Martin's.

McDougall, John N. 2006. *Drifting Together: The Political Economy of Canada-US Integration*. Peterborough: Broadview.

McIlroy, John. 1995. *Trade Unions in Britain Today*. Manchester: Manchester University Press.

McNamara, Kathleen R. 1998. *The Currency of Ideas: Monetary Politics in the European Union*. Ithaca, NY: Cornell University Press.

McQueen, Humphrey. 1983. "Higgins and Arbitration." In *Essays in the Political Economy of Australian Capitalism*, ed. Edward L. Wheelwright and Kenneth D. Buckley, 145–63. Sydney: Australian and New Zealand Book Co.

McVicar, Malcolm. 1990. "Education Policy: Education as a Business?" In *Public Policy under Thatcher*, ed. Stephen P. Savage and Lynton Robins, 131–44. New York: St. Martin's Press.

Mendes, Philip. 2003. "Australian Neoliberal Think Tanks and the Backlash Against the Welfare State." *Journal of Australian Political Economy* 51: 29–56.

Meyer, John W. 2000. "Globalization: Sources and Effects on National States and Societies." *International Sociology* 15 (2): 233–48. http://dx.doi.org/10.1177/0268580900015002006.

Meyer, John W., John Boli, George M. Thomas, and Francisco O. Ramirez. 1997. "World Society and the Nation-State." *American Journal of Sociology* 103 (1): 144–81. http://dx.doi.org/10.1086/231174.

Meyer, John W., David John Frank, Ann Hironaka, Evan Schofer, and Nancy Brandon Tuma. 1997. "The Structuring of a World Environmental Regime, 1870–1990." *International Organization* 51 (4): 623–51. http://dx.doi.org/10.1162/002081897550474.

Meyer, John W., Francisco O. Ramirez, Richard Rubinson, and John Boli-Bennett. 1977. "The World Educational Revolution, 1950–1970." *Sociology of Education* 50 (4): 242–58. http://dx.doi.org/10.2307/2112498.

Meyer, John W., Francisco O. Ramirez, and Yasemin Nuhoğlu Soysal. 1992. "World Expansion of Mass Education, 1870–1980." *Sociology of Education* 65 (2): 128–49. http://dx.doi.org/10.2307/2112679.

Miller, Kenneth, and Mairi Steele. 1993. "Employment Legislation: Thatcher and After." *Industrial Relations Journal* 24 (3): 224–35. http://dx.doi.org/10.1111/j.1468-2338.1993.tb00675.x.

Miller, Raymond. 2003. "Labour." In *New Zealand Government and Politics*, ed. Raymond Miller, 235–50. Oxford: Oxford University Press.

Mills, Stephen. 1993. *The Hawke Years: The Story from the Inside*. Ringwood, Vic.: Viking.

Milne, R.S. 1966. *Political Parties in New Zealand*. Oxford: Oxford University Press.

Minford, Patrick. 1990. "Mrs Thatcher's Economic Reform Programme—Past, Present and Future." In *Thatcherism*, ed. Robert Skidelsky, 93–106. Oxford: Basil Blackwell.

Minkin, Lewis. 1992. *The Contentious Alliance: Trade Unions and the Labour Party*. Edinburgh: Edinburgh University Press.

Mintrom, Michael. 1997. "Policy Entrepreneurs and the Diffusion of Innovation." *American Journal of Political Science* 41 (3): 738–70. http://dx.doi.org/10.2307/2111674.

Mintrom, Michael. 2000. *Policy Entrepreneurs and School Choice*. Washington: Georgetown University Press.

Miskin, Sarah J.M. 1997. "The Political Philosophy of the New Zealand Treasury: An Analysis of Treasury's Briefing Papers to the Incoming Governments, 1984 to 1994." M.A. Thesis, Christchurch, University of Canterbury.

Mo, Jongryn. 1996. "Political Learning and Democratic Consolidation: Korean Industrial Relations, 1987–1992." *Comparative Political Studies* 29 (3): 290–311. http://dx.doi.org/10.1177/0010414096029003002.

Moon, Jeremy. 1993. *Innovative Leadership in Democracy: Policy Change under Thatcher*. Aldershot: Dartmouth.

Moran, Michael. 1977. *The Politics of Industrial Relations: The Origins, Life, and Death of the 1971 Industrial Relations Act*. London: Macmillan.

Morgan, Kenneth O. 1984. *Labour in Power 1945–1951*. New York: Oxford University Press.

Morgan, Kenneth O. 1990. *The People's Peace: British History 1945–1989.* Oxford: Oxford University Press. http://dx.doi.org/10.1093/acprof: oso/9780198227649.001.0001.

Mosley, Layna. 2005. "Globalization and the State: Still Room to Move?" *New Political Economy* 10 (3): 355–62. http://dx.doi.org/10.1080/13563460500204241.

Mowat, Charles Loch. 1955. *Britain between the Wars, 1918–1940.* Chicago: University of Chicago Press.

Muetzelfeldt, Michael. 1992. "Economic Rationalism in its Social Context." In *Society, State and Politics in Australia*, ed. Michael Muetzelfeldt, 187–215. Leichhardt, NSW: Pluto Press Australia.

Muldoon, Robert D. 1977. *Muldoon.* Wellington: Reed.

Muldoon, Robert D. 1981. *My Way.* Wellington: Reed.

Mulgan, Richard. 1990. "The Changing Electoral Mandate." In *The Fourth Labour Government: Politics and Policy in New Zealand*, ed. Martin Holland and Jonathan Boston, 11–21. Auckland: Auckland University Press.

Mulgan, Richard. 1997. "State and Democracy in New Zealand." In *The Political Economy of New Zealand*, ed. Chris Rudd and Brian Roper, 256–72. Auckland: Oxford University Press.

Mulroney, Brian. 1983. *Where I Stand.* Toronto: McClelland and Stewart.

Muppidi, Himadeep. 1999. "Postcoloniality and the Production of International Insecurity: The Peristant Puzzle of U.S.-Indian Relations." In *Cultures of Insecurity: States, Communities, and the Production of Danger*, ed. Jutta Weldes, Mark Laffey, Hugh Gusterson, and Raymond Duvall, 119–46. Minneapolis: University of Minnesota Press.

Murie, Alan. 1989. "Housing and the Environment." In *The Thatcher Effect*, ed. Dennis Kavanagh and Anthony Seldon, 213–25. Oxford: Oxford University Press.

Nadelmann, Ethan A. 1990. "Global Prohibition Regimes: The Evolution of Norms in International Society." *International Organization* 44 (4): 479–526. http://dx.doi.org/10.1017/S0020818300035384.

Nagel, Jack H. 1998. "Social Choice in a Pluralitarian Democracy: The Politics of Market Liberalization in New Zealand." *British Journal of Political Science* 28 (2): 223–67. http://dx.doi.org/10.1017/S0007123498000155.

Nagel, Jack H. 2004. "New Zealand: Reform by (Nearly) Immaculate Design." In *Handbook of Electoral System Design*, ed. Josep Colomer, 530–43. London: Palgrave.

Naughton, Richard. 1997. "Sailing into Uncharted Seas: The Role of Unions Under the Workplace Relations Act 1996 (Cth)." *Australian Journal of Labour Law* 10 (1): 112–32.

Nelson, Joan, ed. 1990. *Economic Crisis and Policy Choice.* Princeton: Princeton University Press.

Nielson, Daniel L., Michael J. Tierney, and Catherine E. Weaver. 2006. "Bridging the Rationalist-Constructivist Divide: Re-Engineering the Culture of the World Bank." *Journal of International Relations and Development* 9 (2): 107–39. http://dx.doi.org/10.1057/palgrave.jird.1800084.

Nollen, Stanley D., and Harvey J. Iglarsh. 1990. "Explanation of Protectionism in International Trade Votes." *Public Choice* 66 (2): 137–53. http://dx.doi. org/10.1007/BF00127798.

Nollen, Stanley D., and Dennis P. Quinn. 1994. "Free Trade, Fair Trade, Strategic Trade, and Protectionism in the U.S. Congress, 1987–88." *International Organization* 48 (3): 491–525. http://dx.doi.org/10.1017/ S0020818300028277.

Ogden, Max. 1993. *Towards Best Practice Unionism: The Future of Unions in Australia.* Sydney: Pluto Press.

Onuf, Nicholas. 1989. *World of Our Making: Rules and Rule in Social Theory and International Relations.* Columbia, SC: University of South Carolina Press.

Onuf, Nicholas. 1997. "A Constructivist Manifesto." In *Constituting International Political Economy,* ed. Kurt Burch and Robert A. Denemark, 7–17. Boulder, CO: Lynne Rienner.

Organisation for Economic Co-operation and Development. 1994. *The OECD Jobs Study: Facts, Analysis, Strategies.* Paris: OECD.

Organisation for Economic Co-operation and Development. 1995. *The OECD Jobs Study: Implementing the Strategy.* Paris: OECD.

Organisation for Economic Co-operation and Development. 1999. *OECD Employment Outlook.* Paris: OECD.

Organisation for Economic Co-operation and Development. Various years. *OECD Economic Surveys: Australia.* Paris: OECD.

Organisation for Economic Co-operation and Development. Various years. *OECD Economic Surveys: Canada.* Paris: OECD.

Organisation for Economic Co-operation and Development. Various years. *OECD Economic Surveys: New Zealand.* Paris: OECD.

Organisation for Economic Co-operation and Development. Various years. *OECD Economic Surveys: United Kingdom.* Paris: OECD.

Organisation for Economic Co-operation and Development. Various years. *OECD Historical Statistics.* Paris: OECD.

Parker, David. 1993. "Privatisation Ten Years On: A Critical Analysis of its Rationale and Results." In *Britain's Economic Miracle: Myth or Reality?* ed. Nigel M. Healey, 174–94. London: Routledge.

Parker, Mike. 2000. *Thatcherism and the Fall of Coal*. Oxford: Oxford University Press.

Parkin, Andrew, and John Warhurst, eds. 1983. *Machine Politics in the Australian Labor Party*. Sydney: Allen and Unwin.

Parliamentary Debates (Hansard), House of Commons. [United Kingdom]. Various years. London: Her Majesty's Stationary Office.

Parliamentary Debates (Hansard), House of Representatives. [New Zealand]. Various years. Wellington: Government Printer.

Parsons, Craig. 2003. *A Certain Idea of Europe*. Ithaca, NY: Cornell University Press.

Pauly, Louis W. 1987. *Foreign Banks in Australia: The Politics of Deregulation*. Mosman, NSW: Australian Professional Publications in association with the Centre for Money, Banking, and Finance, Macquarie University.

Payne, Rodger A. 2001. "Persuasion, Frames and Norm Construction." *European Journal of International Relations* 7 (1): 37–61. http://dx.doi.org/10.117 7/1354066101007001002.

Peet, Richard. 2002. "Ideology, Discourse, and the Geography of Hegemony: From Socialist to Neoliberal Development in Postapartheid South Africa." *Antipode* 34 (1): 54–84. http://dx.doi.org/10.1111/1467-8330.00226.

Pelling, Henry. 1992. *A History of British Trade Unionism*. Harmondsworth: Penguin.

Pennock, J. Roland, and John W. Chapman, eds. 2006. *Coercion*. New Brunswick, NJ: Aldine.

Pepper, Gordon. 1998. *Inside Thatcher's Monetarist Revolution*. Basingstoke: Macmillan.

Pepper, Gordon T., and Michael J. Oliver. 2001. *Monetarism under Thatcher: Lessons for the Future*. Cheltenham: Edward Elgar.

Perkins, J.O.N. 1989. *The Deregulation of the Australian Financial System: The Experience of the 1980s*. Carlton, Vic.: Melbourne University Press.

Perry, J. Harvey. 1989. *A Fiscal History of Canada: The Postwar Years*. Toronto: Canadian Tax Federation.

Pierson, Paul. 1994. *Dismantling the Welfare State? Reagan, Thatcher, and the Politics of Retrenchment*. Cambridge: Cambridge University Press. http://dx.doi.org/10.1017/CBO9780511805288.

Pincus, Jonathan J. 1987. "Government." In *The Australian Economy in the Long Run*, ed. Rodney Maddock and Ian W. McLean, 291–318. Cambridge: Cambridge University Press.

Pliatzky, Leo. 1989. *The Treasury under Mrs. Thatcher*. Oxford: Basil Blackwell.

Plourde, André. 2005. "The Changing Nature of National and Continental Energy Markets." In *Canadian Energy Policy and the Struggle for Sustainable*

Development, ed. G. Bruce Doern, 51–82. Toronto: University of Toronto Press.

Polanyi, Karl. 1944. *The Great Transformation: The Political and Economic Origins of Our Time*. Boston: Beacon Press.

Pollack, Mark A. 2005. "Theorizing the European Union: International Organization, Domestic Polity, or Experiment in New Governance?" *Annual Review of Political Science* 8 (1): 357–98. http://dx.doi.org/10.1146/annurev.polisci.8.082103.104858.

Pollard, Sidney. 1982. *The Wasting of the British Economy: British Economic Policy 1945 to the Present*. London: Croom Helm.

Polsby, Nelson W. 1984. *Political Innovation in America*. New Haven: Yale University Press.

Pope, David. 1987. "Population and Australian Economic Development 1900–1930." In *The Australian Economy in the Long Run*, ed. Rodney Maddock and Ian W. McLean, 33–60. Cambridge: Cambridge University Press.

Powell, G. Bingham. 1982. *Contemporary Democracies: Participation, Stability, and Violence*. Cambridge, MA: Harvard University Press.

Powell, G. Bingham. 2000. *Elections as Instruments of Democracy: Majoritarian and Proportional Visions*. New Haven: Yale University Press.

Prasad, Monica. 2006. *The Politics of Free Markets: The Rise of Neoliberal Economic Policies in Britain, France, Germany, and the United States*. Chicago: University of Chicago Press.

Price, Richard. 1998. "Reversing the Gun Sights: Transnational Civil Society Targets Land Mines." *International Organization* 52 (3): 613–44. http://dx.doi.org/10.1162/002081898550671.

Price, Richard M. 1997. *The Chemical Weapons Taboo*. Ithaca, NY: Cornell University Press.

Puplick, Christopher. 1994. *Is the Party Over? The Future of the Liberals*. Melbourne: Text.

Pusey, Michael. 1991. *Economic Rationalism in Canberra: A Nation-Building State Changes its Mind*. Cambridge: Cambridge University Press.

Pusey, Michael. 1992a. "Canberra Changes its Mind—The New Mandarins." In *Shutdown: The Failure of Economic Rationalism and How to Rescue Australia*, ed. John Carroll and Robert Manne, 38–48. Melbourne: Text.

Pusey, Michael. 1992b. "What's Wrong with Economic Rationalism?" In *The Trouble with Economic Rationalism*, ed. Donald Horne, 63–9. Newham, Vic.: Scribe.

Pusey, Michael. 2003. *The Experience of Middle Australia*. Cambridge: Cambridge University Press. http://dx.doi.org/10.1017/CBO9780511481628.

Quiggin, John. 2001. "Social Democracy and Market Reform in Australia and New Zealand." In *Social Democracy in Neoliberal Times: The Left and Economic Policy since 1980*, ed. Andrew Glyn, 80–109. Oxford: Oxford University Press. http://dx.doi.org/10.1093/acprof:oso/9780199241378.003.0004.

Ramirez, Francisco O., and Elizabeth H. McEneaney. 1997. "From Women's Suffrage to Reproduction Rights? Cross-National Considerations." *International Journal of Comparative Sociology* 38 (1–2): 6–24. http://dx.doi.org/10.1177/002071529703800102.

Reid, Alastair J. 2000. "Labour and the Trade Unions." In *Labour's First Century*, ed. Duncan Tanner, Pat Thane, and Nick Tiratsoo, 221–47. Cambridge: Cambridge University Press.

Reitsma, Alexander Jan. 1960. *Trade Protection in Australia*. Brisbane: University of Queensland Press.

Reynolds, Andrew, ed. 2002. *The Architecture of Democracy: Constitutional Design, Conflict Management, and Democracy*. Oxford: Oxford University Press.

Richardson, J.J., ed. 1990. *Privatization and Deregulation in Canada and Britain*. Aldershot: Gower.

Ritchie, Gordon. 1997. *Wrestling with the Elephant: The Inside Story of the Canada-US Trade Wars*. Toronto: Macfarlane Walter and Ross.

Riddell, Peter. 1985. *The Thatcher Government*. Oxford: Basil Blackwell.

Riddell, Peter. 1989. *The Thatcher Decade: How Britain Changed during the 1980s*. New York: Basil Blackwell.

Riekhokk, Harald von, and Hanspeter Neuhold, eds. 1993. *Unequal Partners: A Comparative Analysis of Relations between Austria and the Federal Republic of Germany and between Canada and the United States*. Boulder: Westview Press.

Risse, Thomas. 2000. "'Let's Argue!': Communicative Action in World Politics." *International Organization* 54 (1): 1–39. http://dx.doi.org/10.1162/002081800551109.

Risse, Thomas, Daniela Engelmann-Martin, Hans-Joachim Knopf, and Klaus Roscher. 1999. "To Euro or Not to Euro? The EMU and Identity Politics in the European Union." *European Journal of International Relations* 5 (2): 147–87. http://dx.doi.org/10.1177/1354066199005002001.

Roberts, B.C. 1989. "Trade Unions." In *The Thatcher Effect*, ed. Dennis Kavanagh and Anthony Seldon, 64–79. Oxford: Oxford University Press.

Rodrik, Dani. 1997. *Has Globalization Gone Too Far?* Washington: Institute for International Economics.

Rogin, Michael. 1962. "Voluntarism: The Political Foundation of an Anti-Political Doctrine." *Industrial & Labor Relations Review* 15 (4): 521–35. http://dx.doi.org/10.2307/2520394.

Roper, Brian. 1993. "A Level Playing Field? Business Political Activism and State Policy Formation." In *State and Economy in New Zealand*, ed. Brian Roper and Chris Rudd, 147–71. Auckland: Auckland University Press.

Roper, Brian. 1997. "New Zealand's Postwar Economic History." In *The Political Economy of New Zealand*, ed. Chris Rudd and Brian Roper, 3–21. Auckland: Oxford University Press.

Roper, Brian. 2003. "Neo-Liberalism: A Radial Critique." In *New Zealand Government and Politics*, ed. Raymond Miller, 578–89. Oxford: Oxford University Press.

Royal Commission on the Economic Union and Development Prospects for Canada. 1985. *Report of the Royal Commission on the Economic Union and Development Prospects for Canada*. Ottawa: Minister of Supply and Services Canada.

Rudd, Chris. 1990. "Politics and Markets: The Role of the State in the New Zealand Economy." In *The Fourth Labour Government: Politics and Policy in New Zealand*, ed. Martin Holland and Jonathan Boston, 83–100. Auckland: Oxford University Press.

Rudd, Chris, and Ichikawa Taichi. 1994. *Electoral Reform in New Zealand and Japan: A Shared Experiecne?* Palmerston North: New Zealand Centre for Japanese Studies, Massey University.

Ruggie, John Gerard. 1998a. *Constructing the World Polity: Essays on International Institutionalization*. New York: Routledge. http://dx.doi.org/10.4324/9780203424261.

Ruggie, John Gerard. 1998b. "What Makes the World Hang Together? Neo-Utilitarianism and the Social Constructivist Challenge." *International Organization* 52 (4): 855–85. http://dx.doi.org/10.1162/002081898550770.

Ruggie, Mary. 1996. *Realignments in the Welfare State: Health Policy in the United States, Britain, and Canada*. New York: Columbia University Press.

Russell, Meg. 2005. *Building New Labour: The Politics of Party Organisation*. Basingstoke: Palgrave Macmillan.

Ryan, Mark, ed. 1995. *Advancing Australia: The Speeches of Paul Keating, Prime Minister*. Sydney: Big Picture Publications.

Safarian, A.E. 1991. "Direct Investment Strategies and the Canada-U.S. Free Trade Agreement." In *The Dynamics of North American Trade and Investment: Canada, Mexico and the United States*, ed. Clark W. Reynolds, Leonard Waverman, and Gerardo M. Bueno, 147–65. Stanford: Stanford University Press.

Sanders, Peter, and Colin Harris. 1994. *Privatisation and Popular Capitalism*. Buckingham: Open University Press.

Sassen, Saskia. 1996. "The Spatial Organization of Information Industries: Implications for the Role of the State." In *Globalization: Critical Reflections,* ed. James H. Mittelman, 33–52. Boulder, CO: Lynne Rienner Publishers.

Sassen, Saskia. 1998. *Globalization and Its Discontents: Essays on the New Mobility of People and Money.* New York: New Press.

Sassen, Saskia. 1999. "Making the Global Economy Run: The Role of National States and Private Agents." *International Social Science Journal* 51 (161): 409–16. http://dx.doi.org/10.1111/1468-2451.00209.

Savoie, Donald J. 1990. *The Politics of Public Spending in Canada.* Toronto: University of Toronto Press.

Savoie, Donald J. 1994. *Thatcher, Reagan, Mulroney: In Search of a New Bureaucracy.* Pittsburgh: University of Pittsburgh Press.

Schmidt, Manfred G. 1996. "When Parties Matter: A Review of the Possibilities and Limits of Partisan Influence on Public Policy." *European Journal of Political Research* 30 (2): 155–83. http://dx.doi.org/10.1111/j.1475-6765.1996.tb00673.x.

Schmidt, Manfred G. 1997. "Politics Does Indeed Matter!" *European Journal of Political Research* 31 (1): 164–8.

Schmidt, Manfred G. 2002. "Political Performance and Types of Democracy: Findings from Comparative Studies." *European Journal of Political Research* 41 (1): 147–63. http://dx.doi.org/10.1111/1475-6765.00007.

Schmitter, Philippe C., and Gerhard Lehmbruch. 1979. *Trends toward Corporatist Intermediation.* Beverly Hills: Sage.

Schmitter, Philippe C., and Gerhard Lehmbruch. 1982. *Patterns of Corporatist Policy-Making.* Beverly Hills: Sage.

Schneider, Mark, and Paul Teske. 1992. "Toward a Theory of the Political Entrepreneur: Evidence from Local Government." *American Political Science Review* 86 (3): 737–47. http://dx.doi.org/10.2307/1964135.

Schofer, Evan, and John W. Meyer. 2005. "The Worldwide Expansion of Higher Education in the Twentieth Century." *American Sociological Review* 70 (6): 898–920. http://dx.doi.org/10.1177/000312240507000602.

Schott, Kerry. 1982. "The Rise of Keynesian Economics: Britain 1940–64." *Economy and Society* 11 (3): 292–316. http://dx.doi.org/10.1080/03085148200000021.

Schwartz, Herman M. 2000a. "Internationalization and Two Liberal Welfare States: Australia and New Zealand." In *Welfare and Work in the Open Economy: Diverse Reponses to Common Challenges,* ed. Fritz W. Scharpf and Vivian A. Schmidt, 69–130. Oxford: Oxford University Press. http://dx.doi.org/10.1093/0199240922.003.0003.

Schwartz, Herman M. 2000b. *States versus Markets: The Emergence of a Global Economy.* New York: St. Martin's Press.

Scott, Peter. 1989. "Higher Education." In *The Thatcher Effect,* ed. Dennis Kavanagh and Anthony Seldon, 198–212. Oxford: Oxford University Press.

Seabrooke, Leonard. 2006. *The Social Sources of Financial Power: Domestic Legitimacy and International Financial Orders.* Ithaca, NY: Cornell University Press.

Seabrooke, Leonard. 2007a. "Everyday Legitimacy and International Financial Orders: The Social Sources of Imperialism and Hegemony in Global Finance." *New Political Economy* 12 (1): 1–18. http://dx.doi.org/10.1080/13563460601068453.

Seabrooke, Leonard. 2007b. "The Everyday Social Sources of Economic Crises: From 'Great Frustrations' to 'Great Revelations' in Interwar Britain." *International Studies Quarterly* 51 (4): 795–810. http://dx.doi.org/10.1111/j.1468-2478. 2007.00477.x.

Seabrooke, Leonard. 2007c. "Varieties of Economic Constructivism in Political Economy: Uncertain Times Call for Disparate Measures." *Review of International Political Economy* 14 (2): 371–85. http://dx.doi.org/10.1080/09692290701203748.

Seabrooke, Leonard. 2010. "What Do I Get? The Everyday Politics of Expectations and the Subprime Crisis." *New Political Economy* 15 (1): 51–70. http://dx.doi.org/10.1080/13563460903553608.

Seabrooke, Leonard, and Eleni Tsingou. 2009. "Power Elites and Everyday Politics in International Financial Reform." *International Political Sociology* 3 (4): 457–61. http://dx.doi.org/10.1111/j.1749-5687. 2009.00086_4.x.

Shannon, Vaughn P. 2000. "Norms Are What States Make of Them: The Political Psychology of Norm Violation." *International Studies Quarterly* 44 (2): 293–316. http://dx.doi.org/10.1111/0020-8833.00159.

Sharp, Mitchell. 1994. *Which Reminds Me: A Memoir.* Toronto: University of Toronto Press.

Shaw, Eric. 1994. *The Labour Party since 1979: Crisis and Transformation.* London: Routledge.

Simmons, Beth A., Frank Dobbin, and Geoffrey Garrett. 2006. "Introduction: The International Diffusion of Liberalism." *International Organization* 60 (4): 781–810. http://dx.doi.org/10.1017/S0020818306060267.

Simon, Craig. 1998. "Internet Governance Goes Global." In *International Relations in a Constructed World,* ed. Vendulka Kubálková, Nicholas Onuf, and Paul Kowert, 147–169. Armonk, NY: M.E. Sharpe.

Simpson, Jeffrey. 1980. *Discipline of Power: The Conservative Interlude.* Toronto: Personal Library Publications.

Singh, Parbudyal, and Harish C. Jain. 2001. "Striker Replacements in the United States, Canada, and Mexico: A Review of the Law and Empirical Research." *Industrial Relations* 40 (1): 22–53. http://dx.doi.org/10.1111/0019-8676.00194.

Singleton, Gwynneth. 1990a. *The Accord and the Australian Labour Movement.* Carlton, Vic.: Melbourne University Press. http://dx.doi.org/10.1080/14662049008447586.

Singleton, Gwynneth. 1990b. "Corporatism or Labourism: The Australian Labour Movement in Accord." *Journal of Commonwealth & Comparative Politics* 28 (2): 162–82. http://dx.doi.org/10.1080/14662049008447586.

Skidelsky, Robert. 1990. "Introduction." In *Thatcherism*, ed. Robert Skidelsky, 1–23. Oxford: Basil Blackwell.

Smith, Peter. 1988. *The Rise and Fall of Monetarism.* Harmonsworth: Penguin.

Snow, David, and Robert Benford. 1992. "Master Frames and Cycles of Protest." In *Frontiers in Social Movement Theory*, ed. Aldon D. Morris and Carol McClurg Mueller, 133–55. New Haven: Yale University Press.

Snow, David, E. Burk Rochford, Jr., Steven K. Worden, and Robert D. Benford. 1986. "Frame Alignment Processes, Micromobilization, and Movement Participation." *American Sociological Review* 51 (4): 464–81. http://dx.doi.org/10.2307/2095581.

Solomon, Ty. 2006. "Norms and Human Rights in International Relations." *Political Studies Review* 4 (1): 36–47. http://dx.doi.org/10.1111/j.1478-9299.2006.00038.x.

Spillman, Lyn. 1999. "Enriching Exchange: Cultural Dimensions of Markets." *American Journal of Economics and Sociology* 58 (4): 1047–71.

Stairs, Denis, and Gilbert R. Winham, eds. 1985. *The Politics of Canada's Economic Relations with the United States.* Toronto: University of Toronto Press.

Stanbury, W.T. 1989. "Privatization in Canada: Ideology, Symbolism or Substance." In *Privatization and State-Owned Enterprises: Lessons from the United States, Great Britain, and Canada*, ed. Paul W. MacAvoy, W.T. Stanbury, George Yarrow, and Richard J. Zeckhauser, 273–329. Boston: Kluwer.

Stein, Janice Gross. 1994. "Political Learning by Doing: Gorbachev as Uncommitted Thinker and Motivated Learner." *International Organization* 48 (2): 155–83. http://dx.doi.org/10.1017/S0020818300028150.

Steiner, Jürg. 1971. "The Principles of Majority and Proportionality." *British Journal of Political Science* 1 (1): 63–70. http://dx.doi.org/10.1017/S0007123400008942.

Stevens, Richard. 2004. "The Evolution of Privatisation as an Electoral Policy, c. 1970–90." *Contemporary British History* 18 (2): 47–75. http://dx.doi.org/10.10 80/1361946042000227733.

Stevenson, John, and Chris Cook. 1994. *Britain in the Depression: Society and Politics, 1929–1939*. London: Longman.

Stewart, Andrew. 2006. "Work Choices in Overview: Big Bang or Slow Burn?" *Economic and Labour Relations Review* 16 (2): 25–60.

Stiglitz, Joseph E. 2002. *Globalization and its Discontents*. New York: W.W. Norton.

Stilwell, Frank. 1986. *The Accord—and Beyond: The Political Economy of the Labor Government*. Sydney: Pluto Press.

Stilwell, Frank. 1990. "Wages Policy and the Accord." *Journal of Australian Political Economy* 26: 197–215.

Strang, David. 1991. "Global Patterns of Decolonization, 1500–1987." *International Studies Quarterly* 35 (4): 429–54. http://dx.doi.org/10.2307/2600949.

Strang, David, and Michael W. Macy. 2001. "In Search of Excellence: Fads, Success Stories, and Adaptive Emulation." *American Journal of Sociology* 107 (1): 147–82. http://dx.doi.org/10.1086/323039.

Strang, David, and John W. Meyer. 1993. "Institutional Conditions for Diffusion." *Theory and Society* 22 (4): 487–511. http://dx.doi.org/10.1007/BF00993595.

Strang, David, and Sarah A. Soule. 1998. "Diffusion in Organizations and Social Movements: From Hybrid Corn to Poison Pills." *Annual Review of Sociology* 24 (1): 265–90. http://dx.doi.org/10.1146/annurev.soc.24.1.265.

Strange, Susan. 1996. *The Retreat of the State: The Diffusion of Power in the World Economy*. Cambridge: Cambridge University Press.

Strange, Susan. 1997. "Territory, State, Authority and Economy: A New Realist Ontology of Global Political Economy." In *The New Realism: Perspectives on Multilateralism and World Order*, ed. Robert W. Cox, 3–19. New York: St. Martin's Press.

Stubbs, John. 1989. *Hayden*. Port Melbourne, Vic.: William Heinemann Australia.

Sugden, Robert. 1998. "Normative Expectations: The Simultaneous Evolution of Institutions and Norms." In *Economics, Values, and Organization*, ed. Avner Ben-Ner and Louis Putterman, 73–100. Cambridge: Cambridge University Press. http://dx.doi.org/10.1017/CBO9781139174855.004.

Sum, Ngai-Ling, and Bob Jessop. 2003. "Pre- and Post-Disciplinarity Perspectives in (Cultural) Political Economy." *Économies et Sociétés* 37 (6): 993–1015.

Sunstein, Cass R. 1996a. "On the Expressive Function of Law." *University of Pennsylvania Law Review* 144 (5): 2021–53. http://dx.doi.org/10.2307/3312647.

Sunstein, Cass R. 1996b."Social Norms and Social Roles." *Columbia Law Review* 96 (4): 903–68. http://dx.doi.org/10.2307/1123430.

Swann, Dennis. 1988. *The Retreat of the State: Deregulation and Privatization in the UK and US.* Ann Arbor: University of Michigan Press.

Taylor, Andrew. 1984. *The Politics of the Yorkshire Miners.* London: Croom Helm.

Taylor, Andrew. 1987. *The Trade Unions and the Labour Party.* London: Croom Helm.

Taylor, Charles. 2004. *Modern Social Imaginaries.* Durham, NC: Duke University Press.

Taylor, Robert. 1993. *The Trade Union Question in British Politics: Government and Unions since 1945.* Oxford: Blackwell.

Taylor, Robert. 1996a. "The Heath Government, Industrial Policy and the 'New Capitalism'." In *The Heath Government 1970–1974: A Reappraisal,* ed. Stuart Ball and Anthony Seldon, 139–160. London: Longman.

Taylor, Robert. 1996b. "The Heath Government and Industrial Relations: Myth and Reality." In *The Heath Government 1970–1974: A Reappraisal,* ed. Stuart Ball and Anthony Seldon, 161–190. London: Longman.

Tebbit, Norman. 1988. *Upwardly Mobile.* London: Weidenfeld and Nicolson.

Teicher, Julian. 1998. *Restructuring the Australian State: Modernisation, Privatisation and National Competition Policy.* Melbourne: National Key Centre in Industrial Relations, Monash University.

Templeton, Hugh. 1995. *All Honourable Men: Inside the Muldoon Cabinet, 1975–1984.* Auckland: Auckland University Press.

Thain, Colin. 1985. "The Education of the Treasury: The Medium Term Financial Strategy 1980–84." *Public Administration* 63 (3): 261–85. http://dx.doi.org/10.1111/j.1467-9299. 1985.tb00905.x.

Thatcher, Margaret. 1993. *The Downing Street Years.* London: HarperCollins.

Thatcher, Margaret. 1995. *The Path to Power.* London: HarperCollins.

Thatcher, Margaret. 1997. *The Collected Speeches of Margaret Thatcher.* New York: HarperCollins.

Thomas, George M., John W. Meyer, Francisco O. Ramirez, and John Boli, eds. 1987. *Institutional Structure: Constituting State, Society and the Individual.* Newbury Park, CA: Sage.

Thompson, James. 1998. "The Genesis of the 1906 Trades Disputes Act: Liberalism, Trade Unions, and the Law." *Twentieth Century British History* 9 (2): 175–200. http://dx.doi.org/10.1093/tcbh/9.2.175.

Thompson, John B. 1984. *Studies in the Theory of Ideology*. Berkeley: University of California Press.

Tomlinson, John. 1991. *Cultural Imperialism: A Critical Introduction*. Baltimore: Johns Hopkins University Press.

Tomlinson, Jim. 2007. "Mrs Thatcher's Macroeconomic Adventurism, 1979–1981, and its Political Consequences." *British Politics* 2 (1): 3–19. http://dx.doi.org/10.1057/palgrave.bp.4200038.

Tomlinson, J.R.G. 1989. "The Schools." In *The Thatcher Effect*, ed. Dennis Kavanagh and Anthony Seldon, 183–97. Oxford: Oxford University Press.

Toner, Glen. 1986. "Stardust: The Tory Energy Program." In *How Ottawa Spends 1986–87: Tracking the Tories*, ed. Michael J. Prince, 119–48. Toronto: Methuen.

Towers, Brian. 1989. "Running the Gauntlet: British Trade Unions under Thatcher, 1979–1988." *Industrial & Labor Relations Review* 42 (2): 163–88. http://dx.doi.org/10.2307/2523352.

Tsebelis, George. 1995. "Decision Making in Political Systems: Veto Players in Presidentialism, Parliamentarism, Multicameralism and Multipartyism." *British Journal of Political Science* 25 (3): 289–326. http://dx.doi.org/10.1017/S0007123400007225.

Tsebelis, George. 1999. "Veto Players and Law Production in Parliamentary Democracies: An Empirical Analysis." *American Political Science Review* 93 (3): 591–608. http://dx.doi.org/10.2307/2585576.

Tsebelis, George. 2002. *Veto Players: How Institutions Work*. Princeton: Princeton University Press.

Tsebelis, George, and Jeanette Money. 1997. *Bicameralism*. Cambridge: Cambridge University Press. http://dx.doi.org/10.1017/CBO9780511609350.

Tupper, Allan, and G. Bruce Doern, eds. 1988. *Privatization, Public Policy, and Public Corporations in Canada*. Halifax: Institute for Research on Public Policy.

Tyler, Richard. 2006. "'Victims of our History'? Barbara Castle and *In Place of Strife*." *Contemporary British History* 20 (3): 461–76. http://dx.doi.org/10.1080/13619460500407186.

United Nations. 1986. *World Economic Survey 1986*. New York: United Nations.

Upton, Simon. 1985. "An End to Insulationism in the New Zealand Economy." *Three Banks Review* 146: 28–42.

U.S.-Canada Automotive Agreement Policy Research Project. 1985. *The U.S.-Canadian Automotive Products Agreement of 1965: An Evaluation for its Twentieth Year*. Austin: University of Texas at Austin, Lyndon B. Johnson School of Public Affairs Political Research Project report, no. 68.

Uslaner, Eric M. 1989. *Shale Barrel Politics*. Stanford: Stanford University Press.

Van Kersbergen, Kees, and Bertjan Verbeek. 2007. "The Politics of International Norms: Subsidiarity and the Imperfect Competence Regime of the European Union." *European Journal of International Relations* 13 (2): 217–38. http://dx.doi.org/10.1177/1354066107076955.

Veljanovski, Cento G. 1987. *Selling the State: Privatisation in Britain*. London: Weidenfeld and Nicolson.

Vowles, Jack. 2002. "Parties and Society in New Zealand." In *Political Parties in Advanced Industrial Democracies*, ed. Paul Webb, David Farrell, and Ian Holliday, 409–37. Oxford: Oxford University Press. http://dx.doi.org/10.1093/0199240566.003.0014.

Waite, Peter B. 1971. *Canada, 1874–1896: Arduous Destiny*. Toronto: University of Toronto Press.

Walker, Peter. 1991. *Staying Power: An Autobiography*. London: Bloomsbury.

Walsh, Pat. 1989. "A Family Fight? Industrial Relations Reform under the Fourth Labour Government." In *The Making of Rogernomics*, ed. Brian Easton, 149–70. Auckland: Auckland University Press.

Walsh, Pat. 1993. "The State and Industrial Relations in New Zealand." In *State and Economy in New Zealand*, ed. Brian Roper and Chris Rudd, 172–91. Auckland: Oxford University Press. http://dx.doi.org/10.1111/j.1467-8543.1993.tb00380.x.

Walsh, Pat. 1994. "An 'Unholy Alliance': The 1968 Nil Wage Order." *New Zealand Journal of History* 28 (2): 178–93.

Walsh, Peter. 1995. *Confessions of a Failed Finance Minister*. Milsons Point, NSW: Random House Australia.

Walsh, Pat. 1997. "From Arbitration to Bargaining: Changing State Strategies in Industrial Relations." In *The Political Economy of New Zealand*, ed. Chris Rudd and Brian Roper, 183–201. Auckland: Oxford University Press.

Walsh, Pat, and Raymond Harbridge. 2001. "Re-Regulation of Bargaining in New Zealand: The Employment Relations Act 2000." *Australian Bulletin of Labour* 27 (1): 43–60.

Walsh, Pat, and Rose Ryan. 1993. "The Making of the Employment Contracts Act." In *Employment Contracts: New Zealand Experiences*, ed. Raymond Harbridge, 13–30. Wellington: Victoria University Press.

Watson, Matthew, and Colin Hay. 2003. "The Discourse of Globalization and the Logic of No Alternative: Rendering the Contingent Necessary in the Political Economy of New Labour." *Policy and Politics* 31 (3): 289–305. http://dx.doi.org/10.1332/030557303322034956.

Wearing, Joseph. 1988. *Strained Relations: Canadian Parties and Voters*. Toronto: McClelland and Stewart.

Weber, Max. 1968. "The Sociology of Charismatic Authority." In *Max Weber on Charisma and Institution Building*, ed. S.N. Eisenstadt, 18–27. Chicago: University of Chicago Press.

Webster, Charles. 1989. "The Health Service." In *The Thatcher Effect*, ed. Dennis Kavanagh and Anthony Seldon, 166–82. Oxford: Oxford University Press.

Weir, Margaret. 1989. "Ideas and Politics: The Acceptance of Keynesianism in Britain and the United States." In *The Political Power of Economic Ideas: Keynesianism across Nations*, ed. Peter A. Hall, 53–86. Princeton: Princeton University Press.

Weldes, Jutta. 1996. "Constructing National Interests." *European Journal of International Relations* 2 (3): 275–318. http://dx.doi.org/10.1177/1354066196002003001.

Weldes, Jutta. 1999. *Constructing National Interests: The United States and the Cuban Missile Crisis*. Minneapolis: University of Minnesota Press.

Weldes, Jutta, Mark Laffey, Hugh Gusterson, and Raymond Duvall. 1999. "Introduction: Constructing Insecurity." In *Cultures of Insecurity: States, Communities, and the Production of Danger*, ed. Jutta Weldes, Mark Laffey, Hugh Gusterson, and Raymond Duvall, 1–33. Minneapolis: University of Minnesota Press.

Weller, Patrick. 1989. *Malcolm Fraser, PM: A Study in Prime Ministerial Power*. Ringwood, Vic.: Penguin.

Wendt, Alexander. 1987. "The Agent-Structure Problem in International Relations Theory." *International Organization* 41 (3): 335–70. http://dx.doi.org/10.1017/S002081830002751X.

Wendt, Alexander. 1992. "Anarchy is What States Make of It: The Social Construction of Power Politics." *International Organization* 46 (2): 391–425. http://dx.doi.org/10.1017/S0020818300027764.

Wendt, Alexander. 1999. *Social Theory of International Politics*. Cambridge: Cambridge University Press. http://dx.doi.org/10.1017/CBO9780511612183.

Whitehead, Phillip. 1985. *The Writing on the Wall: Britain in the Seventies*. London: M. Joseph.

Whiting, Richard. 2007. "The Reform of Working Life in Britain, 1963–1971." *Historical Journal (Cambridge, England)* 50 (2): 423–48. http://dx.doi.org/10.1017/S0018246X07006139.

Whitlam, E. Gough. 1985. *The Whitlam Government, 1972–1975*. Ringwood, Vic.: Viking.

Whitwell, Greg. 1986. *The Treasury Line*. Sydney: Allen and Unwin.

Widmaier, Wesley W. 2003. "The Keynesian Basis of a Constructivist Theory of the International Political Economy." *Millennium: Journal of International Studies* 32 (1): 87–107. http://dx.doi.org/10.1177/03058298030320010401.

Widmaier, Wesley W. 2005. "The Meaning of an Inflation Crisis: Steel, Enron, and Macroeconomic Policy." *Journal of Post Keynesian Economics* 27 (4): 555–73.

Widmaier, Wesley W. 2007a. "Constructing Foreign Policy Crises: Interpretive Leadership in the Cold War and War on Terrorism." *International Studies Quarterly* 51 (4): 779–94. http://dx.doi.org/10.1111/j.1468-2478. 2007.00476.x.

Widmaier, Wesley W. 2007b. "Where You Stand Depends on How You Think: Economic Ideas, the Decline of the Council of Economic Advisers and the Rise of the Federal Reserve." *New Political Economy* 12 (1): 43–59. http://dx.doi.org/10.1080/13563460601068586.

Widmaier, Wesley W. 2008. "'Please Better Shut Their Mouths': German Influence on U.S. Macroeconomic Policy under the Carter Administration." *Germany Policy Studies* 4 (3): 5–30.

Widmaier, Wesley W. 2010. "Trade-offs and Trinities: Social Forces and Monetary Cooperation." In *Constructing the International Economy*, ed. Rawi Abdelal, Mark Blyth, and Craig Parsons, 155–72. Ithaca, NY: Cornell University Press.

Widmaier, Welsey W., Mark Blyth, and Leonard Seabrooke. 2007. "Exogenous Shocks or Endogenous Constructions? The Meaning of Wars and Crises." *International Studies Quarterly* 51 (4): 747–59. http://dx.doi. org/10.1111/j.1468-2478. 2007.00474.x.

Wiener, Martin J. 1981. *English Culture and the Decline of the Industrial Spirit, 1859–1980*. Cambridge: Cambridge University Press.

Winterton, Jonathan. 1989. *Coal, Crisis, and Conflict: The 1984–85 Miners' Strike in Yorkshire*. Manchester: Manchester University Press.

Wood, Greg. 1988. "The Labour Relations Act and Changes to the Structure of Bargaining." *New Zealand Journal of Industrial Relations* 13 (2): 167–77.

Wood, John B. 1975. *How Little Unemployment?* London: Institute of Economic Affairs.

Wooden, Mark. 2000. *The Transformation of Australian Industrial Relations*. Leichhardt, NSW: The Federation Press.

Wooding, Paul. 1987. "Liberalising the International Trade Regime." In *Economic Liberalisation in New Zealand*, ed. Alan Bollard and Robert Buckle, 86–101. Wellington: Allen and Unwin.

Woods, Ngaire. 1995. "Economic Ideas and International Relations: Beyond Rational Neglect." *International Studies Quarterly* 39 (2): 161–80. http://dx.doi. org/10.2307/2600845.

Wyatt, Andrew. 2005. "Building the Temples of Postmodern India: Economic Constructions of National Identity." *Contemporary South Asia* 14 (4): 465–80. http://dx.doi.org/10.1080/09584930600839180.

Young, Hugo. 1988. "The Long Running Premier." *The Guardian,* 2 January.

Young, Hugo. 1989. *One of Us: A Biography of Margaret Thatcher.* London: Macmillan.

Young, Ken. 1989. "Local Government." In *The Thatcher Effect,* ed. Dennis Kavanagh and Anthony Seldon, 124–32. Oxford: Oxford University Press.

Young, Oran R. 1991. "Political Leadership and Regime Formation: On the Development of Institutions in International Society." *International Organization* 45 (3): 281–308. http://dx.doi.org/10.1017/S0020818300033117.

Zahariadis, Nikolaos. 1995. *Markets, States, and Public Policy: Privatization in Britain and France.* Ann Arbor: University of Michigan Press.

Zald, Mayer N. 1996. "Culture, Ideology, and Strategic Framing." In *Comparative Perspectives on Social Movements: Political Opportunities, Mobilizing Structures, and Cultural Framing,* ed. Doug McAdam, John D. McCarthy, and Mayer N. Zald, 261–74. Cambridge: Cambridge University Press. http://dx.doi.org/10.1017/CBO9780511803987.013.

Index